BIO FLOOD

THE
CURT FLOOD
STORY

SPORTS AND AMERICAN CULTURE SERIES
BRUCE CLAYTON, EDITOR

THE
CURT FLOOD
STORY

THE MAN BEHIND THE MYTH

STUART L. WEISS

UNIVERSITY OF MISSOURI PRESS
COLUMBIA AND LONDON

Library of Congress Cataloging-in-Publication Data

Weiss, Stuart L.
    The Curt Flood story : the man behind the myth / Stuart L. Weiss.
        p. cm.–(Sports and American culture series)
    Summary: "Examines Curt Flood's often troubled personal life and explores his possible motives for suing Major League Baseball in 1970. For challenging baseball's reserve system, which he likened to bondage, the St. Louis Cardinals center fielder in time was lionized. But this recognition came at great personal expense"–Provided by publisher.
    Includes bibliographical references and index.
    ISBN 978-0-8262-1740-0 (alk. paper)
    1. Flood, Curt, 1938– 2. Baseball players–United States–Biography. 3. African American baseball players–Biography. I. Title.
    GV865.F45W45 2007
    796.357092–dc22
    [B]
2006102249

⊗™ This paper meets the requirements of the
American National Standard for Permanence of Paper
for Printed Library Materials, Z39.48, 1984.

Designer: foleydesign
Typesetter: BookComp, Inc.
Printer and binder: Thomson-Shore, Inc.
Typefaces: Berthold City and ITC Cheltingham Light

FRONTISPIECE: Flood near the end of his time as the Cardinals' center fielder, 1969. *Courtesy of the Collections of the St. Louis Mercantile Library Association.*

Contents

Acknowledgments

I should like to acknowledge, first, my debt to my wife, Rita, a scholar in her own right, for indulging me in my work or, if you prefer, pleasure of researching and writing this book. I could not have spent the money, done the driving, or left my office a mess without her aid and consent. I should also like to acknowledge the assistance of the several librarians, courthouse officials, and researchers who helped me, including not least those at the St. Louis Mercantile Library, which houses the *St. Louis Globe-Democrat;* those at the *St. Louis Post-Dispatch;* and those at the *Sporting News.* I should also like to thank those interviewed, who are mentioned in the Introduction. And a special thanks as well to both Robert Erickson, whose mention of Flood's death led via a long path to this book, and to Patrick Riddleberger, a former mentor, both professors emeritus of Southern Illinois University at Edwardsville. My thanks as well to those in Oakland who discussed Flood's life there. Further, I must acknowledge the support of everyone at the University of Missouri Press whose cooperation made this book better than it might otherwise have been. At last I would add in all fairness that I have never been stopped by a policeman, refused service in a restaurant, or denied a room at a hotel because of my color. It would be understandable if that has influenced my perspective on Flood's life. Others, men or women of color, African Americans especially, may well find more or better sources than I have, and for these and other reasons find a different Flood than that presented in this book. I welcome those who might make Flood's story more comprehensive and better convey the man behind the myth.

THE
CURT FLOOD
STORY

Members of the 1958 Savannah Reds. Flood, third from
right, stands between Buddy Gilbert, a white player who
made friends with him, and Leo Cardenas, who later
became Cincinnati's starting shortstop for much of the
1960s and played in sixteen major-league seasons.
Courtesy of Drew E. "Buddy" Gilbert.

Flood and his teammate, first baseman Bill White,
are presented with Gold Glove awards prior to a
game at Busch Stadium on May 23, 1965. The two
Cardinals were honored as the National League's
top fielders at their positions in the 1964 season.
Courtesy of the Collections of the St. Louis
Mercantile Library Association.

Flood and Missouri Secretary of State James C. Kirkpatrick (wearing glasses) at the ribbon-cutting ceremony opening Curt Flood Studios, June 3, 1969. Looking over their shoulders is Flood's business partner, Bill Jones. Courtesy of the Collections of the St. Louis Mercantile Library Association.

Flood taking batting practice during the
1969 season. Courtesy of the Collections of
the St. Louis Mercantile Library Association.

Flood with St. Louis Mayor Alfonso J. Cervantes, 1969.
Cervantes appointed Flood the honorary chairman of the
Leukemia Fund's annual door-to-door fund-raising program
after Flood painted a portrait of a St. Louis girl who died from
leukemia and presented it to her parents. Courtesy of the
Collections of the St. Louis Mercantile Library Association.

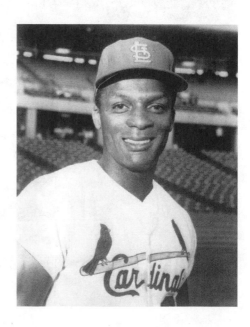

Flood in 1969, his last season with the Cardinals. He
would return to baseball in
1971, but would last only
thirteen games with the
Washington Senators.
Courtesy of the Collections
of the St. Louis Mercantile
Library Association.

Flood reclining during an interview, 1970. By 1970 Flood was
out of baseball, a result of his refusal to accept his trade to
the Philadelphia Phillies and decision to file a lawsuit against
Major League Baseball contesting the legality of its reserve
system. Courtesy of the Collections of the St. Louis Mercantile
Library Association.

Introduction

Can a single misplay by a baseball player lead to a lawsuit that reaches the United States Supreme Court? Improbable, yes! But it happened. The key figure was Charles Curtis "Curt" Flood, a superb center fielder sometimes compared to Hall of Famer Willie Mays.

Flood's misplay occurred during the seventh and decisive game of the 1968 World Series. He was traded by the St. Louis Cardinals after the 1969 season, and he refused to go as required by his contract. The Uniform Players Contract contained the prevailing reserve system, which gave the club that first signed a player the right to sell, trade, or release him without his consent. Flood did not consent to being traded. He launched a lawsuit against Major League Baseball in January 1970, contending that the reserve system required collusion, therefore it constituted a "conspiracy in restraint of trade" prohibited by the Sherman Antitrust Act of 1890. Two years later, Flood's case reached the Supreme Court, and, in a decision tainted with sentiment about the sanctity of the "National Pastime," he lost his battle.

But these bare facts do not tell Flood's story. They do not tell us why he alone of all the many players traded or sold through the years decided to sue. He tried to tell the country his story. In early 1971 he and a ghostwriter published an account of his life that tried to justify his lawsuit and to appeal to public opinion while his case, which had already lost in a federal district court, was climbing the judicial ladder. This account, *The Way It Is*, might as well have been called "I Was Always a Victim." He cites his struggle to rise from the West Oakland ghetto and to contend with racism in the South, in California, and in St. Louis. Sometimes he does so fairly, sometimes not. He also discusses his victimization by the Cardinals' head and Anheuser-Busch brewery president August "Gussie" Busch. Flood claimed that during the 1969 season Busch unfairly picked on him and other members of the team,

1

undermining his and the team's morale and ruining the season. This the boss could do because the players were enslaved by the reserve system. So it was that Flood, portraying himself as a victimized slave of the Cardinals, sued Major League Baseball. Notably, he wrote that he was fighting for principle, not for the millions of dollars he would get if he won, and this is the version of his decision to sue that would evolve eventually into the Flood myth: that he was, as columnist George Will wrote in an essay after his death, "Dred Scott in Spikes," a self-sacrificing martyr in the battle against baseball's reserve system.

Unhappily, if understandably, Flood's self-portrait of himself as a martyred hero is a myth. The reality is that his battle against the reserve system cannot be understood without examining the many factors that precipitated it other than his victimization by the external forces he names. His battle also cannot be rightly understood without considering its cost to others near, if not dear, to him. Furthermore, Flood cannot be fully understood without discussing the complexity of his life from his childhood and youth in Oakland to his self-exile in Palma de Majorca and his death in Los Angeles. This requires discussing the key help given to Flood in Oakland by whites and blacks alike, his talents as an artist and guitarist as well as a baseball player, his battles over alimony and child support with his first wife as they interacted with his play on the field, and his foolishness as a venture capitalist. At last, this book is less about the reserve system and baseball's exemption from the antitrust laws—neither of which it judges—than the inner Flood, a sensitive, brooding, temperamental, and easily manipulated man who seemingly morphed his grievances, real and imagined, against Busch and the Cardinals into his challenge to baseball's reserve system and, almost certainly, the white establishment in general. This broader, deeper treatment of Flood, based on records never before used, is the reason this book is entitled *The Curt Flood Story: The Man behind the Myth,* and not simply "Flood's Challenge to Baseball's Reserve System" or some variation thereof. This book offers new dimensions to Curt Flood's battle, which was the central issue in his life's story, but it is not the whole story. Neither does this book pretend to be the last word. It originated quite by chance, not by design, and if it is provocative—which it will surely be—then I would hope that others will correct such errors in judgment as they think I have made.

I

It Takes a Village

On June 1, 1970, a handsome, well-proportioned, neatly tailored black man waved to reporters from the top step of the federal courthouse in New York City. Charles Curtis Flood, "Curt" to friends and baseball fans, could not have appeared more cheerful to those below, although he was now, most unhappily, out of the game he loved. The previous October the St. Louis Cardinals had traded him to the Philadelphia Phillies, after which sportswriters in both cities evaluated the trade, never thinking Flood might not accept it. He had only one alternative under Major League Baseball's Uniform Players Contract: to retire from baseball, and that seemed highly unlikely given his known love for the game and his handsome salary. But before 1969 ended Flood decided to challenge Major League Baseball in the courts.

Flood knew that the controlling reserve system lodged in the UPC (several contractual clauses commonly referred to simply as the reserve clause, probably because there was one key section, Section 10A) rested on baseball's exemption from the antitrust statutes that bound other professional sports. Furthermore, he had been advised by his lawyer in St. Louis that if he sued Major League Baseball, the clubs might surrender rather than face audits or a battle in the courts. Moreover, late in the fall of 1969 Flood had obtained the financial and legal support of the young but newly assertive Major League Baseball Players Association (MLBPA), which, for obvious reasons, shared his interest in loosening the bonds of the reserve system. Consequently, in January 1970 his lawyers, retained by the Players Association, had taken the first steps in a six-month journey that placed him on those courthouse steps in early June (the trial had begun in May). The key issue to be decided by the judge was now well beyond that posited by Flood's St. Louis lawyer: it was whether the reserve system, by definition involving collusion among the club owners, violated the Sherman Antitrust Act (1890) that prohibited conspiracies in restraint of trade among the several states. So far the courts had decided otherwise. However, if circumstances had changed such that the federal courts now found that the Sherman Act encompassed baseball, as it did every other major sport, then the reserve system would be eliminated, and ball clubs would no longer be able to treat players as mere property to be traded, bought, or sold without any recourse on their part.

Flood's battle for the right of ballplayers to negotiate in a free, open market for their services was to cost him his career and his income. Financially, it would also cost his ex-wife, his children, his mother, a treasured sister, and a dear friend. This he knew was almost certain before he initiated his lawsuit. He had been warned by Marvin Miller, the executive director of the Players Association, that his case was very chancy. Even so, he had taken the plunge. Why? Was it from a personal, deeply rooted sense of injustice, coupled with a righteous anger at Major League Baseball's reserve system? Simply put, did Flood battle for principle? Was he a martyr to the cause of free agency, even to freedom itself? This is the story that permeates the documentaries that have appeared since his death. But is it only a story, a myth, although a very powerful one?[1]

Flood's decision to challenge Major League Baseball did not take place in a vacuum. It will be argued that his decision was a product of an unusually complex personality, character, and set of life experiences—dare one say a sensitive psychological makeup that gave him a sense of victimization. And these underlying characteristics set the stage for a chain of events in which an apparent miscue in the 1968 World Series would cause Flood to unravel, to feud with the Cardinals and be traded a year later, then to react almost blindly by filing his lawsuit. However, as might be expected, Flood did not see the connection between these events; neither has anyone else in the many years since his battle against Major League Baseball.[2]

Flood first discussed his reasons for challenging baseball's reserve system in a book ghostwritten by Richard Carter. Published as *The Way It Is* in early 1971, this slender tome offers an account of Flood's experiences, from his childhood and youth in Oakland through his career with

1. Alex Belth, *Stepping Up: The Story of Curt Flood and His Fight for Baseball Players' Rights* (New York: Persea Books, 2006); Brad Snyder, *A Well-Paid Slave: Curt Flood's Fight for Free Agency in Professional Sports* (New York: Viking Press, 2006).

2. Joseph Durso, *New York Times,* January 1, 1997, wrote three brief paragraphs detailing Flood's failure to catch a line drive in the 1968 World Series.

the Cardinals, his trade, his trial, and a very brief period after. Of course, Flood and Carter attack the reserve system, but they do so without discussing its possible merits as well as its defects, although they imply that it has at least some merit because Flood in his lawsuit wants to modify it, not destroy it root and branch. But in the last analysis, the book is about Flood as a victim, although other than Cardinals' president August "Gussie" Busch, and, of comparatively little significance, racists in general, Flood and Carter are vague about their villains. Yet *The Way It Is* is more dubious on another score: it is seldom "the way it was." Carter did not make a serious effort to corroborate what Flood told him. He was too sympathetic to Flood and his cause, years later rejecting even well-documented statistics that defied his point of view. At last, then, Carter and Flood's book is an apologia, Flood's justification of his battle. Equally, *The Way It Is* is the story of Flood's life as he was about to turn thirty-two, but especially the story of his baseball career and temperament as it set the stage for his reasoning or lack thereof in challenging the reserve system. Despite the fact that the book is something other than it claims to be, and that it was written when Flood was still relatively young, the reader will find it referred to in these pages as a memoir. In any event, it is hoped that what follows is a more detached, more objective, and therefore more realistic portrait of Flood's life, and especially of his lawsuit, than is presently available. It may not be the final word, but it attempts to separate myth from reality in his life, beginning, as it must, with his parentage, his childhood, and his youth in Oakland.[3]

In his memoir Flood ignored his family's history prior to his birth. Only in his recollections near the end of his life would he mention it, and then he depended on the memory of his older half sister, Rickie Riley. Sometimes he or his sister got the details wrong. But he knew where the focus belonged, on Oakland, the City by the Bay, and on his parents, especially his mother, Laura, a "woman with a heart" with whom he shared a certain streak, "not of orneriness exactly, more like 'I just won't take a whole lot.'" Fearless Laura's sensitivity to racial slurs, real or imagined, would lead to instant, sharp attack or retreat; there was seldom a middle way. So it was also with her son Curtis, as young Flood preferred to be called.[4]

3. Curt Flood, with Richard Carter, *The Way It Is*. For Carter's prejudices, see his correspondence to author of December 3, 1998.
4. First of several interviews with Rickie Riley, born Iola Ricks, 1998–2006.

The mother that Flood spoke of was baptized Laura Portis in the black township of Mossville, Louisiana, according to Rickie, but in nearby West Lake according to Flood's application for a passport in 1957. Both Flood and his sister agreed, however, that she was born slightly more than two years before the end of the nineteenth century. Rickie believes her grandparents' poverty explains why, at age four, Laura went to live with an aunt; just as her mother's improved circumstances eight years later—a house was purchased in DeRidder in the west-central part of the state—explains why she could later come home to live throughout her youth. In any event, in Louisiana Laura Portis's last name was mispronounced as Porter so often that eventually she adopted it as her legal surname. Although obviously of chiefly black stock, Laura bore the imprint of mixed racial ancestry in her cheekbones and, some said, her character. Her strikingly handsome face and silken skin, which her son Curtis would inherit, if in a coal-black hue, probably reflected a slice of Choctaw ancestry, though those who knew the family best attributed her character, even her speech, to her Creole grandparents. The family included many strong people, Rickie recalled, and they taught Laura that she was the equal of any woman—or man—and that she should stand firmly against injustice. Also, she must use proper grammar, seek and use the best word choices possible—practicing by doing crossword puzzles would be helpful—and enunciate clearly. Finally, except when truly and rightfully angry, she should speak in a warm, soft voice that said "I am nice." What Laura learned was of no small moment for at least one of her children. Learning to speak clearly if softly and to charm was a lesson young Curtis would learn at her knee. But it was not the only one. He also imbibed her (often temperamental) reaction to perceived injustices.[5]

The value of her grandparents' tutelage notwithstanding, by early adolescence Laura Porter found their supervision confining. Only marriage suggested an escape and, still in her early teens, she found a man who seemed to promise a suitable match. Ivory Ricks was a black man

5. Ibid.; Flood's Passport Application, October 4, 1957, U.S. State Department, Case Control No. 00202860, in an IRS "Request for Inspection of Passport File," November 26, 1974, listed his mother's birth date as October 14, 1897. Curtis was pronounced with a hard "s," as if with two esses, by his half sister, Rickie. Judge Irving Ben Cooper, speaking to Flood on May 19, 1970 (trial transcript, *Curtis C. Flood, plaintiff, v. Bowie K. Kuhn et al.*, 70, Civil Action 202, U.S. District Court for the Southern District of New York, New York City, 10), had to remind him to speak up.

and, unusually for that racist era, a mechanical engineer with a degree from Prairie View College northwest of Houston. At the end of 1913 he had answered an ad and almost sneaked into a position at a lumber mill in Ludington, Louisiana, just a short distance north of DeRidder. Fortunately for Ivory, he arrived at the mill when the owner's need for an engineer prevailed over the region's traditionally strong racial prejudices, and he was hired as the mill's assistant foreman. Shortly after, he met Laura Porter, and in 1914 they married and moved to a small house near his Ludington work site.[6]

Within three years Laura Ricks bore two children. The first, Rickie, baptized Iola, was born in 1915. Rickie never cared for the name, however, and asked one and all to call her by what she thought a minor alteration of the family's surname. A strong, motherly, easygoing woman, Rickie would keep the family's history, outliving two stepbrothers many years her junior, as well as her younger brother, Alvin. When interviewed years later, Rickie, speaking in a smoothly modulated voice typical of her mother and, in time, of her half brother, Curtis, and her other siblings, recalled several fascinating aspects of the family's life in DeRidder, Ludington, and elsewhere, as well as Laura's life with her second husband and their children.

Apparently the Ricks family did not suffer noticeably from racism during their early years in Ludington. Ivory maintained the lumber mill's equipment and, for all intents and purposes, managed the mill itself. His status seemed to shield the family from the terrible problems most southern blacks faced. But that shield was very thin, as Laura learned in 1920. Spiraling prices during and after the First World War were followed by a sharp recession that exacerbated racial tensions in rural Louisiana as in most other places in the country. And perhaps as a result, an incident occurred that forced Ivory, Laura, and their children to flee Louisiana.

One day Laura Ricks was shopping in DeRidder's best department store when a local matron approached her. "Do you know where I can get a nigger to do my laundry?" the woman drawled in a voice loud enough for Laura to hear. Quickly, sharply, and surely unusually for that time and region, Laura said, "No, as a matter of fact I'm looking for a white bitch to do mine." Shocked, the woman struck Laura, who

---

6. DeRidder is only one of three spellings of this southwest Louisiana city, otherwise De Ridder and even Deridder.

slapped her back, and a "cat fight" ensued. The two women grabbed each other, overturned tables, and swept clothes onto the floor before an angry store manager pulled them apart. Then each left quietly.

Laura, quickly gathering her wits, realized that the brawl would not be the the end of the matter: a black woman didn't fight with a white woman in Louisiana in that era and live to tell about it. So she ran to the mill to warn Ivory that they must leave the area. Failing to find him (he already knew about the brawl), she ran home to gather up her children. Hurriedly collecting a few necessities, she put the children in the car, somehow found her husband—or he found her—and they left for a safer haven.

Years later, Laura would tell Rickie, who would eventually tell her youngest stepbrother, that "God pointed them west, toward Oakland." There was more to the story, though, than Rickie told her brother. Laura, her husband, and their children first took a train to her family home, now in Houston. There, Ivory left Laura and the children while he went to Oakland to look for a job. He would send for them, he said, when he found work and a place for the family to live.

Unfortunately for Ivory, he found Oakland gripped by the same postwar collapse and absence of jobs that was crippling Ludington and DeRidder, and he could not find work in mechanical engineering or anything else that paid enough to provide his family a decent living. For a few months he eked out a bare existence for himself and his family as a strikebreaker on the docks, hardly a permanent job. A year went by before he found permanent work as a longshoreman on Oakland's wharves, rented a small apartment for a meager $12.50 a month, and sent for Laura and the children. They soon came to Oakland as Ivory asked, but barely a year later Laura and her husband separated and, soon after, they severed their marriage. Exactly when this occurred Rickie did not know, and if she knew why, she would not say directly. She left little doubt, however, that her mother, soft voice or no, had a very short temper and might have been very difficult to live with. She might have added that Laura's youngest son, Curtis, was just as temperamental and would prove in time to be a difficult marital partner as well.

For the next five years Laura worked and cared for her children, although she received some help from Ivory's parents, including rail passes that his father, a fireman on the Missouri Pacific Road, handed her. The passes enabled her and the children to visit Houston from time to time, and there during one visit she met Herman Flood. He played the guitar in a blues group called the Saturday Night Breakdowns, and he met Laura after one evening's "gig." For several nights afterward, they enjoyed each other's company, but though eight years younger and generally easygoing he was much the more serious suitor of the two and, it seems, too serious for Laura. She went back to California without giving him an address where he could write to her. But Herman did not give up, not even when Laura's parents said they did not know her address in Oakland. Something of a romantic, he decided to see if he could find her. He moved to Oakland, and shortly after his arrival he devised a plan. He knew that some day she would take a ferry to San Francisco, so he found a job on a boat he hoped she would board and waited.

Four months after Herman Flood rode his first ferry, Laura Porter boarded the boat. Soon after, they thought themselves in love, and in 1928 they were married. Unfortunately, the times did not favor them. By 1931 the American economy had collapsed and jobs in Oakland, as elsewhere in the country, had disappeared. Unemployed, the two decided to return to Houston to find work and to live with his parents. What Herman did there is unknown. Laura, however, developed two careers. She opened a successful beauty parlor, and she bore four children. The couple's first child, Herman, Jr., was born in 1931; their second, Barbara, in 1933; their third, Carl, in 1935; and, finally, Charles Curtis, or "Curtis," as he preferred and the family always called him, on January 18, 1938.

Though he was born in Houston, young Curtis and his family returned to Oakland shortly after his birth. His older half sister, Rickie, had moved there in 1939. She could not abide Houston: it was a pestilential swamp colonized by swarms of mosquitoes. Yet as much as she preferred racially mixed Oakland with its moderate climate, she also wanted to have her parents and siblings nearby. In 1941 she found them a four-bedroom house that they could rent for thirty dollars a month, and Herman, Laura, and their children traveled by train to Oakland and moved in. For a few years the city was very good to the Flood family. Herman brought home good money earned as a welder in the booming shipyards where Liberty (merchant) ships were being built in legendarily rapid succession, and Laura did her bit for the family and for the war effort, minding the house and the children while folding parachutes in a nearby factory. Thus although both Floods did work very hard, and perhaps, as their son asserts, it was drudgery, the couple made enough money for not only life's staples but also Barbara's piano lessons.

Unfortunately, there were racial problems in this neighborhood with its overwhelmingly white population and, thus, its white-dominated public school. One incident involved the Floods' youngest son, and Rickie found it so fascinating, not to mention revealing, that she easily recalled every detail half a century later. In December 1943, five-year-old Curtis came home from school of an afternoon to tell his mother that his teacher wanted him to play a role in the class's Christmas play. He was to say: "I'm little black Sambo, ain't I sweet, take me home and put me on your Christmas tree." Laura reacted sharply, her voice dripping with sarcasm: "Well, isn't that cute?" She knew very well that the lines were racist and that Curtis, because of his color, had been demeaned before the class. However, she quickly turned the incident into a positive, telling one and all about it, concluding with more than a little pride: "No one had to tell Curtis that's wrong."

The following summer the family left their home in East Oakland. Rickie had married and, with her husband, wanted her own house. Alvin had also left earlier. But neither departure explains the move. Laura wanted to buy their East Oakland home, not leave it. Cheap as the rent was, she believed there was no reason to pay rent when buying the house would enable her to build equity. To her great surprise, she found that the house was not for sale. Hearing this, she reacted in character, sharply, informing her family that night that they would look for another house that was for sale. Immediately. She believed the absentee owner did not want to sell to a black family, and she would not accept this slap in the face. Laura was probably right about the owner's reasons for refusing to sell. Before the Japanese attack on Pearl Harbor, Oakland had lived fairly comfortably with a relatively small number of blacks spread throughout the city; after what President Franklin Roosevelt called that "day of infamy," however, the city's vast majority of whites became increasingly hostile. Doubtless they were reacting to the great number of blacks moving from the rural South to take the many new, well-paying wartime jobs available. In any event, this "in-migration," as it became known, took its toll on the city's tolerance.

In 1944, Laura and Herman bought a sturdy two-story duplex in one of the less desirable sections of Oakland, an area their youngest son later would harshly—perhaps too harshly—label the West Oakland ghetto. Rickie, now Rickie Riley, and her husband, Harold, rented the first floor, while her mother, stepfather, and their four children lived on the second. Though a fair-sized house, it was not built for two families, and the three boys and their sister slept on bunks in the same second-story room. Curtis later said he did not have a problem with this arrangement, but he was otherwise confused and conflicted about his childhood and youth. At times he recalled his family's life as desperate. In fact, his hard-working family was more than comfortable even after the high-paying war jobs disappeared. After the war, his father and mother secured jobs at Fairmont Hospital, and though the jobs were menial and paid little, his mother was able to run a small restaurant where a seat was always available for someone truly down on his luck to eat free of charge. The family also owned a car and truck, they still could pay for a piano and lessons, and they could send their children to camp for the summer.[7]

Young Curtis's adolescence was by no means perfect, of course. There was intense acrimony now in his parents' marriage. The marriage was impaired by differences in their personalities, but this was much less important for their children than the long, hard, stressful days that Herman and Laura worked. Herman, usually tired and out of sorts, often hurried directly to his bedroom after work, but neither in his memoir nor later did Curtis complain: his father worked a twelve-hour shift, six days a week. Neither did he complain then or later that his father came home, was told by his mother that a child had misbehaved, and, without listening to the child's side of the story, simply "whipped [that] somebody's ass"—or so he wrote later. One is inclined to believe, however, that if Flood says he was forgiving and did not complain when describing his father's harshness, it was because he expected his children to understand when he acted the same way. But there was another reason as well: the circumstances that forced his father to work so hard for so little. His father was, as he was, a victim. As for his mother, he recalled that she worked so hard that at times she appeared dazed by her exertions. But Flood's claim that his parents had to work so hard, implicitly just to scrape by, does not explain his comment after stealing fruit from a nearby cannery: that it was just for fun, not because he was hungry; there was always fresh fruit and enough food otherwise. And Rickie agrees: fresh fruit and vegetables were readily available in their home. If there appeared to be a money problem at times, it was because

---

7. Flood, *The Way It Is,* chap. 1. I have tried to reconcile Flood's version of his family and neighborhood with what I heard from his sister Rickie, what I saw in Oakland, and what I heard from others who had known him and the area.

Laura and Herman were not only workaholics but also alcoholics. Both traits would be passed on to their youngest son.

Although there was conflict and tension in young Flood's home, he recalled many positives as well. His father took time after Christmas to show his children how to lacquer, preserve, and hang their Yule tree, so that it might last three or four years before it became totally bald and had to be discarded. Furthermore, his father taught him to play the guitar, and he quickly became proficient at it. Then, too, his father taught him to sketch and to paint, helping him develop artistic talents that he would market later. So, while it cannot be doubted that Herman passed on hurtful personality traits to his youngest son, he also bequeathed him a diverse array of artistic talent and helped him to develop it.

In his 1971 memoir, Flood recalled with great sadness, some bitterness, and perhaps a dollop of self-pity that his parents taught him that even if he worked hard and lived a moral life, a quite modest future was probably the best he could hope for. He did not blame them for conveying this sense of limited expectations. His family, like other blacks, lived amidst the lingering effects of slavery and segregation that made the color of their skin a "badge of ineligibility," while a "white mindset" still asserted that European immigrants had "made it," so "what's your problem"? If his parents were a bit better off than most people in their neighborhood, as they were, he asserted that they should be viewed as an island in the dark but often enticing and always powerful and dangerous sea that was the black West Oakland ghetto. Flood also insisted that the "conventionally squalid ghetto" where he grew up was rife with "mean streets" that were strewn with "abandoned furniture, broken glass, and stripped automobiles." Worse, perhaps, they were dangerously rife with "noisy, smelly bars, disheveled whores, loveless sex," and "thoughtless violence." And worse yet from his perspective thirty-odd years later, every child in the grammar and junior high schools was black, but the white teachers prattled on about slavery, freedom, and opportunity as if the students sitting before them had only themselves to blame if they later failed in life's struggle. "We had once been slaves," the teachers reminded, "but now we were free. If anything went wrong, we had only ourselves to blame." And his teachers' ignorance of the black man's harsh heritage was not the only problem Flood recalled from his youth. He never met any white men in West Oakland who were "bearers of joy." All the landlords, shopkeepers, teachers, cops, and bill collectors were "enforcers." All this he had accepted as natural. So had his neighbors, which showed that the ghetto not only warped its victims but also lulled and isolated them. Thus the Supreme Court's 1954 decision in *Brown v. Board of Education* (of Topeka, Kansas), and, the next year, in Brown II, requiring desegregation of the public schools "with all deliberate speed," prompted little discussion in the ghetto. He was sixteen at the time, and he believed that he would have been aware if *Brown* had been a subject of discussion. Given these circumstances, the plight of a black child in a white-dominated society, Flood recalled that the probabilities had been very slight that a boy could grow to manhood in the ghetto with any real hope for his future and a healthy view of love and life. In sum, Flood saw himself, as he saw his neighbors in this West Oakland ghetto, as victims of their badly degraded environment and the white establishment that dominated it.

In fact, except that it was heavily black by Flood's youth, the West Oakland ghetto was probably not as desolate and isolating as Flood later painted it. Admittedly, it was an older section of Oakland, a highly industrialized Pacific Ocean port housing a variety of foundries, shipyards, mills, and railroads. Before World War II families that could afford to live elsewhere left behind its noise, smell, and dust. Those that left were either professionals or simply upper-middle-class, native-born, and white; those that came into the ghetto were mainly black, but they were complemented by approximately equal numbers of first-generation Americans from Portugal, Italy, and China. After Pearl Harbor, because of the arrival of many hundreds of migrants from the South, West Oakland became blacker, but it was neither a ghetto nor as squalid as Flood painted it. Of course, it was not an idealized suburbia either, but it had no walls and it was not a slum. Rickie recalls that new jobs appeared at nearby military bases and a shipyard, and West Oakland was home to the usual stores and services, as well as a nightspot comparable to Harlem's fabled Cotton Club.

In addition, Flood's very close and long-term friendship with Jim Chambers, his white art teacher, belies to some degree his criticism of the "ghetto's" schools. In fact, many of the white teachers were liberals who (rumor had it) were exiled there. Others saw it. Frank Robinson, a future baseball Hall of Famer and another of the West Oakland ghetto's "victims," later praised the white teachers working there as compassionate, motivated, skilled, and ever ready to give young blacks a hand. Robinson also recalled as special the university-educated black recreation directors (and mentors) who worked at the DeFremery recreational center a short walk from Flood's home. So did Bill Russell, the future Hall of Fame center for basketball's Boston Celtics, who was another of DeFremery's outstanding graduates. Russell recalled—and honored—its directors who had given him and other youngsters not only the opportunity to reach for their dreams as athletes but also many essential lessons for living. In sum, the "ghetto" may have been a dead end for many who lived there—what area is not—but it was also a village, ready and able to embrace those, like Flood, who were willing and able to help themselves.[8]

Flood acknowledged this when in his later, alcohol-free years he again recalled his youth in Oakland. He knew then that during his youth it was not the squalid ghetto he had earlier labeled it. He knew, as his sister Rickie did, that homes could be left unlocked and that children could safely roam the streets. He also knew even earlier that at least one "enforcer" among those he condemned was black and had helped his family deal with a very serious problem. Furthermore, he knew other "enforcers" whose skin was white but about whom he had no reason to complain. Finally, of greatest importance for his future in baseball, he could not have forged a path out of West Oakland into professional baseball but for the coaching, counsel, and support of white and black men alike. Interestingly, even in his memoir, he gave all but one of them their due—and that a black mentor—in the process belying in his own words his generalized claim of bleak isolation in the West Oakland ghetto.[9]

Whatever West Oakland's effect on Flood, no one influenced him more for ill in his youth—or later—than his beloved but troubled brother, Carl. Carl was intellectually and athletically gifted, but he was a truly serious problem in the neighborhood, as he would be elsewhere for other neighborhoods and his younger brother in later years. When only thirteen, Carl was sent to a juvenile home. Under California law his family was required to provide part of his upkeep, and his mother on one occasion failed to send the money. Laura was hoarding pennies for Barbara's music lessons. The Floods avoided a penalty for missing the payment only because Harold Wilson, a *black* probation officer and surely an "enforcer" in the sense that Flood used the term, heard about the problem from young Curtis and used his connections at city hall on the family's behalf.[10]

8. Dorothy W. Pitts, *A Special Place for People: The DeFremery Story,* 60–61.
9. The exception was Bill Patterson, a recreation director at DeFremery then (and Oakland recreation director later, as well as a political force in the city).
10. Harold Wilson, interview, Oakland, June 2, 1998.

Harold Wilson and Curt Flood had met earlier when the boy, ten years old, had his first and only scrape with the law. Following misguided suggestions from Carl, young Curtis had found a parked truck with the keys in the ignition and, after nervously "driving" it two blocks, lost control and plowed into a car parked at the curb. Quickly collared by the police and locked up that night, Flood, by his own account, began to question his readiness to listen to his brother and to take risks for a bit of fun. He also said that the next morning when his parents came to get him (and Carl, who had stolen the bike that sent him to juvenile detention), "I banished bravado forever." Curiously, except that he was developing a foundation for his life's later decisions, he blamed the "whole goddamned environment" for this evidence of his own childish folly. Flood portrayed himself as a victim, but somehow he recognized that he would have to find more constructive means of impressing his family and his neighborhood. Somehow he could hold two conflicting ideas in his head simultaneously: deterministically blaming his problems on the environment while acknowledging that he could employ his will and talents to overcome them.[11]

In fact, he had already found much more constructive means of favorably impressing both his family and his neighborhood. His brother Herman led the way: when Curtis was only two and a half years old, Herman carried the little boy two blocks to Poplar Street Park, where he could watch his older brothers play baseball and try to copy their swings. A few years later at age six or seven (in his memoir, Flood did not recall which), young Curtis discovered that he "could outrun any kid on the block," and a few years after that he found, and would say, if a bit immodestly, that he "could catch and throw a ball as expertly as boys twice my age. I was precociously coordinated and mightily impressed [with myself]." So he played baseball whenever the opportunity presented, hoping to improve his swing, in large part because he hoped to be almost as good as his taller, stronger brother, Carl, "the only better athlete in the immediate vicinity." It was not that young Flood really believed he could match Carl's ability—he was too small for that—but he had internalized his parents' message to strive for success, and that he did. His intensity, then, while not especially unusual, may be viewed as a sign that Flood, if only because he would always be smaller than his fellow athletes, would find himself consumed by a need to prove himself,

11. Flood, *The Way It Is,* 22.

and not just on the playing field. But beyond these positive characteristics lay Flood's personality. He wanted to be liked, and he was. He looked vulnerable, and he was. He was able to charm, and he did. Throughout his life he had an almost magical ability to attract and sustain warm, close, long-term relationships with men and women alike, all of them ready to give freely of themselves, but few if any asking anything of him in return.

Long before Flood's many other talents were developed, baseball emerged as his very breath of life. With Carl and Herman he walked the few blocks to neighboring Emeryville and sneaked into the ballpark of the minor-league Oakland Oaks (of the Pacific Coast League). There, in the hours before the game, the three boys would take in the smell of hot dogs and roasting peanuts, gaze longingly at the neatly manicured grass, the countless sharply painted rows of seats, and the colorful logo-emblazoned uniforms, and hope no one noticed them: if they escaped attention, then they could watch the game without paying for tickets.

Young Curtis was mesmerized by these visits to the Oakland Oaks' ballpark. One visit and he knew he wanted to be a professional baseball player, presumably playing for the Oaks. And his parents did as much as they could to help. They gave him a glove, a cap, and other essential pieces of baseball equipment every Christmas, and for several summers they sent him to a baseball camp. Then, too, when he was only an adolescent but playing American Legion baseball away from Oakland, they found money for his hotel rooms and food so he could compete in those cities and towns. That their efforts on his behalf belie his reports of their impoverished state goes without saying.

Flood was just nine years old when he joined Carl, a pitcher for Junior's Sweet Shop team, in a police-sponsored midget league. He was probably the smallest player, he recalled; that meant that he had to try the hardest. He hoped that if he did so baseball might be his ticket to the better life on the other side of San Pablo Avenue, playing for the Oaks. He was not thinking as yet of the major leagues. That would have amounted to wishful thinking or ignorance—it was not until three months after his ninth birthday that the first black man, Jackie Robinson, was given a chance to play in the big leagues. But as a boy and a teen, Curt, as he was known first at nearby Poplar Street Park, then at the larger Bushrod Park two miles away where Junior's Sweet Shop played, was favored by fortune. George Powles (pronounced Poles), the brilliant baseball and basketball coach at nearby McClymonds High School who also managed two national-champion American Legion teams, coached midget-league players such as Flood after his day job ended.[12]

Flood would never forget what he and numerous other young athletes in West Oakland owed Powles. In later years he would reel off the names of numerous young players Powles had coached—among them Joe Morgan, Frank Robinson, his close friend Vada Pinson of the Cincinnati Reds and, eventually, the Cardinals, and Billy Martin of the New York Yankees. Two of them—Morgan and Robinson—would enter baseball's Hall of Fame. And there were other men in other sports—the Boston Celtics' Bill Russell, and National Football League superstars Ollie Matson and John Brodie—whom Powles had helped as well.

Coach Powles taught technique and he taught theory, but he also gave readily of his time and displayed a warm concern for his players. Many years later, Flood recalled that during winter's long nights Powles would hit him grounders on McClymonds High School's hardwood basketball floor, all the while yelling at him, "Stay down! Stay down! Keep your butt down! You're not keeping your eye on the ball! Keep your hands out in front where you can see the ball go into the glove! Soft hands! Glide into it! Anticipate! Don't fight it! Let it happen naturally!" And there was more to Powles' work with Flood than coaching him how to field properly. He was a surrogate father. He gave Flood confidence, he taught him about people, and, hardly least, as Flood recalled, he "would caution me to get my homework done, after which he would say: 'Same time tomorrow.'"

That was only part of a story Flood would tell very fondly but also to make a point, if one at variance with his condemnation of the ghetto in which he had lived. Powles was white; most of the young men he fed into professional baseball and other professional sports as well were black. Flood found Powles an exception among whites: "The beauty . . . was that you did not have to adulterate your blackness to win his confidence and approval." Flood seemingly meant that Powles did not judge on the basis of color; his judgments were based solely on performance. The coach, Flood added, "neither preached nor patronized. He emitted none of the smog of the dogooder embarked on a salvage operation." When after games Powles "brought the whole gang of ragamuffins to his pleasant home (a palace!) to plunder his wife's refrigerator," he never tried to inspire in them glimpses of a larger life: "it was just kids in for ice

12. Belth, *Stepping Up.*

cream and cookies." Why Flood suggests that a coach should avoid inspiring young men, a concept that intuitively seems most appropriate, he does not say. Also, if Powles was an exception among the whites that Flood knew, might not there have been other whites he had not met who were of the same caliber? In fact, as shall be seen, he would come to know other exceptions as well. The specifics of Flood's endorsement of Powles point up a problem that recurs in his life' story: what he condemns in general he praises in the particular.

From Flood's first year at Bushrod Park, Powles watched him closely. Years later the coach told a sportswriter, "Even as a kid he had power. His small size fooled people." He also noted that the young man had always been poised and articulate, and said that even then he thought Flood might go places. What position he might play, however, was unclear until his mother offered a nudge. One day while her son was behind the plate as a catcher, Curt was hit on the wrist by a foul ball, and she screamed at Powles that unless he played Curtis in a different position she would forbid him playing at all. So Flood temporarily became an infielder. But it soon become evident to Powles that Flood was so quick that he should play center field permanently.

Of course, not every minute of Flood's time revolved around baseball, and nearby Poplar Street Park was no longer the primary place where he played ball. When he was not doing school work, helping with household chores, or earning money painting neighbors' porches, he was coupling baseball with powerful lessons for a life well and properly lived, learned from a larger arena—the DeFremery Recreation Center a few blocks farther from his house.[13]

DeFremery was more than a large, well-equipped recreation center; it was Oakland's successful answer to the great in-migration of southern blacks during the war, and, for students at McClymonds at least, it provided guidance, without which their aspirations would be limited. At DeFremery teenagers found an opportunity to engage in well-supervised sports, including swimming. They also found classes ranging from dancing to art, drama, and rhetoric, and recreation directors who seemed always ready to help adolescents with any interest in preparing for college or job interviews. But these mentors taught other lessons that were valuable as well. Years later Bill Russell recalled that Bill Patterson, then

---

13. Flood to Bill Patterson, April 6, 1988, regarding the DeFremery Historical Research Project, letter in author's possession.

a part-time recreation director attending California State University in San Francisco, taught him the art of transforming a potential fistfight into a peaceful exchange. For his part, Flood recalled Patterson as the director who "taught me how to dance; maybe he taught me how not to dance." Surely more seriously, if perhaps immodestly, he recalled that Patterson quickly recognized Flood's varied talents—that he was not only articulate but eloquent at times, that he could draw, that he could write poetry, and that he could play the guitar; in fact, he could do anything he worked at— and the recreation director had given him special attention. Almost daily Patterson had taped Flood's voice, listened to it with him, and coached him to speak more clearly and grammatically. Then, too, he all but forced Flood to put on a shirt and tie before they attended church. And always, too, Patterson discussed baseball strategy, play at its various positions, and teamwork with his teenage protégé. Also, he encouraged Flood to dream, to work hard, and to use his brains rather than to fight, but in any case to stand firm for his beliefs.[14]

One day Flood would acknowledge his debt to McClymonds High School (although he played longer for Oakland Technical) because Powles coached there and his good friend Vada Pinson, his hero Frank Robinson, and many other notable sports stars played there. He also commended DeFremery, including in his commendation his only refer- ence to Patterson: "Many accomplished men came from . . . DeFre- mery," he wrote. "Bill and other recreation leaders were responsible for that. We were fortunate to have men . . . who were sincerely interested in the welfare of youth and saw to it that you went on to achieve great things in life." They had the "patience to take time out and help channel the energies of myself and many other young people years ago at DeFremery Center." Except for such men, "I would have easily become just another victim of the meanness of the streets."[15]

The influence of DeFremery's staff in strengthening the skills and self- esteem of West Oakland's teenagers, in socializing and polishing them and readying them for the larger world ahead, can hardly be exagger- ated. But in Flood's case, as with other lives DeFremery constructively impacted, there was a seed to be nurtured. He was an appealing boy. Like his siblings, he had his mother's soft, disarming, even melodious

14. Pitts, *A Special Place for People*, 60–61.
15. Flood's letter to Bill Patterson of April 6, 1988, stresses the debt he owed both him and DeFremery. Unfortunately, he nowhere mentions the debt, no less great, that he owed Patterson for his help in later years when he was down and out.

voice, and both Patterson and Powles noted that he was "very easy in meeting people." Understandably, then, both men personally encouraged Flood, making certain that he had opportunities to burnish his skills, confidence, and self-esteem.[16]

When Flood was only ten and still playing for Junior's Sweet Shop, Powles picked him to be the mascot and batboy of the powerful Bill Erwin Post American Legion team he coached, and gave him an opportunity before home games to show off his budding skills. At first Flood caught pitchers during warm-ups. After that, he was able to demonstrate his prowess gathering up grounders in the infield, and still later he patrolled center field. Twenty years later Powles told *Sports Illustrated,* "We'd put on a little show with him, because the customers couldn't help noticing the little guy and how clever he was. We gave him the nickname Flash—you know Flash Flood. But the name never stuck (thank goodness)." Even so, for Flood the pleasant memories did stick. He loved the attention. He recalled later, "The applause warmed me. If I had ever been short of self-esteem, the problem disappeared in the recognition I got for doing something socially acceptable and doing it well." Why not? Unfortunately, Flood's need for applause to sustain his self-esteem, while natural in some degree, would become absolutely essential to his success. Conversely, should he make a significant error on stage, he would not readily recover, if he recovered at all.

By adolescence baseball had become an obsession for young Flood. The only exception, if that, was his desire to sketch and paint. His interest, early kindled by his father, became a passion after he met Jim Chambers, the young, outspoken white art teacher the Board of Education had sent to West Oakland's Herbert Hoover Junior High School after the war. In later years, Flood would describe Chambers as "fervently unorthodox," appalled by "pomposity, inhumanity, and pretension, an illuminating figure who taught me art not as technique alone but as one of the great resources of the human spirit." Flood further recalled that Chambers awakened his "sensibilities" to life as well as to art, even valuing rather than ignoring his blackness. What this last part about not ignoring his blackness meant Flood did not explain, but obviously he and Chambers understood one another, as they kept in close touch for at least a decade, discussing the most intimate subjects. And most important, one day Chambers would introduce his former student

16. Bill Patterson, interviews, Oakland, 1998–2006.

to a married couple whose friendship would greatly influence Flood's life thereafter.

Although Flood continuously broadened and burnished his artistic talents, baseball was his life. Except for a few hours taking small jobs to put some change in his jeans, doing enough school work to get by, and pursuing girls, he played baseball at every opportunity he had, and that meant year-round in Oakland's usually mild climate. Sometimes he played the outfield with other talented teenagers such as Vada Pinson. Increasingly, both men played alongside the larger, older (by three years) Frank Robinson, who was then and later a more powerful hitter. Flood later recalled, "I did not hit the ball as hard as Frank Robinson, and I was not as fleet as Vada, but I had not yet seen a team for which I could not play."[17]

It was true; Powles, his coach during his single year at McClymonds, knew it. So did Sam Bercovich, who with two brothers ran E. Bercovich and Sons, a furniture business that sponsored the Bill Erwin American Legion Post junior team, a club in the semi-pro Alameda Winter League, and teams in other sports. Bercovich first saw Flood when he was ten and amazing everyone with his pregame fielding prowess as the Erwin Post team's mascot. Thereafter, he kept a close eye on the boy. Flood impressed him with his solid skills as a player, but also with his very courteous manners, gracious nature, and artistic talent. So Bercovich was eager to help when Powles informed him in 1954 that he wanted Flood to play for the Bill Erwin Post, but that acquiring Flood posed a problem. American Legion teams were organized by school district, and Flood lived in a district that belonged to a different legion post. He could transfer to Oakland Technical High School within the Erwin Post's sector only by moving in with a sister, Barbara. Fortunately, she was very fond of him. She also was in need of a babysitter since she was separated from her husband. But her house was too far from school to walk, and he would need a part-time job.[18]

Bercovich had a ready answer. He was then watching Flood play for his E. Bercovich and Sons team in the Alameda Winter League, where

17. William Leggett, "Curt Flood of St. Louis: Baseball's Best Centerfielder," 21.

18. Reports concerning the year that Flood became a regular and his status with the team vary depending on the source. According to Powles (in William Leggett, "Curt Flood of St. Louis: Baseball's Best Centerfielder," 21), Flood was team captain by 1955, suggesting that he was a regular by then, if not a year earlier when he was just sixteen, while the *Oakland Tribune*, January 27, 1956, says he was a regular at age fourteen.

Flood was more than holding his own with veterans from the minor-league San Francisco Seals and Seattle Rainiers. He was swatting the ball to all fields, often for distance. Moreover, he was "a mighty fine boy." Bercovich told Powles to inform Flood that he would give him a job in the family's store and buy him a bicycle to ride to school if he would play for the Bill Erwin Post in the summers following his sopho-more and junior years of high school.

Of course, Flood agreed to play for the Bill Erwin Post, move in with his sister, and work at Bercovich's furniture store. He acknowledged some qualms about leaving his good friend Vada Pinson behind at McClymonds and hoped that someday they would play on the same team again, but he knew he must follow where his coach and mentor wanted him. Powles, along with Patterson and Bercovich, was now Flood's surrogate father. Powles encouraged Flood and helped him along his career path, but he also advised him to be realistic about his prospects as a major-leaguer. Two years earlier he had warned Flood of the difficulties and disappointments he would almost certainly face as a small (only about 5'6" and 140 pounds) black man seeking a professional baseball career. But Flood had met every test to date. He had even grown. By the time the Bill Erwin Post called, he was 5'8" and apparently had put on weight, although no one thought it necessary to weigh him, so reports of how much he had gained varied with the observer. What-ever the truth of the matter, Flood had solid upper-body strength and in the small parks where he played could hit for distance as well as average. Whether he was strong enough to play baseball in major-league parks, clearly his goal, remained to be seen. But Powles and Bercovich were thrilled with Flood's play that summer of 1954. Batting for average, laying down a bunt when called upon, and hitting the cut-off man, he displayed skills that clearly proved their decision to lure him in had been wise, and he attracted a few Oakland sportswriters looking for a "local boy shows promise" story. Powles was outspoken when discussing Flood, but Bercovich was positively effusive. He told all who would listen that the "kid could do everything. He hits to all fields and with all kinds of pitch-ing. He can field like an angel, throw like a Willie Mays, and run bases with the savvy of an old-timer." He added that Flood was very "artistic" and was learning to "dress" windows at the furniture store. He did not mention that he had become yet another surrogate father to the young man, that he often invited Flood to his home, and that he encouraged

Flood's artistic talents. And he did not say, obviously because he did not know as yet, that he would remember Flood more fondly than any other youngster who had ever played for him, that he would help him early in his career and in his time of need later, and that he would turn a room in his home into a memorial to his career and life.[19]

In 1954 Flood hit .440 for Bercovich's American Legion team, but he really came alive at the bat the following summer. Perhaps the Erwin team strengthened his confidence when it named him its captain for 1955; perhaps, too, he hit for a greater average because he felt more comfortable fielding when Powles moved him permanently from third base to center field, but Flood batted a notable .620 in twenty-seven games that season and hit nine home runs, five triples, and a dozen doubles. Suddenly he was a local celebrity. One sportswriter glowed that "many fans," remembering he had been the team's mascot and batboy at age ten, "are drooling over Curt Flood today." So, too, he reported, were scouts from "at least six" major-league clubs. In fact, however, the sportswriter was dreaming when he wrote in January 1956 that the scouts were waiting breathlessly for Flood's high school graduation at the month's end so that under Major League Baseball's rules they could sign him to a contract—going so far as to say that one of them had tagged the young center fielder as a future Willie Mays.[20]

With one exception, the scouts who saw Flood play had come and gone. They had turned up in serious numbers three years before to scout the Erwin team because of Frank Robinson. As for Flood, they admired his hitting and fielding, but they believed that he was too small for the majors. Only Bobby Mattick, who scouted for the Cincinnati Reds and would eventually sign Flood, remained to watch him play game after game, and that was because he lived nearby. Many years later Mattick would say that he could not remember "any scouts hiding in the bushes" and watching Flood in January 1956. He had no competition as he waited for Flood to graduate so that he could consummate negotiations with him and his parents. Mattick alone saw in Flood qualities that might well compensate for his slight size: at the very least, intensity, intelligence, and determination. And Flood was aware that

19. *Oakland Tribune,* January 27, 1956; my visits to Bercovich's home in Oakland, California, 1998–2002.

20. *Oakland Tribune,* January 27, 1956.

other scouts had turned their backs on him because they thought he was too small: in his memoir he jested that perhaps Mattick "thought I would grow."[21]

Perhaps, although Flood had just passed his eighteenth birthday, and there was no reason to believe that he would grow much more. But Mattick had seen Flood play since he signed Frank Robinson, and he had watched him hit the ball for distance often enough to recognize that while Flood was not big, he was stronger than he at first appeared. He had also seen that Flood could field superbly. In congratulating Mattick later, one sportswriter said that he "didn't see only size. He saw speed, aggressiveness, and an instinct for the ball that reminded him of a beagle sniffing his prey." These were, of course, the characteristics that had reminded Bercovich and other observers of Willie Mays, and always would. But Mattick also saw that Flood was anxious to please, that he worked hard at improving his skills, and, not least, that he was "a nice kid" from a nice family. Mattick knew. He had visited the Flood home on several evenings, talking to his parents and discussing his future. Later, Mattick recalled that a bond was formed. But even if other clubs had wanted Flood, he probably would have signed with Mattick and Cincinnati; he dreamed of playing once again with Frank Robinson, who was already in the Reds' fold.[22]

On January 30, 1956, just three days after Flood graduated from high school, Mattick offered him a salary of $4,000 to join the Cincinnati Reds organization. And Flood signed. According to a report in the *Oakland Tribune,* Mattick said that he offered Flood a bonus, but that "the boy decided against it." However, such an offer seems unlikely: Mattick would have known that it was not in Flood's best interests to accept a bonus. Major League Baseball required that a "bonus baby" remain on the roster of the big-league club that signed him for at least two years. That meant Flood would ride the bench; he would not get the coaching and gradual development of his skills and confidence that Mattick knew a raw prospect needed. That development was to be found in the minor leagues. Mattick may have told Flood that the Reds were unlikely to send him to the bottom of the minors; he would almost certainly be offered an opportunity to play for a Class B farm club, a few steps up from the lowest-level minor leagues. And Flood, probably after consult-

21. Bobby Mattick, telephone interview, February 28, 1999.
22. Ibid.

ing Powles and Bercovich, and perhaps even Patterson, found that arrangement acceptable. Money was money, whether as a bonus or a salary. Furthermore, he knew that Frank Robinson, his idol, had started in Class C, a rung below B, and had grown into a likely member of the Reds' major-league roster for the coming season. That example was enough to convince Flood that he would get a serious chance to play professional baseball.[23]

Spring training was still a month away, and Flood had time to thank the many people who had helped him get his chance. That included his parents, of course, who had helped finance his development and had given him the time free of work to perfect his skills. That also meant Harold Wilson, the probation officer who interceded for his mother when she ran into problems with the juvenile authorities regarding Carl. And it meant Bill Patterson and the rest of the DeFremery family that pointed out life's choices—the juvenile home on one side of the street, and school, church, and a future of various constructive options on the other. It also meant men who were white and from outside Flood's West Oakland "ghetto": George Powles, his coach; Jim Chambers, his art teacher; Sam Bercovich, the fatherly furniture company owner and ball club sponsor who made it possible for him to play for the Bill Erwin American Legion Post team and attract notice; and Bobby Mattick, who took a chance that his overpowering drive to succeed would readily compensate for his lack of size. Doubtless there were others Flood also specifically thanked that February for helping him along the road to the major leagues, but obviously he owed a community much larger than the "ghetto" in which he grew up. He owed a village, black and white, one that Frank Robinson was heard to recall, if curiously, as "interracial" Oakland.[24]

23. *Oakland Tribune*, January 31, 1956.
24. Frank Robinson, interview, Phoenix, mid-October 1998.

II

Alone among the Peckerwoods

In late February 1956 Curt Flood peered through the window next to his seat on the Boeing airliner sitting on the tarmac at Oakland's Metropolitan International Airport. He would be gone for many months, and he wanted one more look at his mother, brothers, sisters, and surrogate family—George Powles, Bill Patterson, Jim Chambers, Bobby Mattick, and Sam Bercovich. Each in various ways had nurtured him, honed his talents and manners, and tried to prepare him for the world outside Oakland. "Tried" is the operative word because no one could prepare an eighteen-year-old, much less a black eighteen-year-old, for what he would find in the outside world. Even so, because of his mentors as well as his own innate talent, in ten hours he would land in Tampa, Florida, almost three thousand miles away, and soon after arrive at the Cincinnati Reds spring training camp.[1]

Flood was seldom if ever bored during the long flight. He read and read again the fancy brochure the Reds had mailed him. Complete with pictures, it readily suggested baseball heaven. Flood could see himself residing at the Reds-leased Floridian Hotel pictured in the brochure. There he would mix with the team's veterans, including Frank Robinson. Perhaps he dreamed that he and Frank would room together, paint the town in the evenings, and just possibly they would end spring camp taking the train north to the majors and opening the regular season as teammates. But there must have been times during the lengthy trip when Flood could not help but reflect on a less romantic side of his prospects in Florida and after. He was not built like Robinson, who was bigger and stronger, and despite many years playing American Legion ball in Oakland and other towns and cities as far away as the Midwest,

---

1. Rickie Riley, interviews, 1998–2006; Bobby Mattick, telephone interview, February 28, 1999; Flood, *The Way It Is,* 33.

he lacked Robinson's experience on the field and off. He was, in fact, just a teenager, away from home unchaperoned and unprotected for the first time, and at some point during his flight he must have wondered if his romantic dreams squared with what he would find. But he does not record any anxieties. Later, he recalled himself as "sophisticated" as he started on a wonderful adventure.[2]

In the Tampa airport Flood's sophistication and expectations were to meet their first real test: the harsh reality of segregation, commonly known as Jim Crow. He had heard of Jim Crow before, but although he later called West Oakland a ghetto, he then viewed segregation and the burgeoning Civil Rights movement as abstractions with little import for his own life. This perspective, although in some respects curious, is understandable. When his American Legion team played in other cities in California or in other regions of the country, the black players were well protected by their coaches cum chaperons from the "separate but [not] equal" practices and various other forms of discrimination they might find. Now, walking into the baggage section at the Tampa airport alone, he saw separate water fountains, one marked "white," the other "colored." For the first time he came face to face with the harsh reality of the South's laws and customs, and he was shocked. But he was not yet aware of Jim Crow's full extent. He thought that however evil and dispiriting the scene in the baggage room, it was not the Reds' spring training camp. Still an innocent, he reminded himself that he was just passing through the airport. He would be staying at the Floridian with the other players. There would be no problem there. Or so he thought.

Of course the Reds' hotel had no reservation for him. Indeed, the desk clerk turned white or, as Flood put it, "whitely," when asked the question. After recovering from his shock, the clerk looked at Flood's new suit and asked, "You with the team?" When Flood very proudly acknowledged that he was, the clerk handed him over to a black porter, who took him to a side door, waved him into a cab, and told the black driver, "Ma Felder's." The taxi deposited Flood at Ma Felder's boardinghouse almost five miles outside Tampa, duly segregated from his white "comrades" at the Floridian, and there he lived for the duration of the Reds' training camp. Later, he asserted that he felt upon arriving at the

---

2. Flood, *The Way It Is,* 34ff. A January 31, 1956, story in the *Oakland Tribune* seems to claim that Flood had a guarantee from the Reds that he would not start the season any lower than Class B in the minor leagues.

boardinghouse that the white man had sent him offstage until his athletic talents were required. He recalled being bitter: "Officially and for the duration, I was a nigger." He also remembered other, more complicated feelings upon entering Ma Felder's house. Her other "guests," all black players, welcomed him with "thoughtful grins and soft handshakes." So "I choked back my revelations about the drinking fountains and the white hotel." Somehow, if perhaps at odds with his stated ignorance of segregation, he understood the plight of the men greeting him. He saw "the scars in their eyes." He saw them, in a sense that might remind one of Shakespeare's Henry V at Agincourt, as "aging gladiators weeping over one another's wounds." And he recalled, with obvious sentimentality, that he had felt "bound to them in the outraged tenderness of brotherhood." At the same time he recognized that he must prepare "to fight them for my own survival." Baseball was a team game, to be sure, and it required cooperation, but he had no illusions about the difficulty of achieving his dream of going to the major leagues: the road to Cincinnati's Crosley Field flowed through a veritable Darwinian jungle of tough competition. He must fight off the "trembling numbness" that seized him upon entering Ma Felder's. He must pull himself together or his professional career would not get off the ground.

Flood had reason to worry. True, many players did. But he was untested and had to perform well if he hoped to take the train north to the majors that spring, or even, perhaps, if he wanted to assure himself of ending up with a Class B or higher minor-league club. Although he would one day report that he had "won mention in a few newspaper stories" during spring training and that he was "clearly the best fielder on the squad," it was obvious to key observers that he was not ready for major-league pitching. Almost a decade later, *Sport* magazine's Al Stump reported that when Flood was used by Cincinnati manager Birdie Tebbetts in exhibition games, he "kept lunging for the outside curve and kept striking out." His report was echoed by another writer: "Birdie Tebbetts . . . looked him over, said a few kind words like: 'I don't recall seeing an 18-year-old, who has the poise of Flood,' [then] sent him out to see the baseball world, beginning with High Point–Thomasville in the Class B Carolina League."[3]

In point of fact, Flood was first sent to the Reds' minor-league training camp at Douglas, Georgia. There, at a former air base, several hundred

3. Al Stump, "Curt Flood in the Midnight League," 79.

candidates for Cincinnati's farm clubs were lodged in barracks, awakened at 7 a.m. with reveille, and marshaled throughout the day as if they were army recruits in basic training. But from dusk to dawn Flood and the other black players found themselves on their own. They bunked in a separate barracks, of course, but Flood had to admit that their segregation, however demeaning, brought with it some benefits that had helped him make do in Tampa. Boarding at Ma Felder's, black players had come and gone in the evenings free of the curfew that limited the hours of their white counterparts, and they had seized that opportunity to drink at the local nightspots. According to Frank Robinson, commenting forty-odd years later, the black players could easily afford these nights out: the club supplied the essentials of room and board, they had some thirty dollars a week in expense money, and they did not drink very much. But his pleasure on those nights—as undoubtedly was Flood's—was limited in one vital respect, Robinson recalled: he missed mixing with his white peers. But he did not emphasize this form of segregation. Like (possibly) every other black player except Flood, Robinson did not expect to socialize with white players. Furthermore, he had a tough skin and a go-along-to-get-along attitude, pluses that Flood lacked. Whether it was these differences in their native temperaments and experiences, different interests outside of baseball, or a difference in status—Robinson was headed for the major leagues at spring training's end, Flood for the minor leagues—the "veteran" did not socialize with his teammate of one year at McClymonds High School. Although Robinson's aloofness is understandable, it could not help but embitter Flood, who idolized him and expected to be mentored by him. That, coupled with his segregation at Tampa and, realistically, his newly awakened anxieties about his future as a baseball player, help to explain why Flood said he found his only comfort in Tampa was that being "with a major league club . . . kind of whitened me a little bit."

Douglas, Flood's interim stop, was no better. In Georgia, the only compensation for being a black man was that "white overseers did not enter the black neighborhood, much less patrol its bars." Even that, however, was a dubious benefit as the taverns sold cheap bootlegged moonshine and were frequented by prostitutes more often diseased than not. Fortunately, Flood knew, he would soon be headed to a classier city. Some players, black and white, would be sent to a lowly Class D league; he was headed for the Reds' club in High Point–Thomasville, North Carolina, in the Class B Carolina League. Rightly or wrongly, he attributed his assignment to the strong impression that his hard work and quality of play had made at Douglas, even though it was reported that the contract he had signed included a guarantee that he would start no lower than at Class B. Whatever the truth of the matter Flood saw a season with the Hi-Toms as a reward for his superb training camp, and he expected to find a "nice apartment" in High Point, to "establish himself in the community," and, much like Frank Robinson, to proceed in a year or two to "the fame and riches that awaited" him. He meant, of course, the major-league Reds. The likelihood, even the possibility, that racial prejudice might be an acute problem in the North Carolina piedmont, he did not recall giving a minute's thought as he traveled a bus northeast. Ahead he saw certain success in High Point–Thomasville, followed by a climb in a year or two to the majors. Then he would return to those cities a hero, with girls waving at him, substantial citizens slapping him warmly on the back, and the mayor asking him to lunch and to dedicate a new library, even perhaps to endow a hospital wing. Then, too, when he returned as a heroic figure, a great success in the major leagues, he would give every child in High Point and Thomasville a ride in his new Rolls-Royce.

Whether Flood actually entertained such fantasies as his bus drove through the southern pines to hilly North Carolina is at least questionable. How could he? Even if, as he later claimed, there had been little mention among his peers or family of segregation or of *Brown*, Rosa Parks, and Martin Luther King, Flood had seen Jim Crow at first hand in Florida and Georgia. And if his real, personal experiences with segregation in those southern states did not offer a sufficient education, then he must have heard many dark stories from the veterans at Ma Felder's and in Douglas about their demeaning experiences, not only in the South, but as far west as Arizona and as far north as Utah. Perhaps even the usually aloof Robinson, who had spent a year in South Carolina, offered Flood a vision of the racism he would find in towns like High Point and Thomasville. Somehow, though, Flood was unprepared for the shrill expressions of racism and the segregated facilities he would find in his new home.

High Point, where Flood would actually live and play ball—at Finch Field, named after the city's leading family, owners of the nearby Thomasville Furniture Company—was clearly a southern city, but it was not one of the racist hell-holes to be found in Mississippi or Alabama. That is, no one was lynched there. But not even a semblance of racial equality, much less a readiness to judge blacks fairly, existed in High

Point or North Carolina in general. The state's legislature had approved the "Southern Manifesto" symbolizing its determination to resist *Brown v. Board*'s order to desegregate its schools and, it was feared, eventually move toward racially equal policies in every aspect of public life. Yet even though North Carolina's racism was similar in some respects to that of the Deep South, the racism of High Point was, as locals said, more "civil" than that nearer the coast. There were reasons, of course: the proportion of blacks to whites was smaller than elsewhere in the state or the Deep South, and therefore blacks were seen as less threatening; however, equally important, if not more so, High Point was more than just a small town in the North Carolina piedmont.[4]

Founded in 1856 at a junction where a road linked what is now Winston-Salem with Fayetteville, and where a new railroad linked Goldsboro and Greensboro, High Point soon had a furniture factory. In a matter of twenty years the city became the site of the Southern Furniture Market. After that, the local elite, especially furniture men, began to worry about the city's image. Those concerns increased measurably after 1921 when the city became the location of the International Home Furnishings Center and began receiving visitors from every state and, soon enough, 110 countries. For High Point's leaders, then, protecting the city's image as a stable and friendly place required that they handle their racial problems in a civil, moderate manner, hemming and hawing, but giving ground when integrationist pressure became too strong to sensibly resist, and sometimes even when that pressure was not apparent. Blacks had voted for many years, a sharp contrast to the situation in most of the South where they were banned from the polls. Though they rarely influenced elections, in 1943 blacks did help elect a mayor who promptly rewarded them by appointing two black police officers. Sometimes even the slightest bit of pressure brought other racial progress. In 1954 two black doctors demanded the right to play golf at a public course, and before long that course became the second in the state to be integrated, if with the "understanding" that only black professionals would ask to play. Class and race tended to intersect in High Point–Thomasville to lessen or increase divisiveness or acceptance. Unfortunately for Flood, he would arrive at a point in time, after *Brown* II, when the Supreme Court insisted on desegregation of the country's schools in a clumsy manner ("with all deliberate speed") and

4. William H. Chafe, *Civilities and Civil Rights*, 67ff.

the issue of complying or resisting, and by what means, was raising racial divisiveness to a higher level than the city and the state had seen for many years.[5]

In April 1955, the North Carolina legislature, hoping to escape a lawsuit against the state that might force its school systems to desegregate, enacted a Pupil Placement Act that cities such as High Point could use as a basis to maintain racially separate schools while concealing that race was the criterion for the separation. Recognizing the legislature's obvious attempt to circumvent *Brown,* that summer High Point's NAACP chapter submitted a petition asking for the admission of black students to the city's all-white public schools. When the petition was put before the school board, two Quaker members voted to admit blacks, but the majority rejected the petition. They said the time was not right; integration would threaten public order. It was one thing to let two black professionals play on a golf course; they were gentlemen much like the middle-class whites then on the course. It was a very different matter to make the city's poor white furniture, textile, and hosiery workers send their children to public schools with black children. It would rile them, a major problem for a city with an image to protect. Consequently, the board's majority finally asserted that segregated schools were essential, at least temporarily, to protect High Point's business interests from the disquiet the white working class or, as they were often called, "rednecks," might create if their children were forced to attend schools with blacks.[6]

Probably no one in High Point knew the local "rednecks" better than George Erath, then the business manager of the Hi-Toms, the city's minor-league baseball team and afterward the successful owner of a company specializing in wood veneers. He knew them as the poor, often illiterate working class, derisively named for the impact on their skin of the sun and wind when they were farmers plowing High Point's hinterland. He knew them also as descendants of the tough-talking, tobacco-chewing moonshiners who once built the first fast stock cars, and perhaps still did, to outrun the Treasury's "revenue men." He knew the "rednecks," or, as he sometimes called them, "crackers," if for no other reason than that their attendance at the Hi-Toms games was essential.

5. Ibid.

6. A cynical variation of this explanation is that High Point's business elites endorsed segregation as a tradeoff to the city's impoverished working class for not forming or joining unions. The Ku Klux Klan was infiltrated by the state and was not a threat. Neither, apparently, were the North Carolina Patriots (White Citizens Councils in North Carolina).

Though often so poor they could not or would not buy school lunches for their children, the "rednecks" somehow found dollars enough to buy most of the thousand tickets that the Hi-Toms needed to sell on any given day. They could not be ignored or slighted. Neither could the other clubs in the Carolina League ignore them, and for the same reason. Typically, however, these men, and at times their wives and children, screamed racial epithets. Although their shouts were directed primarily at visiting players, even so, Erath admitted, the downside of running a baseball team in High Point was listening to their ugly language spewed in varied accents throughout every game at home and away.[7]

The High Point "rednecks" and their counterparts, on the field and off, throughout the Carolina League would turn Flood's bus-ride fantasies upside down. He did not find himself living in a wonderful apartment and forming great friendships. He would not be cherished by the town, or treated respectfully by the Hi-Toms' manager, as he had expected. Flood's experience in High Point, as he describes it in his memoir, was miserable to say the least. But was it? Or to what extent? Was he not in some part a lonely, adolescent victim of his own naïveté? Was his personality such that he perhaps embellished the darker aspects of his "Adventures in the Bush" and ignored the brighter side, if only to fit his memoir's needs when, more than a decade later, he was challenging Major League Baseball?

Notably, in *The Way It Is* Flood does not mention the housing he was assigned. His mother, concerned about him because of his age, had phoned Erath and asked him to see that her boy had a decent place to live—almost certainly knowing it would be in a black section of High Point—including some warm motherly supervision if possible. Erath, in turn, asked some of the leading members of the black community to suggest homes. They pointed to Estelle Nelson's boardinghouse, and a good choice it was. The white-frame house was well kept, large, and had a substantial screened porch that provided a bit of escape from the summer's heat. Nicely located in a middle-class neighborhood, it may have offered better lodgings than any other Hi-Toms player had, excepting possibly those players who lived in the area throughout the year. Moreover, Mrs. Nelson, a kind schoolteacher, would treat Flood like he

7. Interviews with George Erath and *High Point Enterprise* sports editor Tom Berry, October 4, 1998, in High Point, North Carolina. Berry showed me Mrs. Nelson's boardinghouse and, like Erath, discussed life in High Point as he thought it had been in 1956.

was her son. Well aware that he could not eat out with his teammates after the evening games, she readied food for him and Bo Bossard, another black player who roomed with him, as well as for the Cuban Hi-Toms who lived there. Flood may also have benefited somewhat from the conversation at the dinner table of some of Mrs. Nelson's other boarders, all but two of them teachers, although they may not have appreciated his presence and that of the other ballplayers eating at the house. The two Cubans had eaten so much meat and chicken the year before that Mrs. Nelson had raised the weekly rent, from fifteen dollars to twenty. Of course, the raise worked no hardship on Flood with his relatively big salary of $4,000 a year. All in all, he should have made a point of blessing Mrs. Nelson when in later years he discussed his season in High Point. But that would have detracted from his portrait of himself as a victim, which of course in some very real ways he was.[8]

Flood, like every other black player in the South in those days, had no trouble detailing the racial slurs that rang out in a constant barrage at every field where he played, and there can be no doubt that the taunts left "enduring memories." Recalling the Hi-Toms' tour through the ballparks of North Carolina and southern Virginia, he noted, "Wherever we played in that league, at home or away, the stadiums resounded with 'nigger, eight-ball, jigaboo,' and other pleasantries." Sometimes, as Flood recalled, the litany of shrill racial epithets that streamed to his position in center field came not only from the "crackers" but also from a few "demoralized" blacks "who seemed to enjoy echoing their oppressors." After one "cracker" bawled out: "Move yo' ass, snowball," a "boozy voice" from the otherwise quiet Jim Crow stands would shout, as if attempting some semblance of equality, "Move yo' ass, snowball." Given such ranting, it is not to be wondered that during Flood's first months with the Hi-Toms, he did not know how to deal with the fans or even, at times, his teammates, many of whom were themselves piedmont "rednecks." He admits that at first he just took it. "During the early weeks of the season I used to break into tears as soon as I reached the safety of my room. I was too young for the ordeal. I wanted to be home. I wanted to talk to someone." Of course, he had someone he might have talked to about the slurs, Bo Bossard, his roommate, but Flood does not mention him. Of course, it was not Flood's style to discuss his problems with anyone other than family members. He

8. Erath and Berry, interviews, October 4, 1998.

was more likely to brood and play his guitar or pick up his sketch pad and pencils. As Bill White, a good friend among his future Cardinals' team-mates, would later comment, Flood was moody, introverted, and, for a baseball player of that era, well-read and mostly inclined to rely on him-self. "When Bob [Gibson, the Cardinals' All-Star pitcher in Flood's and White's years with the Cardinals] and I were reading the *Sporting News*, Curt was reading novels. We were listening to rock and blues, Curt was lis-tening to classical music. We tried to play the harmonica, Curt had mas-tered the guitar." If, as Flood said, he was playful in the dugout and clubhouse, for the most part he preferred his own company—and per-haps that of a woman—to his fellow Hi-Toms. So, perhaps it is understand-able that he was not inclined to discuss his problems with Bossard. But it is curious, and perhaps significant, that in his memoir he did not mention his roommate at all.[9]

Racist taunts from the stands were not the only headache for Flood while playing and residing "among the peckerwoods," and possibly not the most serious. That honor came in the form of separate but unequal facilities, which were to be found everywhere in the South. It was espe-cially troublesome for Flood that when the bus took the team to other towns on "day trips," he could not eat at restaurants with the others or use the restrooms. For him life riding the bus meant seeking food at a rear entrance, and urinating in a back alley, or, if on the highway, wait-ing for the driver to stop, then hiding from the traffic "as best I could while wetting a rear wheel." Whatever the form, segregated facilities were as disgusting in their way as taunts from the stands in the ballpark, and humiliating besides. They were, however, the law, which every black playing in the South had to accept if he hoped to climb to the majors. Some players, including Henry Aaron, born in Alabama and accustomed to Jim Crow, accepted it calmly; Bill White, who brought some college maturation to Danville (Virginia) in the Carolina League, at times roared back at his tormentors in the stands but otherwise awaited a more favorable chance to unseat Jim Crow; Frank Robinson, Flood's neighbor in Oakland, rebelled, if such is the right word, only by remaining in his room at night rather than sitting in the balcony of a seg-regated theater as required of blacks. In general, then, Flood's experi-ences in the Carolina League were typical for a black player in the South

9. *St. Louis Post-Dispatch,* January 28, 1997, reporting Flood's funeral.

and often elsewhere in the 1950s, and probably for some years after. What distinguished his reaction, as Jackie Robinson's biographer has argued, and even Flood eventually admitted, was his thin skin.[10]

Other than his unusual sensitivity and tendency to brood rather than discuss his problems with others, it would seem that Flood's experiences with Jim Crow stand out because fifteen years later, in the midst of his legal challenge to Major League Baseball, he wanted to strengthen his image as a victim. Not all his experiences were negative, however. He wrote to Jim Chambers, his former art teacher in Oakland and still a close friend, bragging about the women he dated. He noted that he did not have to chase women; they were "always scratching at my door." Of course, such braggadocio is understandable in an adolescent, but although Flood's letters discuss women only briefly, they gratuitously record more than notches in his belt: "I . . . expended rage in forbidden beds. I did not want to marry the peckerwood's sister." Presumably, by "forbidden beds" Flood meant the beds of white women. At the century's end at least one white woman in High Point still recalled his biracial taste in the female sex. She also recalled that Flood was "cocky" and often looked to the stands "with open arms" as if greeting one or more of his favored women. Indeed, she heard from another Hi-Tom she dated that endless women desired Flood's company. Flood's oldest sister, Rickie, agreed: "My brother did not chase women; they chased him." And Chambers readily understood. Women not only found Flood very handsome—his skin silky smooth, his face neatly and finely sculpted, his body compact and hard—but vulnerable, sending a message that he needed a good woman to take care of him. Why not? He could be as charming as any woman might wish.[11]

Flood's womanizing rings true as part of his life in High Point not only because more than one woman has testified to it, but because far from hiding it, he regarded these relationships with great pride and as one of the more important benefits of a player's life. His complaints about his manager, however, do not ring quite so true or fair. Alleging a discussion (of what he does not say) with Bert Haas, the Hi-Toms' manager, Flood recalled in his memoir fifteen years later, "The manager, whose name mercifully escapes me, made it clear that his life already was sufficiently

10. Jules Tygiel, *Baseball's Great Experiment: Jackie Robinson and His Legacy* (New York: Oxford University Press, 1997), 265–84 (esp. 283); Flood, *The Way It Is*, 18.

11. Joanne Black, interview in High Point, October 4, 1998; Connie Reilly (formerly Jones), interview, St. Louis, June 19, 2003.

difficult without contributions from me." It is a sad reflection on Flood that he should speak so harshly of a manager who said of him during the season: "Curt Flood has certainly come through wonderfully. He's been worth his weight in gold." It might be wondered, too, why Flood should have expected a manager with many years of major-league experience to pay serious attention to a rookie's "contributions." There is a possible explanation for his anger, however: he had wanted Haas to deal with his problems with his teammates. "I was entirely on my own," he lamented later.[12]

Flood's early complaints about his High Point teammates during the 1956 season were typical of those made by black players throughout the South in that pre–civil rights year. "Most of the players . . . would not talk to me when we were off the field," he complained in his 1971 memoir. This was probably true, and most likely it simply reflected southern racial mores, but it need not have. Flood was cocky and he was earning $800 a month, an amount that greatly exceeded the $350 a month that was the average for a Hi-Toms player, and his teammates probably resented the rookie's pay scale. Whatever the reason, though, Flood was probably right about his race being the defining factor. Other black players throughout the South faced the same problem; he just took it harder, doubtless because of his youth, inexperience, and the something-like-orneriness that he thought came from his mother. However, Flood's specific complaints alleged unusual racial abuse. He wrote later, "My teammates despised and rejected me as subhuman. I would gladly have sent them all to hell." Whether this charge was fair or not, and probably not, Flood often phoned his sister, Barbara, and his mother in those early days to inform them how unhappy he was. Precisely what they told him is not recorded, but given Laura Flood's well-known fighting spirit, he probably heard her insist that he not quit, that he fight back, in this case with his bat and glove. Those were his weapons. And just a few days into the season Flood himself recognized that self-pity was a dead end. He could not allow his teammates to ruin his career and life. He was, he told a sportswriter almost two decades later, Baptist-reared to believe "that persecution from the outside can be a measure of a man's inward strength." To that he added, "Pride was my resource. I solved my problem by playing my guts out." And so he did.[13]

12. Flood, *The Way It Is*, 38
13. Stump, "Midnight League," 79.

A little past the sixth week of the season Flood was batting .300 with 11 home runs, and, for such a short span of time, an exceptional 53 runs batted in. Sports pages flattered him. After one night's brilliant performance a *High Point Enterprise* sportswriter compared him favorably with the prior year's most valuable player, a Hi-Tom since departed to Class A Savannah. From that time forward, pictures of him became commonplace in the Thomasville and High Point newspapers, and accolades continued as his batting average soared and his feats in center field dazzled. By July 5, Flood topped the balloting for the league's All-Stars. As his batting average rose to .347 and his other statistics climbed accordingly, the Friend News Service labeled his play "brilliant." His manager, whose name he had said "mercifully escapes me," told the *Enterprise* that Flood "was invaluable on the base paths and there isn't a better defensive outfielder in Class B ball than that 18 year old kid," while twenty-three-year-old Joanne Perry, a white woman, yelled along with her friends: "Go Curt Go." Or such was her memory forty years later. "We had a lot of respect for him. He was such a gentleman," she recalled. If Flood was, properly, the beneficiary of such comments by midseason, and perhaps earlier, it is hardly to be wondered that Flood wrote his mother one day: "The home fans are swell to me"; it was the fans on the road that were on him all the time.[14]

Well before the summer's end Flood had a fan club in High Point, chiefly white women who passed him (and other players) messages through cracks in the dugout's wood-planked ceiling. Black fans were segregated in stands farther away. He had another fan club, too. Significantly, he posed for (unofficial) pictures with some of the teammates he later would write "despised and rejected" him as "subhuman." And he had another reason for pride as well: in September at Finch Field a local jeweler awarded him a watch as the "people's choice" on the Hi-Toms squad. The acclaim was appropriate. Flood ended the 1956 season batting .340 with 29 home runs and 128 runs batted in. In sum he may not have realized every element in his fantasies the previous spring when on his ride to High Point, but he could hardly have made a better beginning. And there was more to come.

Flood's almost miraculous year with the Hi-Toms was capped at season's end by his being named the Carolina League's most valuable player. But the honor almost turned tragic for him when the civic leaders of

14. Joanne Black, interview in High Point, October 5, 1998.

Thomasville and High Point scheduled a gala dinner at one of High Point's nicest downtown hotels to hand out the team's awards—unhappily, no one gave much thought to the fact that the hotel was segregated. According to Hi-Toms business manager George Erath, Flood understood the situation, but decided to get on the bus to the hotel that evening anyway. He did not explain, but apparently he intended to test segregation in High Point and its environs one last time. He had nothing to lose. Wearing his only suit, he took his seat in the team bus, and off it went. When the bus arrived and he got out, the doorman came over, blocked his path, and said, "Hey boy, where are you going? We don't serve no Nigras in here." It was hotel policy. Flood complained to his manager that as he was to be the primary honoree, he should be allowed to enter, but Haas said, "There's nothing I can do, I hope you don't mind." Then Haas volunteered to accept the award for him, but Flood told him where he could "stick it" and returned to the bus to wait for the gala to end.[15]

There Flood sat, fuming, the more so after one of "the guys" (suddenly a friend) brought him a program with his name listed for the big award, when the bus door opened and a well-dressed man stuck his head in and asked, "Curt, Curt Flood?" At that point, his anger reaching fever pitch, Flood snapped, "I'm already at the fucking back of the bus. What else do you want from me?" Much to his surprise, Flood heard the man yell back, "No, no, no," then identify himself as James Finch. However, it is more likely that it was James's brother, Tom. Tom Finch had done business with Sam Bercovich's furniture store in Oakland for some thirty years, and he had met Flood there when the boy was dressing windows and been impressed with his artistic talent, charm, and fluid speech. Perhaps advised by Bercovich that Flood was playing in High Point, or perhaps on his own—it is not clear—Tom Finch, one of the wealthy and powerful owners of the Thomasville Furniture Company, had sent Flood, anonymously, a 1956 Chevrolet to use during his time in High Point—some said he had also rented Flood an apartment. And the night of the gala he had heard that Flood was waiting on the team bus and decided to come get him. When Finch called out to him on the bus, Flood thought he heard this powerful man apologize for the town's bad manners, then he clearly heard himself asked to join Finch at his table,

15. Undated clipping from Joanne Black's scrapbook, High Point; "Tom Berry's Sunday Forum," *High Point Enterprise,* August 31, 1956, and February 2, 1997; Stump, "Midnight League," 79; Curt Flood and Kenneth Turan, "Outside-Outside: A Life That Changed Baseball," 18–19.

and together they walked "literally arm and arm" into the gala event. That was not the end of the matter, however. Although Finch was not listed on the program, he got up at the right moment and personally presented Flood his award. "He got up and began reading my stats," Flood recalled some forty years later, and Finch had added: "'Flood he did this, he did that, he won the league's most valuable player trophy.' Finally, he told those in the ballroom, 'he's the first Negro to eat in this goddamn restaurant.'" Having listened to those words, it is no wonder that Flood recalled that night in the hotel ballroom as the most thrilling he had ever known. It was a moment he would never forget. As he put it in later years, "I wish I had taped that. God almighty."[16]

However great Flood's memory of his MVP award and Tom Finch's grand gestures at the ceremony and before, it did not heal the hurt he had felt during the season. And the passing years—after his lawsuit failed, after his memoir was published, even after he had no agenda to pursue— did not heal his wounds. Forty years later, even as he recalled his MVP night, he spoke of an episode in Danville, Virginia, that he said revealed the hatred embedded in the system of segregation. The city, he began, had an ordinance that forbade whites and blacks from dressing in the same facility. So he had to dress between games of a doubleheader in a sun-drenched tin shack connected to the whites-only dressing room by a hole in the wall. Worse, when he threw his dirty uniform through the hole, the clubhouse boy picked it up with a stick, knowing who had worn it—and not wanting to touch it—then took it to a black-owned laundry two blocks away. By the time it was returned, Flood said, the rest of the team was on the field. He had to run out alone, humiliated. And he never forgot. Whatever the generosity of a Tom Finch, his gesture was an aberration. One man's generosity could not relieve, much less undo, the humiliation and hurt of the South's system of segregation.[17]

At first glance Flood's story sounds reasonable. Danville, Virginia, just north of the North Carolina state line, lay deep in the heart of tobacco country; it had witnessed the last cabinet meeting of the Confederacy, and it might have had the ordinance Flood mentions: it might have required that blacks and whites dress separately. But the evidence is to the contrary. In 1951, Danville featured the first black player in the Carolina League. Then, too, Bill White, who had played there earlier, denies

16. Flood and Turan, "Outside-Outside," 18–19.
17. Ibid.

the existence of any ordinance of that kind when he was there. Also, the *Danville Register and Bee* and city officials cannot find the governing ordinance. Furthermore, if Flood dressed in that hot, separate tin shack, what of his black roommate, Bo Bossard, and the Cuban players? Finally, while Flood told the *Los Angeles Times'* Kenneth Turan that this obviously disgusting example of segregation occurred in Danville, which would have placed it in 1956, he told Geoffrey C. Ward and Ken Burns for their book, *Baseball: An Illustrated History,* that he had to face this humiliating situation in 1957 when he was no longer in the Carolina League and no longer playing in Danville. It would appear, then, that Flood invented the Danville episode. More than that, he did what he could to propagate it. What Flood told Turan, he told his wife; after his death she would spread the story in an HBO special for *Real Sports* produced by Spike Lee, and, after that, she would discuss the incident in a documentary, standing by a dugout (although one without the attached tin cubicle her husband had described).[18]

That Flood concocted this story of his humiliation in Danville seems apparent. Surely, if true, it would have served him better had he written it in his 1971 memoir, stressing his victimhood. As it was, in 1971 he wrote enough about racism when with the Hi-Toms to produce a shock in High Point. Gratuitously, he asserted, "I believe I would have quit baseball rather than return there." Forty years later, discussing the matter, George Erath asserted that Flood's harsh comment did not square with what he remembered of Flood's days with the Hi-Toms. Erath told the *Enterprise,* "In no way did [Flood] show it [his bitterness] in his actions, words, or deeds; he had a really good attitude about things. He was most gracious to fans and everybody." Erath had a right to be shocked; evidence from that period proves his point. When Flood left High Point after receiving his MVP award, headed for an end-of-the-season shot with the Reds, he could be pretty certain that he would not return to High Point, and he had no reason to say anything gracious about the town, but he told a

18. Ibid., 14–16; Geoffrey C. Ward and Ken Burns, *Baseball: An Illustrated History,* 339. Flood told the story in an HBO documentary produced by Spike Lee for HBO's *Real Sports* (in author's possession). To further the question of authenticity, in Flood, *The Way It Is,* 43, he mentions a somewhat similar scene in 1957 when he was with the Savannah Reds, but did so in two sentences. And even that sketch is denied by his acknowledged white friend, Drew "Buddy" Gilbert, in a telephone interview of November 1998 and letters of December 3, 1998, and April 19, 1999; also Al Jennings, interview in Savannah, Georgia, October 6, 1998.

reporter, "I've enjoyed the year very much and I'm very happy to be getting this break."[19]

Flood's "break" did not turn out as well as he obviously hoped: he would get just a few days with the Reds at the end of the 1956 season. He managed to get into only four games, and then only as a pinch runner or a pinch hitter. Flood did not worry much about his failure to play more or to get a hit. He enjoyed the limelight and had an opportunity to play at Crosley Field, the Reds' home. At least equally important, he played in New York, where he and "the entire team stayed at the Biltmore Hotel, as if blacks were members of the human race." Then, too, he enjoyed writing family and friends long letters on hotel stationery, bragging in some imaginative but harmless ways of the "privileges and pleasures of being big league."[20]

There was a singular hitch in Flood's otherwise grand entrance into the big leagues. Gabe Paul, the Reds' general manager, called him into his office one afternoon in the season's last days. Flood says he led off by reminding Paul of his statistics in the Carolina League and arguing at some length that he was entitled to a raise in pay. This argument, however, only produced a "melancholy" negative sweep of the head from the Reds' general manager. Paul was solicitous of the young man's ego. He told him as gently as possible—even, Flood recalled sardonically, with apparent sadness—that the Reds could not afford to pay him more. While he had done a fine job in the Carolina League, he was not ready for the majors. He should keep working hard and exercise some patience. That meant accepting the same salary for a second season along with a promotion to the Reds' Class A Sally League team in Savannah. Meanwhile, Paul told Flood he wanted him to play a season of winter ball in the Dominican Republic. Although Paul did not say so at the time, the Reds wanted to move him from center field to third base—they had enough outfielders, among them Frank Robinson, with Vada Pinson waiting in the wings—and Flood would need more than a little schooling at the new position. Spending part of the winter in the Dominican Republic was the way to get it.[21]

19. Joanne Black, interview, High Point, October 5, 1998, with partial scrapbook clipping, September 1956.

20. Flood, *The Way It Is,* 40.

21. Curiously, Flood first applied for a passport in 1957, to go to Venezuela, at which time he noted that he had been in the Dominican Republic for a month and no more the previous year. Passport obtained by FOIA, December 19, 2003, U.S. Department of State, Case Control No. 0202860.

Flood did not stay very long in the Dominican Republic. As he put it later, "neither spirit nor flesh was willing." His harsh adventures "among the peckerwoods" had tired him out. He wanted to return to Oakland and sleep away the winter, and soon he was given the opportunity. Perhaps Flood was truly exhausted, perhaps it was his failure to handle third base acceptably—he had a second-rate arm (despite Bercovich's comparison with Willie Mays)—but the Dominican team released him after only a couple of weeks, and without objection from the Reds, he returned to Oakland.[22]

Apparently rest was what Flood needed. The next February he returned to Ma Felder's in Tampa feeling like a "tiger," and, also apparently, this time with full recognition, if not acceptance, of Jim Crow. Perhaps to his surprise, he went north with the Reds once again to play briefly at Crosley Field. He did not stay long, however. On April 11, one week into the season, Flood was sent down to Savannah, as Paul had intended all along. Again, as with his assignment in the Dominican Republic, Flood had no real choice. Although he almost certainly did not understand the reasons, he knew that his contract with Cincinnati, like those of every other player contracted to a major-league club, bound him to his club as long as it wanted him. He would remain in the Reds' organization until the team decided to sell, trade, or release him. He must go to Savannah and learn to handle third base or forgo any hope of playing in the major leagues. Also, though Flood may not have been aware of it, he had at least one obvious hitting problem. Like other minor leaguers, he feasted on the fastballs thrown to him, but he had a problem when the better pitchers served up curveballs. The Reds hoped he could deal with the problem if he spent another year in the minors.

Flood's season in Savannah was marked again by both the racism and the loneliness he had known in High Point, but with a few differences, some significant. Again, at his mother's request, the Savannah Reds found him a place to live, this time in a dormitory at black Savannah State College. Unhappily, Flood found that the dormitory, unlike Mrs. Nelson, did not afford him snacks after night games. He was on his own, and there was only one place where a black could eat after a night game, a grimy, distant bus station that served questionable food. In 1965 he told a sportswriter that he had to cook on a hot plate in his room or

---

22. See page 45 for his problems as a third baseman with the Savannah Reds.

go to bed hungry, but he reported it with a laugh. He may have laughed because the story was not entirely true. A black woman who rang a cowbell when one of the Reds hit a home run brought him and the other black players in the dugout food, and a black-owned café a few blocks from the college served barbecued chicken and greens. Of course, these two sources may have been inadequate. In any event, Flood had far more serious food problems when the Reds went on the road. Mrs. Nelson was not around to provide him with a box lunch, and finding food meant a humiliating walk to the back door of a restaurant. Also, the bus rides in the Class A league were longer: several hundred miles, over bumpy two-lane roads, sitting in a sun-baked oven of a bus. It was boring and tiring. As Flood recalled, the only difference between road games with the Reds and those the year before was that "the cries of 'nigger' and 'snowball' were not as frequent or loud as in the Carolina League." Of course, the racial slurs, even if less prevalent in the more urban South, still hurt. Indeed, he would say later, "Cincinnati arranged another full dose for me." And in later years, he refused to drive his car through the Southland to the St. Louis Cardinals' spring training camp at St. Petersburg, Florida. He had friends drive it for him.[23]

In the end it must be said that, although Flood was surely one of the many victims of southern racism, and the impact of that peculiar sickness cannot be stressed enough, he was also a victim of his youth and temperament. He was lonely, and it would seem that he was lonely by choice. He roomed alone at Savannah State College, but unnecessarily; he could have shared a room with Bo Bossard, his roommate at High Point that he had failed to mention before. He might also have associated himself with some of the militant civil rights–minded students; they were plentiful in Savannah. He did not. He preferred his own company, joined, of course, by his guitar, sketchbook, and paints and brushes. Drew "Buddy" Gilbert, also a Savannah Red player and an acknowledged white friend from Knoxville who often brought Flood food when the bus stopped, recalls that though they sometimes joked a bit, Flood "wasn't outgoing." Indeed, Flood was so closed up that he did not tell Gilbert where he lived. Reds broadcaster Al Jennings noticed the same thing. Flood was usually warm and gracious when he was talking to sportswriters and superiors, but he was usually diffident and withdrawn

23. Stump, "Midnight League," 79; Riley interviews; Jennings interview, October 6 1998; Jones interview, June 19, 2003, the last regarding driving Flood's car to Florida.

in his relations with his peers. Jennings also noted that when Flood had his easels out and was asked to show his sketches and paintings, he refused. It seems fair to say, then, that if Flood was lonely when in Savannah, as he says he was, it was as much because of his sensitivity and brooding as the city's racist climate.[24]

Why Flood was moody and a loner is not clear, though some years later he acknowledged that he was a worrier, often painting or lying awake at night and brooding over his play that day while thinking about the game or games ahead. Manager Jimmy Brown had welcomed him to Savannah in April. "He'll make us a good ball player," Brown told the *Morning News*. And if being named on the South Atlantic League's All-Star team is a criterion, Flood easily confirmed his manager's hopes. Although his batting average fell to .299, it was good enough for fourth place in the Sally League, and he ranked second in runs batted in. On the other hand, he developed a hitch in his swing as he tried to hit pitches harder in order to match his home runs at High Point. Years later, after dealing with the problem, Flood admitted that when he was in Savannah and even when in High Point, "I thought I had to be Babe Ruth." Meanwhile, he was performing miserably at third base. While he was known to make tough plays now and then, he booted too many easy grounders, and his throws to first base had all the speed of a mule treading in quicksand. Flood admitted as much years later: "The only way I could get the ball to first base was to carry it there. The manager used to beg me to throw to second anytime I got my hands on a ground ball. 'That way we can hold it to a single.'" Clearly, Flood would have to make it to the majors at another position, if he was to make it at all.[25]

At the end of the 1957 season Flood found himself called up once again to the Reds. This time, he got his first major-league hit. Again, he entered Gabe Paul's office. Again, he thought he deserved a raise. Quickly, he reports—again sardonically—that Paul banished the thought of a raise from his mind; after all, his average had dropped forty-one points. Moreover, the Reds no longer needed a third baseman. If Flood wanted to make it to the majors with the club, he must now learn to play second base. That meant he would have to spend part of the winter with a team in Venezuela playing at second. Paul said nothing about his

24. Jennings interview, October 6, 1998; Drew "Buddy" Gilbert, letter to author, April 19, 1999.

25. *Savannah Morning News*, April 13, 1957; *Los Angeles Times*, July 7, 1968.

returning to the outfield, the position at which he had starred with the Hi-Toms.

Flood was not happy in Venezuela. He feared the food and water, which greatly irritated his intestines, and for a month he felt sick. Beyond that, management policed the players' relationships with women. He also lived with some fear because he could not play second base acceptably despite his manager's efforts to give him the benefit of his experience at the position. Happily, considering his problems, Flood was not in Venezuela very long. Within weeks the Reds' general manager sent him a cable saying that he had been traded to the St. Louis Cardinals and could go back to Oakland, which, to Flood, meant much-needed rest. Better yet, although he could not have known it then, he would find in his association with the Cardinals a faster road to the major leagues. The Cardinals would prove to be a wonderful home for many years and, eventually, would become his destiny.

III

A Minor in the Majors

December 5, 1957, was a fateful day for Curt Flood, one he would long remember with mixed emotions. It was the day he heard that Cincinnati had traded him to the St. Louis Cardinals. He could see a more promising future for himself with the Cardinals, but he regretted that he would not have an opportunity to play alongside his idol, Frank Robinson, now a star in Cincinnati's outfield; he also would not be playing alongside Vada Pinson, a McClymonds classmate and good friend who was about to join the Reds' outfield that summer. But those thoughts were not Flood's only negative reaction to the trade. Perhaps signifying his insecurities and his tendency to brood, he wondered how he, a recognized All-Star in two minor leagues, had failed to impress the Reds' management. He was bitter about it, and he would have been more so had he known that the Cardinals had slipped the Reds a pittance in return: he had been traded for three pitchers who would prove to be ineffective and seldom-used. Even so, Flood lodged no objections with the Reds' management, and thirteen years later when he was challenging his trade from St. Louis to Philadelphia and reporters were asking him why he had not fought his earlier trade from the Reds to the Cardinals, he said the idea of rebelling never occurred to him. He did as every baseball player then did when traded—he went where the club that "owned" his contract sent him, without questions, much less threats. When asked years later why he had accepted being traded by the Reds so readily, he responded, "I was a nobody."[1]

Some years after Flood went to the Cardinals, word circulated on the baseball grapevine that race was the decisive factor in the Reds shipping him out. It was whispered, none too softly, that the Reds' general manager, Gabe Paul, had looked to the field from his private box in

1. Phil Pepe, "How Flood Finally Made It," 45.

Crosley Field one day near the end of the 1957 season and seen too much black—there was the prospect of Robinson, Pinson, and Flood playing side by side in the same outfield—and had worried about the impact it would have on ticket sales. Also, after Flood's rather dismal performance as an infielder the summer before with Savannah, Paul could not visualize him as a second or third baseman. Thus, one of the three men, Robinson, Pinson, or Flood, had to go. This story, however reasonable for that era, was denied by Birdie Tebbetts, the Reds' field manager. He offered a different rationale for letting Flood go. Race was not a factor: Robinson was a star, but it was not really clear that either Pinson or Flood would make the team. And Flood appeared the least likely. He had a "hitch in his swing"; he pulled his bat back "in a kind of windup" as the pitcher was about to release the ball, which meant that he was not ready to meet the ball when it arrived. It was a problem that might take years to correct (and did). Furthermore, the Reds desperately "needed pitching help," which the St. Louis Cardinals were offering. Thus Paul traded Flood because the trade helped him to get what he could to meet his foremost needs. It was a baseball decision pure and simple, not a racially influenced one as some alleged. At least that was the Reds' answer.[2]

In the mid-sixties, Flood addressed the issue and agreed with Tebbetts's version. "Birdie was right about the hitch. As far as the Negro situation at Cincinnati," Flood went on, "I never felt that was why I was traded." This was not, however, precisely what he felt, or at least said, when discussing the same issue in 1970, the traumatic year in which he sued Major League Baseball. His stated position was more complicated by then; it was not "either or," but "both and." He recalled that Pinson was "the bigger of us, and because they no longer needed me for third base nor cared particularly for an all-black outfield [black being the new politically correct terminology], they unloaded me to the Cards." Surely, Flood was right on both counts: he was an erratic infielder, and while he had hit well at Class B High Point, his batting average had fallen forty points at Class A Savannah, so it was not clear that he could hit big-league pitching. Also, the Reds' need for pitching and the race of the players traded were not mutually exclusive. What Flood did not discuss as he looked back on the trade in 1970 was his good fortune in leaving Cincinnati. Baseball's reserve system enabled a club to "park" a player

2. Ibid.

on a farm team in case one of their roster players was injured; if no one was injured, then "parked" players remained in the minors. So the Reds, by retaining Flood, could have foreclosed his chance for a career in the major leagues.[3]

In late 1957 Flood was too young to realize that he should have been altogether pleased with his trade, that with the Cardinals he might make it to the major leagues more easily, and sooner. Otherwise, why would they trade for him? And he had to feel somewhat reassured when the Cards mailed him a contract for 1958 with a 25 percent raise, to $5,000. But after spring training at the Cardinals' St. Petersburg camp in segregated Florida—discrimination which Flood quietly accepted at the time—he was sent to a farm team where he would be able to play center field every day. Happily for him, the club was not in the South, which he had feared, but in Omaha, with St. Louis's AAA club in the American Association. Furthermore, although Flood could not have been aware of its significance at that time, he found himself playing (he preferred the word "working" as properly defining what ballplayers did) for manager Johnny Keane, whose fatherly friendship and appreciation for his "work" would one day prove essential to his major-league career. And except when he patrolled Omaha in his new Thunderbird coupe, work is what Flood did—and did well.[4]

Whatever his problems had been with the bat during his previous year in Savannah, they were not evident in Omaha. He got off to an excellent start, in early May hitting .340. By then the Cardinals had moved Ken Boyer, a superb hitter, from the outfield to third base, where he proved a better fielder, but it was soon clear that Bobby Smith, Boyer's heir in center field, could not handle major-league pitching. That brought the Cardinals' general manager, Vaughn P. "Bing" Devine, to near panic, and he phoned Keane in Omaha, seeking help. Did he have an outfielder who could field and hit? When Keane heartily recommended Flood, Devine told him to send the young man up forthwith.

Flood heard the good news that he had been called up from Omaha's general manager, Bill Bergesch. Flood, obviously thrilled at the news, said "That's great, Bill"—but he also said he had a problem: "What am I going to do with my car?" Flood knew he had to fly, which he would do

---

3. Flood, *The Way It Is*, 47. The Detroit Tigers did not have even one black ballplayer until 1958, so the Reds' worries are understandable.
4. Pepe, "How Flood Finally Made It," 45.

although he feared and hated it, but how was he going to get his new Thunderbird to St. Louis? His worries were needless, though, as Bergesch said he was going to St. Louis and offered to drive the car there. Flood happily accepted the offer, an offer that Bergesch half-jokingly recalled a bit sorrowfully after reaching St. Louis. Bergesch, who was 6'2" and 240 pounds, had not been aware that the car was a coupe and too small for him. By the time he appeared in St. Louis after driving 450 miles, he "couldn't straighten up for a week."[5]

Once in St. Louis, Bergesch listened to an amusing story, if one whose likelihood had probably occurred to him earlier. Flood said he had arrived in St. Louis and, knowing no one, had found that it was impossible for a twenty-year-old kid to find a room for the months remaining in the baseball season. Making matters worse, St. Louis was a segregated city, and that meant looking for a room only in the black community, where no landlord would rent a room without a three-year lease. And the Cardinals' management did not offer any help. Fortunately, or so it appeared, Sam "Toothpick" Jones, also known as "Sad Sam," a slim, veteran black pitcher in his second year with the Cardinals who was known for a scarily wild curveball and a penchant for booze, agreed to help. When Flood approached him with his difficulty in finding living quarters, Jones drawled, "No problem baby, got plenty of rooms where I am." It turned out that Jones lived in a Victorian mansion somewhat grandly called the Heritage Arms. Much too grandly, it turned out. Flood quickly found out that he and Jones were the only males living at the Heritage Arms who were neither pimps nor johns. "Toothpick" wanted women available to him. So when Bergesch arrived in St. Louis with Flood's car, he found his former center fielder living in one of the city's most notorious bordellos.[6]

Six weeks passed before Flood found other quarters, but they were no better than the ones he had left. Naively, he had wandered into a bordello again. Many years later, when it meant nothing except to posterity, he would complain that the Cardinals had not volunteered to help him find more acceptable lodgings. He might have asked, but as a rookie he was very shy, especially when he was the subordinate, and did not feel comfortable asking for help by going to the Cardinals' front office. So he stayed at this second whorehouse the remainder of the season. Fortu-

5. Ibid.
6. Ibid., 78.

nately for Flood and the Cardinals, his problem finding lodging did not impair his performance on the field during those first hectic months. On May 2, playing in his first game as a Redbird, he managed to get hit by a pitched ball and hit a double before, unfortunately, hitting into a double play later in the game. Within a month he was hitting a quite decent .280, prompting extravagant praise from Cardinals manager Fred Hutchinson, who told Pittsburgh sportswriters before a night game that he thought Flood's hitting was quite remarkable for a young man only twenty years of age. And that night in late June there was solid support on the field for Hutchinson's praise: his young center fielder went four for five, raising his average to .294.[7]

Flood's performance brought him celebrity status in St. Louis. In July the "Whiz in the Outfield" had a full-page pictorial in Sunday's *St. Louis Post-Dispatch*. The accompanying story marked him as a "rookie of the year" candidate, the best Cardinals center fielder since Terry Moore a decade earlier, and, according to Hutchinson, second best only to Willie Mays as a National League center fielder. As Hutchinson saw it, Flood appeared to know instinctively most of the moves on the base paths and in the field, and if he did make the wrong play once he did not have to be told again. Furthermore, he was not just a baseball player. The *Post-Dispatch*'s pictorial staff probably thought it emphasized Flood's other talents and interests more than adequately when it showed him typing answers to some of his dozens of fan letters at a remarkable seventy-five words a minute, when it noted that he enjoyed listening to progressive jazz in the clubhouse, and when it further pointed out that he took pictures with either a candid camera or a movie camera, usually from the dugout between games of doubleheaders. Curiously, the *Post-Dispatch*'s story failed to note, much less stress, that Flood sketched and painted with unusual skill, that he played the guitar, some said well enough to give lessons, and that he enjoyed classical music as well as jazz.[8]

Unhappily for Flood, the *Post-Dispatch* display came at the peak of his season's work, a peak from which he would descend precipitously in the two months left in the season. When the article appeared, he was hitting a surprising .314; when the season ended in late September he

7. *St. Louis Post-Dispatch*, May 3, June 24, 26, 1958; Flood and Turan, "Outside-Outside," 20.

8. *St. Louis Post-Dispatch*, July 27, 1958.

was hitting .261, fifteen points below what Hutchinson had thought essential for him to be of value to the team. When Flood mentioned his fallen average in later years, it appeared that he had not taken it very seriously. He said he thought it "pretty good for a little rookie—not nearly bad enough to convince [him] that something was amiss." He was unwilling to admit that he had a hitch in his swing, that he lunged at curveballs, and that pitchers seeing him for a second or third time by midsummer had discovered his weaknesses.[9]

After his 1958 season, Flood returned to Oakland basically intending to rest and paint. Relaxation was his reward for "working" during the baseball season, but it was also necessary to repair his tired body. That meant rest and painting. Neither then nor at any other point in his career did he follow a season with the sort of conditioning program—running, weight-lifting, and other exercises—that would become so common among athletes as the years wore by.

More important at the moment and forever after, Flood decided to get married. His bride was Beverly Collins, a petite, sophisticated teenager, surely beautiful but with two children. He had met her during the summer at her parents' St. Louis nightclub, "The Talk of the Town." Once reputedly the city's most prestigious black nightspot, the club had featured such famous entertainers as singer Ike Turner and trumpeter Louis Armstrong in the forties and early fifties, and apparently it was a source of considerable income for Bill and Nwassa, Beverly's parents. By 1958, however, it was only a cocktail lounge connected to a small snack shop (and about to disappear altogether). Nevertheless, Flood found it a very enjoyable place to drink, the more so after he met Beverly. Presumably, he courted her that summer and fall, but surely he did not have to work very hard at it. He was his usual charming, boyishly winsome self, and a rising star even though a new member of the St. Louis Cardinals. Beverly, according to Flood's half sister Rickie, was looking for a man to support her in the manner to which, as the daughter of comfortable parents, she had been accustomed. She had expensive tastes and her family would not pay for her fancier personal needs. Not when she had two children—Debbie, who was almost three, and Gary, nearing two—who both needed a father; also, Gary would proba-

9. Flood's problem was noted even when he was hitting so well for the Hi-Toms, as pointed out in the *Winston-Salem Journal and Sentinel,* undated clipping from scrapbook of Joanne Black of High Point.

bly need surgery soon. Thus, according to Rickie, Beverly saw Flood as the answer to her several needs, and she was leading him even as he was pursuing her. Flood, for his part, later admitted that he quickly thought himself in love: "I was twenty-one; Beverly was a couple of years younger and absolutely beautiful. We mistook an immediate attraction for love." And the obvious followed. Given the immaturity and charged hormones common to their youth, the question was not whether they would marry, but when. That time turned out to be February 1959, in Tijuana, Mexico, far from her parents' home and much to their dismay. They wanted Beverly married in St. Louis. Consequently, they were married again when they returned to Missouri.[10]

It is probable that the marriage began happily because Flood quickly adopted Beverly's very young children. Then they had a son and daughter of their own, Curtis Christopher Flood, Jr., and about two years later Shelley Susan Flood. Four years after that Beverly bore a fifth child, Scott Charles Flood. Such are the bare facts, and for most marriages they would readily suffice: it would be needlessly invasive to discuss their good times and their bad. But the marriage's eventual collapse, Beverly's efforts to secure alimony and child support, and Flood's resistance to making the payments demand our attention. Flood's challenge to Major League Baseball's reserve system cannot be understood without reference to these issues.

Notably, in his memoir, Flood freely discusses his and Beverly's marital problems. On the one hand, he makes standard excuses for the failure of their marriage: the charged hormones and innocence of youth had masked sharply different personalities, needs, and aspirations. They rushed into an ill advised marriage, which is so common as hardly to be noted, and Flood writes about it at first impartially, "We knew little worth knowing about love, sex, responsibility, raising a family." But then he finds a complicating scapegoat: baseball. "Whatever handicaps we brought to the marriage were intensified by the tense comings and goings of the baseball season. We didn't have a chance." But it was not just baseball. Flood describes the problem fully in a chapter titled "The National Pastime's Pastime." The primary pastime for most players was

10. Flood, *The Way It Is*, 111; Rickie Riley, interviews, 1998–2005; the exact date of the marriage was February 13, 1959, according to *Beverly A. Flood vs. Curtis Charles Flood* (Flood, "Complaint for Divorce," January 17, 1966, case no. 356589, Superior Court of the State of California, Alameda County). Why the Floods were first married in Tijuana is unclear.

sex, or, as Flood put it, "wenching" or "beaver-shooting," especially during but not limited to the three months per season the players spent traveling from city to city, plus another half month if counting spring training. Although Bill White, who came to the Cardinals in 1959, later described Flood as a loner, happy in his room with his books, paints, and guitar, Flood asserts that living "on the road" with the team meant endless hours of wretched loneliness and boredom, complicated by great tension, worrying about a game the next day or the day after that. A player could watch only so many movies and so much television before such diversions became repetitive and boring. In any case they failed to alleviate the fear that someone in the minors might grab your job if you failed to hit on a regular basis, and they failed to reduce the tension one felt when keyed up after a game and unable to sleep until well into the wee hours.

It was precisely this pressure that accounted for the emphasis not only on sex but also the various pills that players took—from laxatives to antacids, aspirin, and even pep pills, the last presumably for a day game after a night game with little or no sleep following. Another tension release involved alcohol. Many players, even superstars, drank, often to excess, but the better players knew they were likely to play erratically if they drank heavily. Flood admitted that he drank, and not only because of the tension before, during, and after a game, or the many parties on off-days. Flying frightened him, Gussie Busch and the Anheuser Busch brewery supplied endless free beer on the team plane, and the players were given a case at their home whenever they asked for one—or more. How much Flood drank this early in his career cannot be said. Probably he drank moderately; he was smart enough to know he had not yet "made it." He had to take care of himself. In any event, he said, part of his brain—and hormones, no doubt—recognized that the groupies, the women who gathered around ballplayers, offered better, safer therapy than alcohol or pill-popping. And most ballplayers, he thought, agreed with him; they were "more interested in pennants and copulation than in alcohol, a formidable antagonist of both."[11]

This being understood, that girls were the ultimate therapy for loneliness, boredom, and tension on the road and even during home stands, Flood asked the readers of his memoir to sympathize with the problems of a young ballplayer with the normal amount of hormones. "Girls are

11. Flood, *The Way It Is,* chap. 6, "The National Pastime's Pastime."

more therapeutic. They are more fundamental. The ballplayer uses them medicinally, like an apple a day." In this respect ballplayers were no different in their basic needs than other men with less romantic jobs; the difference lay in the abundance of women eager to accommodate their "playful appetites." And Flood joyfully admitted having [had] the very "appetites" (as he still did). "To me, any nonviolent manifestation of sex is an expression of joy, real or potential. I am for it. I do not claim to have been the foremost beaver shooter in the history of organized baseball, but I was big league all the way." Flood elaborated on the Cardinals' wenching (and by extension that of almost all ballplayers) as well as their voyeurism at some length. He might have labeled this section of his book "how to find them, except that they did not have to be found, they found you." This was the good side of being a ballplayer, of traveling to different cities during the season. Fortunately, too, an abundance of eager women was not limited to "the road." Flood knew at first hand that eager women were readily found in his hometown, just as undemanding, just as consoling.[12]

Unhappily for every married player, there was another side to this life on the road, and it was not just the certainty that his wife would suspect him of being unfaithful even if he was not; it was that his wife might be seeing another man while he was gone. "Shorty," as Flood called the man visiting the player's wife, lived in the same city as the player's family and had been watching his charming, sexy wife and the team's schedule. When the player left the front door for a road trip, "Shorty" came in the back. And when the player returned to his home and heard the back door closing, it was "Shorty" leaving. Possibly, Flood understood this problem from personal experience. Clearly he could have found little if any justification for complaint.

Despite his lengthy discussion of the "National Pastime's Pastime," Flood recognized at last that the sex life of the married, traveling ballplayer must be seen in perspective: "It is not the root cause of marital disgruntlement, but compounds it." What, specifically, were the root causes—other than his and/or Beverly's sexual promiscuity—of their marital problems, Flood does not say. However, it is clear enough that their personalities and needs clashed. Other than easy hit-and-run sex, Flood was "very fifties," very traditional. He demanded—the word is not too strong—a well-kept home, quiet children, and a wife who carefully

12. Jody Kramer, telephone interview, August 10, 2001.

minded both. Furthermore, although he (presumably) found Beverly her modeling job with Anheuser-Busch, he wanted her to wear conservative clothes. Even in St. Louis's hot and humid summers she was not to wear shorts, not even around the house. In the same traditional vein, he expected her to manage the household's bill payments and other chores. Indeed, according to his stepdaughter, Debbie, in Flood's mind Beverly existed only to support his baseball career. In sum, Flood's high-strung, brooding temperament and inability to handle pressure reminded her of Flood's father's problems with pressure. If Debbie's assessment is correct, and it would appear so, her father required a world he could control, or else someone he trusted who could relieve the pressures he could not handle. An inability to handle pressure, not extramarital sex, seems to have been Flood's root problem. It threaded through his marriage, his baseball career, and led in time to his challenge to baseball's reserve system.[13]

Unhappily for Flood's marriage, Beverly was not raised to be the quietly reserved, supportive wife he needed. According to Rickie—who was partisan to be sure—Beverly "was raised with a silver spoon in her mouth." She loved to shop at Saks Fifth Avenue in suburban St. Louis, buying expensive clothes and accessories, and her spending habits as well as her failure to pay the bills in a timely fashion kept the family broke and her husband out of sorts. Rickie's story is countered, as might be imagined, by Debbie's. Debbie, who was very young, indeed only eight, when her parents separated, nonetheless insists that Flood unfairly charged her mother with extravagant spending. Much of what she spent at Saks and elsewhere went on the backs of her children—and his. The battles over Beverly's spending, Debbie believed, followed from the fact that her father was very much like her grandfather, Herman Flood, whom she had heard called "the king of frugality." Pennies had always been pinched and saved in the Flood home in Oakland. That, she was told, was Herman's doing.

Again, of course, one sees an obvious case of he said, she said, one by a sister who knew only what her brother told her, the other by a girl probably too young to fully understand the source(s) of the family's financial problems (which included Gary's medical bills), let alone where responsibility lay. On the other hand, Debbie could see and hear

13. Debbie Flood, interview, Altadena, California, March 5, 1998, and with her brother, Curtis, Jr., in 1999.

what was in front of her. Again, her father reminded her of her grandfather. She recalls that Flood no sooner came through the door than he yelled at her mother, condemning her for some apparent failure on her part. Fistfights followed at times, after which her father would go off by himself to the garage to sketch or paint, tinker with models of one kind or another, play his guitar, or work on his sports car. Of course there was a positive side to the family scene. Some mornings, Debbie recalls, her father would give her and her brothers and sisters a portrait or something else he had crafted during the night. That was his notion of affection and its limits. Her father was too self-absorbed to be truly nurturing. Yet Debbie had to admit that when her father lived with her and her brothers and sisters, they saw him as "cool"; they adored him as their "hero."[14]

While Flood's marriage started with great hope only to sour over time, the reverse was true of his career with the Cardinals. For the 1959 season, his first as a married man, the Cardinals doubled his salary to $10,000. It was twice the major-league minimum and probably much more than Flood expected. Apparently the club liked his prospects. He did, too. Although he had struggled at the bat in the second half of the previous season, he could not have been more optimistic when he went to spring training camp in St. Petersburg in early March of 1959. "I came to spring training on a cloud," he would note in his memoir a decade later. "I now was an established major leaguer en route to the big chips. [Newly appointed manager Solly] Hemus would appreciate my all-out style of play. Perhaps he would clap his hand on my shoulder and say: 'Young man I like you. Glad to have you aboard.'"

Perhaps Hemus did clap him on the shoulder and welcome him warmly, but Flood did not produce as either he or the Cardinals had expected. For the season he batted just .255, and he did not hit the sizable number of home runs and knock in or score the runs that teams usually expect from their center fielder. Consequently, he found himself playing in the same number of games for the Cardinals in 1959 as in 1958—121—even though he had been in the minors for all of April in 1958. He also went to bat only half as many times in his second major-league season: he had 422 at bats in 1958, but only 208 in 1959. Much the same

---

14. Debbie Flood, interview, March 3, 1998, in which she tended to minimize Flood's sins. She probably did so because of her mother's lawsuit. Five years later, her son said that he disrespected his grandfather.

thing happened the following year, 1960. He went to bat 396 times in 1960, but that was still far short of the norm of 600-plus at bats for an everyday player. Either he was yanked from games early for a pinch hitter or, more typically, he did not enter a game until the late innings, and then only because he had the speed and agility required by a pinch runner and because he was something special in center field. These latter two qualities were, in 1959 and 1960, his salvation as a major-leaguer, probably all that kept the Cardinals from sending him back to Omaha to either regain his early 1958 form as a batter or fade away.

During those two years Flood gradually began to grapple with some of his problems at the plate that he had refused to admit when he said, after his first season, that he had a "pretty good year for a little rookie." He realized even during the 1959 season that he needed help as a hitter. He was attempting to hit home runs, perhaps because he had hit so many playing in Oakland and at High Point, but also because the Cardinals' young player-manager, Solly Hemus, wanted more power from his outfielders. But major-league parks were larger than those in Oakland or in the Class B minors, and trying to hit home runs meant overswinging in an effort to compensate and satisfy Hemus. Consequently, Flood had the old hitch in his swing. Beyond that, he was lunging at pitches outside the strike zone and he was upper-cutting when swinging, which led to either strikeouts or easily caught fly balls or pop-ups. Struggling at the plate and playing less often than he wished and needed to if he hoped to remain with the Cardinals, Flood eventually recognized that he had a serious problem and became receptive to help. Naturally he turned to his teammate Stan Musial, one of the greatest hitters ever to play baseball. But all the future Hall-of-Famer could give him, Flood recalled a decade later, were useless bromides that went: "Well, you wait for a strike. Then you knock the shit out of it." Continuing to reflect on Musial's advice, Flood said, "I might as well have asked a nightingale how to trill." This last was fair, but it was also a sad commentary, the more so as Flood had advised *St. Louis Post-Dispatch* sportswriter Bob Broeg several years earlier that "Hutch helped me and especially Stan. Stand [*sic*] pointed out that by waiting on a pitch to go to the opposite field, you not only get a better look at the ball, but you also keep the defense spread." Musial's advice was superb on its face, but it went further by implication: to spray the ball to all fields, Flood had to change his swing to meet the ball for singles and doubles rather than trying to hit it out of the park, which he could not naturally do because of his limited strength. Whether or to what extent Flood took Musial's advice is unclear, but it is a notable characteristic of his 1971 memoir that Flood was reluctant to acknowledge this great Cardinal's help.[15]

A decade later, Flood chiefly credited teammate George Crowe for helping him correct his hitting problems. Fifteen years older than Flood and nearing the end of his career, Crowe had come to St. Louis in 1959 as a pinch hitter. Easygoing "Big Daddy," as *Sports Illustrated* labeled him in 1960, could communicate so well with other black players that the magazine called him their leader in the majors. And whatever "Big Daddy's" actual theoretical knowledge of hitting, Flood thought "Big George" "knew more about batting theory and was more articulate about it than anyone else on the Cardinals team." Later, in the autumn of 1964, after Flood had hit .311 and tied the Pirates' Roberto Clemente for the National League lead with 211 hits, he informed a St. Louis sportswriter: "I have always tried to follow George's advice. Big George would emphasize two things—a short stride and a level swing. He would say that whatever else happened [involving a batter's swing] those two things would compensate for them." Flood was surely right about Crowe's advice—that a short stride and a level swing would compensate for many of the worst mistakes a hitter might make—how could it not help—but Crowe's advice was probably most beneficial because Flood trusted him. Yet Cardinals' hitting coach Harry Walker was probably as effective as Crowe. Flood admitted that Walker "got me to choke up." Walker helped him refocus as a hitter, placing greater emphasis on just making contact with the ball and spraying hits to all fields for singles and doubles (just as Musial suggested), adjusting his hitting to his size and strength rather than swinging for the fences at every turn.[16]

In the end, however, as every athlete knows, even the most knowledgeable of coaches or players can only point out a player's problems, demonstrating or suggesting measures that might correct them. Coaches could alter Flood's stance somewhat, but they could not keep him from shifting his feet, from lunging at balls he should ignore, or from overswinging. Teachers might teach, but there was no way a player could correct his problems at the plate other than by practicing endlessly to cure them. In this sense, Musial taught by example. Flood saw

15. Flood, *The Way It Is*, 64; *St. Louis Post-Dispatch*, June 26, 1964.
16. Neal Russo, "Crowe Can Crow about Flood," *St. Louis Post-Dispatch*, October 14, 1964.

"Stan the Man," great hitter that he was, taking batting practice every day. Although Flood later said he thought Musial was unfortunately naive because he endorsed the front office at every turn, and, worse, did so in the most unctuous manner, he viewed "the Man" as "an awesome sight in the batting cage, sweat pouring, brows knit in concentration . . . hammering twenty or thirty balls to the fences and beyond—polishing, polishing, polishing." And he knew this: Musial set an example he must emulate if he was to stay in the major leagues. He had no choice. "Satchel" Paige, the great black pitcher from the Negro Leagues, often was quoted as having insisted: "Don't look back. Something might be gaining on you." Flood knew what that meant in his case: work endlessly on his hitting. The Cardinals had young players in their farm system waiting hungrily for him to fail so they could take his place in center field. So he followed Musial's example in the batting cage. Larry Jackson, a Chicago Cubs' pitcher who studied Flood closely, later recalled that "Curt would always concentrate in the batter's cage. Why, he would bear down as if he were in an actual game." Flood's memory was that "I did not play baseball, I worked at it hard. I brought to baseball the same intensity I lived my life with. I want to be the best. . . . This has nothing to do with the greenness of money. . . . I'm a black guy, someone who has been told so many times that he's too small, a wise-ass, the wrong color. I had a lot of people I wanted to show things to."[17]

The one person Flood most desperately wanted to "show," of course, was the Cardinals' manager, Solly Hemus. He had to do that if he wanted to remain with the Cardinals, but Flood also wanted to "show" Hemus because he could not stand him as a person and did not respect him as a manager. According to Flood, few of his fellow Cardinals did. The word was that Busch had appointed Hemus, a thirty-six-year-old utility infielder, to succeed Hutchinson in part because he was "scrappy," but more importantly because he sent the boss a subservient letter pleading for the job. In any event, the prevailing view, including that of Musial, was that Hemus lacked every quality essential in a manager except the capacity to cater to Gussie Busch. Unfortunately for Flood, Hemus would remain in Busch's stewardship for more than two years.[18]

Flood does not mention having such negative thoughts about Hemus when he arrived at spring training in March 1959. He thought of himself

17. Ibid.
18. Flood, *The Way It Is*, 67; James N. Giglio, *Musial: From Stash to Stan the Man*, 240–56.

as an established major leaguer and expected that the Cardinals' newly appointed manager would greatly appreciate his "all-out style of play" and install him as his regular center fielder. But it was not to be. Hemus, he soon found, "did not share the widely held belief that I played center field approximately as well as Willie Mays. He sat me on the bench, preferring to use men such as Gino Cimoli, Don Taussig, Don Landrum, and even the miscast Bill White in center field." Flood was right about White being miscast in center field—he belonged at first base. But Hemus was trying to keep Musial's still-powerful bat in the lineup, and Musial lacked the legs to continue playing in the outfield, so Hemus put him at first and White in center. More generally, the issue for Hemus was not who played center field or the other outfield positions as well as or better than Flood. He was looking for power hitting, and the four players Flood mentioned had real power—at least when they managed to hit the ball. So it turned out that Flood played irregularly and at a variety of positions—at second, third, and, sometimes, center field—and he believed that this policy of moving him around, as well as his lack of playing time, were the reasons his batting average suffered in 1959 as it had during the second half of the 1958 season.[19]

Flood may well have had a point: he needed to get into a rhythm. But, he complained, Hemus did not give him a serious opportunity to find his rhythm by playing him on a regular basis at the same position. This is understandable, of course, given Hemus's emphasis on winning with run production. Power hitting is usually the best means of producing runs, and Flood was not hitting for distance, he was not sending men all the way around the bases; he did not fit into Hemus's strategy. As Johnny Keane, Flood's manager in Omaha who had joined the Cardinals as a coach, explained, Hemus was "always looking for another Willie Mays. They [Hemus and Devine] wanted somebody who would bat .350 and hit 40 home runs." Years later Hemus partially admitted that Keane was right: "I thought we needed more power than Curt could give us. I realize that [his defense] helped our pitching, but we had everything else. I tried to give Don Landrum and Jim Beauchamp a chance because their minor league records showed they could hit for power."[20]

Hemus's emphasis on power hitting, justified or not, and his persistent efforts to find a center fielder who could hit for power, exacerbated

19. Flood, *The Way It Is*, 67.
20. Pepe, "How Flood Finally Made It," 44–45.

Flood's problems at the plate. He was not built for power, and all his practicing could not cure that plain fact. If he were to try to hit home runs to comply with Hemus's strategy, he would have to swing too hard, which would probably not produce the desired runs batted in and, at the same time, would cripple his batting average, in both cases a disastrous outcome. So it was that, trapped between Scylla and Charybdis, Flood sat on the pines for much of the 1959 season. Flood recognized the problem—when he did play, he had no chance to get into a rhythm—but he had no answer to it. And his manager only made matters worse, digging at him, saying that "he wouldn't make it" if he did not improve. It is not to be wondered, then, that Flood was cursed with insomnia and chronic indigestion. He was frustrated, and one may guess bitter, which had to adversely affect his play on the field and may account, as well, for many of his angry fights with his wife. Who would not be frustrated in those circumstances? Quite naturally Flood feared being farmed out, perhaps even released if he did not produce, and all the while he believed that he could hit for a decent average if he played every day. If only Hemus would give him a chance, he would write later. One might think that Flood would have discussed his need to play on a regular basis with Hemus or with the front office at the time. But pride would not permit him to speak with Hemus, and as a second-year man he did not dare bypass his manager by asking the front office to intervene. As for Hemus, the manager correctly saw Flood as temperamental, someone who expressed great resentment at the mildest rebuke, one example being his acid reaction when he missed a plane leaving for a road trip and was handed a relatively small fine. Just a month into the 1959 season, then, there was bad blood between the two men, and Flood was frustrated, bitter, and chewing on antacids, as he believed many other Cardinals were, because of Hemus.[21]

Flood's hostility toward Hemus ripened as he came to the conclusion that his manager's failure to let him play regularly extended well beyond his problems at the plate. He came to view Hemus as a racist. Was he? It is a label that Hemus would deny forty years after. But times had changed by the century's end: overt racism, and even comments that appeared to be unintentionally and uncharacteristically racist, had

21. Flood, *The Way It Is,* 67–68; Solly Hemus, telephone interview, December 9, 1998. After the 1968 World Series, Hemus sent Flood a compassionate, complimentary letter (Flood, *The Way It Is,* 73), admitting that he had not evaluated him properly, but it did not appease Flood. On the contrary.

become not only unacceptable but also grounds for firing. (One example was Al Campanis, the Los Angeles Dodgers vice-president who despite a history of hiring minority players was fired for making racially insensitive remarks on ABC's *Nightline.*) Thus Hemus's denial at the century's end might be discounted in part as a reasonable response to what had become socially and politically acceptable. At the same time, Flood had some reasons for convicting Hemus of racism, although his anger regarding his lack of playing time hardly made him an objective observer.[22]

The facts, as best they can be told, are these. In 1959, Bob Gibson, a fire-balling black pitcher, came up from Omaha, and quite soon he and Flood became fast friends and eventually roommates. "Hoot," as Gibson soon came to be known, would one day be voted into baseball's Hall of Fame, but at this early point in his career the strong-armed right-hander still had serious control problems. This Flood admitted. But he thought Hemus shuttled Gibson back and forth between St. Louis and Omaha too often and unnecessarily in the 1959 season (and again the following year), that he never used him if he could find another pitcher to work a game, and that he liked to "put Gibson down" at team meetings. One might easily gather from Flood's memoir that he thought Hemus misused and abused Gibson at least in part because Gibson was black.[23]

But Gibson's problems with Hemus did not constitute the only or most important support for Flood's charge that his manager was a racist. During a game in Pittsburgh, Hemus, a player-manager, inserted himself into the lineup as a pinch hitter against Bennie Daniels, a black pitcher. Daniels threw close to Hemus, forcing him to fall back; when Daniels threw the next pitch just as close, Hemus responded by throwing his bat toward the pitcher's mound. Daniels then hit Hemus with his next pitch. "Nothing wrong with that," Flood recalled of the battle between the pitcher and batter. Intimidation was part of baseball. What inflamed him were the words Hemus shouted at Daniels as he trotted to first base, even though he did not hear them when they were spoken; he heard them only the next day when Hemus said at a team meeting, "I want you to be the first to know what I said to Daniels yesterday. I called him a black son of a bitch." Flood asserts that when Hemus told him,

22. Ibid., 70. The Campanis story is available at <http://en.wikipedia.org/wiki/Al;Campanis>. Solly Hemus (telephone interview, December 9, 1998) denied that he was or had been a racist.
23. Flood, *The Way It Is,* 68.

Gibson, Crowe, and White what he had said to Daniels and failed to add a word of regret or explanation, they decided that was the last straw. "Until then," Flood recalled, "we had detested Hemus for not employing his best line-up. Now we hated him for himself."[24]

Lest it be said that Flood misstated or made too much of Hemus's remarks, Gibson in his book *Stranger to the Game* tells the story with slightly different details that offer both a bit of context and, with the addition of one word, are more damning. Gibson implies that other Cardinals heard Hemus call Daniels a "black bastard" not the next day but during the struggle between the two on the mound. More important, Hemus felt it necessary to call a team meeting to explain his actions, and in the process of explaining he referred to Daniels as a "nigger." Thirty years later, at a Cardinals reunion, Hemus approached Gibson and said that, despite what he and Flood had thought, he was not a racist. Gibson then reminded him of the Daniels incident, only to hear Hemus say that he was just trying to motivate the team. In his telling of the story, Gibson admits that the club was not hitting and needed a spark, but he still thought Hemus's explanation was "bullshit."[25]

However serious and pervasive the racism felt by Flood, Gibson, White, and other black players in the fifties, and whatever its sources, the most obvious forms of racism diminished significantly in the sixties, in one situation even before federal legislation. Indeed, the Cardinals' first steps toward dealing with racial discrimination were to produce what Flood thought a new, stronger cohesion and spirit that helped the team become one of the best clubs of the sixties. Together with a fortunate trade, the emergence of untapped talent, and the appointments of new managers, the Cardinals would reach three World Series and win two of them.

Flood would later tell the Major League Baseball Players Association board in San Juan, Puerto Rico, that he was not a black activist. And whatever being an "activist" means, it would not seem that he was one. He played at best an incidental role in the racial transformations he thought contributed so much to the team chemistry critical to the triumphs of the sixties. An opportunity to fight Jim Crow arose in 1961 during spring training in an incident involving the Cardinals and the St.

24. Ibid., 67–68; Hemus interview, December 9, 1998.
25. Bob Gibson and Lonnie Wheeler, *Stranger to the Game: The Autobiography of Bob Gibson,* 52–53.

Petersburg Yacht Club. Every year this yacht club hosted a breakfast for members of the Cardinals and the New York Yankees, who also trained nearby. In 1961, as in the past, the club sent out invitations to most team members; as in years past, the black players on both teams were bypassed. This time Flood, Gibson, White, and Crowe saw that a white rookie had received an invitation while they who were veterans had not, and decided that they could not accept the insult without protest. They may have been inspired by the sit-ins at lunch counters in Greensboro, North Carolina, the year before, by other signs of an emerging black activism, or perhaps by President John F. Kennedy's inaugural address just the month before. Flood does not comment on the protest in his memoir or elsewhere. However, Gibson wrote that he and his three black colleagues were inspired by the growing number of black stars who were becoming so important to baseball: it gave them some confidence that their concerns would be addressed.

It was the veteran Bill White who initiated the protest against the St. Petersburg Yacht Club's invitation policy, perhaps because he had grown up in a northern, white community and was polished and polite, but firm. He brought his painful exclusion, and that of the other black players, to the attention of Joe Reichler, an Associated Press writer. Reichler wrote a story about the protest that was picked up by a black newspaper in St. Louis. The paper quickly called for blacks to boycott Anheuser-Busch's beers if the company did not deal with this deeply offensive problem. Gussie Busch and Bing Devine responded very quickly. First they spoke to the yacht club's board, which was composed chiefly of St. Petersburg's leading businessmen. After one or both emphasized that the Cardinals could move their spring training camp to newly booming Arizona, with a significant loss in dollars to the Florida city, the yacht club's board said that all the black Cardinals would be invited to its breakfast. As it turned out, though, none of the four men decided to go. White said, "Going to breakfast at seven o'clock in the morning didn't really appeal to us . . . But in speaking up, it was a chance to put a spotlight on some of the things that were going on down there, and it worked."[26]

Numbers and a spotlight worked not only in the case of the St. Petersburg Yacht Club's breakfast but also in desegregating the Cardinals'

---

26. Peter Golenbock, *The Spirit of St. Louis: A History of the Cardinals and the Browns*, 439–40.

spring training camp. Busch, who did as much as any club leader other than Branch Rickey to bring blacks into Major League Baseball, told the St. Petersburg Baseball Committee that if the Cardinals could not have all their players staying together, then they would not come back to St. Petersburg the following spring. The committee quickly responded, "Don't worry about that," and the Cardinals leased two of the best motels in the city so that in 1962 and after black and white players lived in the same accommodations. That change initiated an even more significant step toward improving the morale of black players (and white players as well): the veteran superstars, including Musial, gave up their splendid private beachfront accommodations and moved in with the rest of the team. Furthermore, the Cardinals' black players now found themselves receiving "star" treatment from some restaurants and nightclubs that had previously barred them altogether, and diners in some establishments applauded when they saw the black players enter.

Although Flood played only a minor role if any in this second significant transformation in St. Petersburg, he wanted it to appear otherwise. He asserts that earlier in the spring of 1962 Bing Devine asked him whether his accommodations were OK, and he responded, as if Devine were blind: "No," they were segregated and inferior to those of the white players, and that was wrong. When Devine reminded him that "segregation was Florida law," Flood says he asserted that St. Louis and other clubs should move their spring training camps to Southern California, and when Devine said making that move would take considerable time and money, Flood says that he exploded in fury: "Shit, you've had a hundred years and money you haven't even counted." However, there was, by Flood's own admission, probably little if anything to this story. Indeed, it sounds like a story he concocted because he surrounds it by acknowledging that "you can only talk that way when everyone thinks you are the next Willie Mays." And at that point he was not. But whatever part Flood did or did not play, he loved the amenities that became available with the end of Jim Crow in Florida. Yet he was loath to admit it. He wanted his readers to know that he found some of the new amenities "unsettling," because the only other blacks in the restaurants were bus boys.[27]

The Cardinals' success in dismantling segregation in Florida did not end Jim Crow in southern-oriented St. Louis, at least not during the

27. Flood, *The Way It Is*, 79.

fifties and early sixties. Decent housing continued to be the serious problem Flood had found upon his arrival in 1958. Eating in St. Louis's prestigious Chase Park Plaza hotel in midtown was out of bounds to blacks for many years, then opened only in part—with a curtain separating blacks from white patrons—until the Civil Rights Act of 1964. But it was not alone; many restaurants, not least the city's greasy spoons, discriminated in various ways against black patrons. One could not sit at the counter. Flood often heard the waitress cry out, "bacon and eggs to go!" He says that he learned soon enough where he could go and where he could not, or he thought he had, until a night when he and his date were turned away from Stan and Biggies, a very tony St. Louis restaurant owned in part by Stan Musial.[28]

When this happened is uncertain, but it might have been 1958, when segregation was the rule in St. Louis, and Flood's date would have been Beverly. As Flood told of the event, he thought the two of them might have been given a table had he told the "bastard"—the maître d' who greeted them at the door—that he was a teammate of Musial. He did not, however. His telling of the episode suggests that he did not want to be treated in a special way, differently from other blacks. He was a victim; they were victims. This did not stop him, however, from complaining to Musial the next afternoon, "Stan, what kind of eating place are you running there?" Musial replied, "What do you mean?" Flood told him about being turned away from the restaurant, at which point "Musial turned livid" and said he would look into the matter. Such is Flood's tale, with no mention of Musial's follow-up inquiry and response. As for Musial, he referred to the alleged incident only after reading about it in Flood's memoir in 1971. Then he told *St. Louis Globe-Democrat* columnist Bob Burnes that he could not understand why Flood was writing about it. "In the first place, that was a long time ago. What point is there in bringing it up now?" In any event, Musial told Burnes, Flood was wrong about what had happened. Musial recalled that he, not the restaurant's maître d', met Flood at the door at twenty minutes to one in the morning and said, "Our kitchen closes at twelve thirty." Musial added, "I was the one who told him he couldn't come in, and I told him the reason why. I felt bad about it because he was a friend—and a teammate—but I've had to do the same thing many times. Biggie and I always had that rule. It applied to everybody." Sorrowfully, Musial asked, "Why would he write about

28. Ibid., 77.

that for any reason—and why would he tell only half the story?" Musial's rhetorical question was well put, although it is quite possible that he and Flood were referring to different occasions. However, there is no way of knowing the truth of the matter. What is known, however, is that Flood returned to Stan and Biggies in the mid-sixties and was treated graciously. However, it might be noted as a reflection on Flood's anger when writing his memoir in 1971 that he did not discuss this second occasion with due grace: "I accepted the adulation with practiced grace, as if it were my due. I assume I would have been treated courteously even had I been a menial on the night out. Times had changed." This much Flood admits: times had changed. But if Flood was, in this instance, a victim of the times, then why did he pin what was by then the dirty tag of racism on Musial and his restaurant? This is even more curious because Flood admired Musial as a great player; as a potential manager (if only because he would not hurt the team, which Flood really seems to have believed the main virtue in any manager); as a star who had surrendered his own quarters in St. Petersburg to help integrate the Cardinals' spring training; and because in his most desperate days, when Hemus advised him that he would "never make it," Musial "was one of the guys who picked me up." Obviously, there is no easy answer to Flood's story about his treatment at Stan and Biggies. However, the only meaningful one is that by the time Flood related the story, he thought his baseball career was behind him, he had lost his challenge to the reserve system in a federal district court, his business enterprises had gone sour, and he was ready to turn on anyone, including one of his favorite drinking buddies.[29]

The drinking buddy was Harry Caray, the sportscaster of the Cardinals, who was beloved by (most) fans, not least because of the bravura manner in which he cried "Holy Cow" when a Cardinal hit a home run. Flood admitted liking Caray personally, which was understandable if he drank with him, but he somehow discriminated between Caray as a drinking partner and Caray as a sportscaster, whom he did not like. When a ballplayer made a bad judgment, Caray was too likely to ignore the cumulative effect on a fielder when a drive was smashed, men were running the bases, and a crowd was screaming. He would cry out: "Oh, no! Flood missed the cutoff man again." While Flood did not care for such criticism coming from an announcer he believed did not under-

29. Bob Burnes, "The Bench Warmer," *St. Louis Globe-Democrat,* April [n.d.] 1971.

stand the turmoil present in such situations, it was the word "again" that the ultrasensitive Flood could not abide. The word implied that he or another Cardinal fielder had failed in another such situation, or several. Perhaps. But that player's mistake did not need to be advertised to thousands of fans. Flood felt failure's sting without criticism from a carping broadcaster. Furthermore, Caray's carping could impair Flood's or another player's livelihood. That is true, but as Flood reluctantly admits, Caray always called his audience's attention to the great plays that various Cardinals made as well. (Ironically, Caray would be fired by Anheuser-Busch as the Cardinals' sportscaster in the same fall that Flood was traded, but if there is a link it has yet to be noted.)[30]

Flood would never have had the opportunity to claw at Caray or Musial or Hemus had the Cardinals' manager not been fired several years before. During the first half of the 1961 season, Flood was neither hitting well nor playing regularly, and the former was largely due to the latter, or so he thought. For this, it may be recalled, Flood blamed Hemus, who left him sitting on the bench, surely because he was black, but there was more. Hemus, Flood wrote, "acted as if I smelled bad. He avoided my presence and when he could not do that he avoided my eye." As long as Hemus managed the Cardinals, "I was an outcast." But fortunately for Flood all that was about to change.[31]

30. Flood, *The Way It Is*, 93–95; Bob Broeg interview, St. Louis, June 16, 1999.
31. Flood, *The Way It Is*, 67–68.

≡ IV

The (Almost) Golden Years

During the winter of 1960–1961 Curt Flood pondered what future, if any, he might have with the St. Louis Cardinals or any other club in the major leagues. Behind him lay another dismal season. Although he had paid close attention to the advice of his team's veteran hitters and batting coach, studied other hitters, and endlessly practiced what he heard and saw, he had hit a miserable .237. His average had dropped below that of his mediocre sophomore year. And it was not because he lacked playing time: for all his complaints about Hemus not letting him play, he had made almost twice as many plate appearances in 1960 as in 1959. And he played in a reasonable 140 games, in part to rest the aging Musial, in part because the Cardinals' front office could not find any other player with anything like his prowess in center field and his ability to fill in at second or third base when absolutely necessary. Presumably this very flexible combination of skills accounts for the Cardinals having offered him a better contract for 1961 than his numbers at the plate would suggest as reasonable.[1]

Fortunately for Flood, he received a raise of $2,000 in his 1961 contract, and his salary was now $12,500. He needed every penny of it. During the winter, he had moved his family to Pomona, California, just outside Los Angeles. Gary, his adopted son, had required heart surgery, and Beverly had argued that some of the best work was done in Los Angeles. Neither of the Floods then or later detailed the specifics of the surgery or the extent of its success. Whatever the outcome, however, heavy hospital costs, along with the obvious expenses of moving, renting, and moving again, must have weighed heavily on the family. In any

1. *St. Louis Post-Dispatch,* May 21, 1970. Salaries and batting averages readily available at http://www.baseball-reference.com/f/floodcu01.shtml, and in the *Baseball Encyclopedia,* 10th ed., and surely any other edition since 1972.

event, by March the family—which now included baby Curtis Christopher, Jr., and with Beverly pregnant again—was back in St. Louis, taking up residence in a black section of the city not far from Beverly's parents. As for the twenty-one-year-old father, he had serious problems other than the family's expenses. He was not a regular in the Cardinals' lineup, he was still an "outcast" in Hemus's eyes, he worried constantly that one day he would be sent back to the minors, and he blamed his racist manager.[2]

Whatever the reason—Hemus, or his own glitches in the batter's box— Flood started slowly in the 1961 season. By May 28 he was hitting a measly .222 and had gone to the plate a meager fifty-five times. However, during the following week he registered a substantial improvement in his playing time. He started several games when Hemus finally decided that Carl Warwick, then playing center field, could not handle the job well enough. With twenty at bats in that one week, Flood raised his average sixty points to .282. But again his opportunity to display his wares was frustrated. Hemus, ever hopeful of finding a center fielder who could hit for power and average, brought up Don Taussig from Omaha and sent Flood back to the bench. In the next two weeks Flood made just six appearances at the plate to pinch-hit, and by June 14 his average had dropped to .263. From his perch on the pines, he could only despair. But he might have seen some real reason for hope had he been able to look in on an awards dinner that night at the Glen Echo Country Club.[3]

That evening Cardinals owner Gussie Busch spoke at a dinner sponsored by the Knights of the Cauliflower Ear to honor Bob Broeg, the highly esteemed sports editor of the *St. Louis Post-Dispatch*, and Bob Burnes, his equally respected counterpart at the morning *Globe-Democrat*. At a time when the Cardinals were in sixth place, eight games out of first and with apparently no serious prospects for bettering their position, Busch said to the otherwise celebrating diners, "I wish I could be more jovial on this occasion, but my heart is bleeding over the Cardinals. [And] you fans deserve more, too. I am going to call on these fellows [Broeg and Burnes] for advice." The next day *Post-Dispatch* sportswriter Robert Morrison commented with unsuspecting accuracy:

2. For children's names and birth dates, see *Beverly A. Flood, Obligee vs. Curtis Charles Flood, obligor,* December 8, 1997, registry no. BL0028957, Superior Court of California, Los Angeles; *St. Louis City Directory,* 1961.

3. *St. Louis Post-Dispatch,* June 1, 1961.

"Hold onto your hat, Solly. Everything will be all right now. Boss Gussie is going to get to the bottom of what ails the Cardinals. He's going into a huddle with the two Bobs."[4]

Morrison was prophetic if a bit premature in suggesting that Busch was going to deal with the Cardinals' ills, perhaps including Hemus among them. On July 1, just a few days prior to the All-Star game, when the Cardinals were still in sixth place but now twelve games out, Busch said about Hemus: "I'm quite sure he'll finish the season." But the brewery king's words turned out to be "the kiss of death." At 11 a.m. on July 6, Cardinals' General Manager Bing Devine announced at a hastily called press conference that Hemus had been dismissed as manager. Johnny Keane, who had managed for seventeen years in the Cardinals' organization, the first fifteen with its farm clubs, the last two and a half as a Cardinals' coach, would replace Hemus at the helm of the parent club.[5]

Keane approached his new task with a different style toward both his players and the way he wanted the game played. He was not more lenient than Hemus. He cut a player who missed a curfew. But older and more experienced than Hemus, Keane was warm and fatherly. He would hold the hand of a player who needed support. And the Cardinals reacted warmly to his promotion. Years later, Bob Gibson, then a young, struggling pitcher, remained so pleased about Keane's promotion that, deliberately or not, he twisted a bit of baseball history to make the changeover more dramatic. He recalled "struggling" on the mound in the first half of 1961 and blamed it on Hemus for shuttling him between the starting rotation and the bullpen. It is no wonder that in his memoir, *Stranger to the Game,* Gibson recalls July 6, the date Keane was made manager, as a "red-letter day." He writes that Keane walked up to him in the clubhouse, gave him the ball, and said, "You're pitching tonight, Hoot." Also, according to Gibson, Keane sent Flood to center field and restored Bill White to his best position, first base. And the results were almost magical: Flood hit a home run, White hit three, and Gibson allowed only one earned run as the Keane-managed Cardinals crushed the Dodgers 9-2.[6]

Happily, White and other Cardinals did slug their way to a lopsided victory over the Los Angeles Dodgers one night in early July; unhappily

4. Ibid., June 14, July 6, 1961.
5. Ibid.
6. Gibson and Wheeler, *Stranger to the Game,* 64–65; *St. Louis Post-Dispatch,* July 6, 1961.

for Gibson's memory, newspaper records reveal that the Cardinals blasted the Dodgers on July 5, not the next day, on which the Cardinals lost by an equally decisive margin. Furthermore, it was not Keane but rather Gibson's bête noire, Solly Hemus, who was still managing the Cardinals on the fifth and who handed him the ball and allegedly said, "You're pitching tonight, Hoot." Then, too, Flood was not plugged into center field or anywhere else that night. He did not play at all on July 5. But if there are some serious problems with Gibson's treatment of Keane's replacement of Hemus, his reason for telling the story may illustrate the significance he attached to the change: Keane's appointment opened "a whole new world for the black players."[7]

In his memoir nine years after Keane replaced Hemus, Flood recalled the managerial change far more briefly than Gibson, but with the same warmth. In Flood's recollection, Keane had quickly said, "You're the center fielder, Curt," and Flood recalled playing regularly after that. The facts, however, are otherwise. On July 6, Keane's first night as manager, Flood pinch-ran for Musial late in the game, no more. He did the same the next night and many other nights during the always hot, humid St. Louis summer. One week after Keane replaced Hemus, Flood was hitting .284, but he had batted just ten times in that seven-day stretch, a certain measure of his limited playing time early in Keane's tenure. And there was little or no change in the next month and a half. By late August Flood was hitting for a .300 average, a quite respectable number, but even then he was not playing daily. Almost certainly his recollection that Keane said in early July when he became the Cardinals' manager, "You're the center fielder, Curt," is incorrect.[8]

Gradually, during the summer, Keane came to see Flood as an important piece in his strategy for building the Cardinals, a strategy that stood Hemus's emphasis on power hitters and big innings on its head. In his two-year stint as a Cardinals' coach, Keane had pored over the team's win-loss record and the players' individual statistics. And in the first half of the 1961 season he had looked for clues that might reveal why the team was losing more often than in 1960. By July, he thought he had the answers and was ready to remodel the Cardinals' lineup and style of play. He concluded that Hemus had not paid sufficient attention

7. Gibson and Wheeler, *Stranger to the Game,* 65.
8. *St. Louis Post-Dispatch,* July 7, 8, 9, 1964; for Keane's comment, see Stump, "Midnight League," 78.

to the Cardinals' defense. They were scoring runs, but the opposition was too often scoring even more. The solution, he hoped, might be to use quicker and better, if possibly smaller, fielders, which would necessarily mean relying on a different method of scoring as well. Shortly after taking over, then, Keane asserted that he wanted to install a different type of offense. Soon, if not then, it would be known as "small ball." Runs would be "manufactured." This process would begin with a single or a walk, followed by a sacrifice or a stolen base. That would place a runner in position to score from second base on a hit to the outfield, or even on a bunt, wild pitch, long fly out, or error if the runner had stolen third. "Small ball," then, was to be the new model for the Cardinals.

Keane knew that none of the Cardinals fit his "small ball" playing style better than Flood. When he began to hit consistently, Flood would often single through the center of the diamond and, after reaching first base, steal second, then score on another base hit. His quickness would serve the team well. But in July of 1961 that was a calculated guess which would become reality only if Flood began to hit. There was far less question, however, of Flood fitting into Keane's plans to improve the team's defense. Flood was naturally a great center fielder, a defensive gem able with his speed to run down balls other fielders could not, saving runs. But speed was not the only key to Flood's strength as an outfielder. According to Cardinals' catcher Tim McCarver, Flood's greatest asset as a center fielder, other than his speed, was his "extraordinary anticipation," which reflected his almost uncanny focus. Flood always knew the count on the batter, who was pitching, what type of pitch he was throwing, and how hard he was throwing. Flood, according to McCarver, was "awesome"; his mind was a computer, always factoring in the signals that enabled him to know what to look for from a pitch and from a batter, and that enabled him to lean either to the right or the left as the situation required, gaining what appeared to be a running start on drives hit into right or left center. Hardly less important, Flood combined his early recognition of a ball's direction with an equally crucial early recognition of its distance, checking its position, so he said, by whether it was above or below the brim of his cap.[9]

9. Tim McCarver with Danny Peary, *Tim McCarver's Baseball for Brain Surgeons and Other Fans*, 241–43.

All Flood's mental and physical qualities—his study of batters, his ability to concentrate, his natural speed, and his sharp reflexes—contributed to his great and persistent success over the years in "getting to the ball," as recognized by his winning several Gold Glove awards. But there was more to Flood's success than the "hard" qualities mentioned. He studied his position with an immeasurably fierce determination and played it with an immeasurably fierce intensity. He dominated center field as few others have before or since. But the characteristics that made his play so great also left him vulnerable to the danger that a singularly critical misplay, perhaps as a result of momentary loss of focus, might undermine his psyche. And that damage could compound over time, leading to ever more serious, even deadly, mistakes in judgment. Whatever the advantages in Flood's mental approach to the game, hypothetically it also posed grave danger, as one day's performance seven years later would reveal.

Keane knew from his years as a coach that Flood was an extremely talented center fielder, just what the Cardinals' defense needed; but he also knew that Flood's brittle temperament did not augur well for his hitting in the clutch. Keane recalled, for example, that Flood had reacted bitterly when Hemus fined him for even a minimal amount after he missed a team plane. That aside, Keane believed Flood failed to hit for an acceptable average—at least .280—during his predecessor's term as manager largely because Hemus's emphasis on power hitting placed too much pressure on the young man to overswing in order to meet the manager's expectations. What seemed obvious to Keane from just watching was clearly supported by the statistics he had compiled; hitting well with men in scoring position was anything but the center fielder's best quality. A month after Keane took over, Flood stood at the bottom of a list of Cardinals in the key statistic "Opportunity to Bat in Runs," or OBR. He was averaging just .222 in that category; a reasonable number was .400, and the team leader, Ken Boyer, was at .462. Keane saw very clearly what Flood could and could not do. He played center field better than anyone in the majors except future Hall of Famer Willie Mays, and thus having him play there regularly would eliminate a defensive weakness. But Keane also required a steady offense, and as of August 1 Flood, a right-handed batter, was hitting a superb .347 against left-handed pitchers, but at .240 he was having difficulty against right-handers. It was true that Flood appeared to be ready to hit both left- and right-handers equally well, thanks to Crowe's insistent advice that he shorten and level his swing and his own unusually fierce determination to succeed and to practice constantly. But being on the verge and actually realizing his potential were two different things.[10]

Given that Flood had not shown any real evidence that he could hit right-handed pitchers, it is understandable that Keane rarely played him when one was on the mound. But it was hardly the decisive factor: Keane's other right-handed batters were doing no better against right-handed pitchers. He had two other reasons for not playing the young center fielder regularly. Keane felt that Flood would shorten his swing more consistently when he fully recognized the remodeling of the Cardinals' style of play, which made it unnecessary to swing for the fences; Flood would feel less pressure. He also feared that Flood would get too weak if he played regularly in the dog-days of July and August in St. Louis. During Keane's first two years as a Cardinals' coach, he had watched Flood wilt in those midsummer days, losing as many as five pounds a game, and he believed that might account in part for Flood's batting average "tailing off" in those months. Flood admitted as much to sportswriters. He had a serious problem when the summer's "misery index" numbers climbed. Weakened, he lost bat speed, and he could not roam center field with his normal speed; eating more and taking vitamins did not help.

Even so, Flood thought he could play more, and he seized his limited opportunities. In an August 5 game he outran a ball slammed into the gap and made a backhanded stab before skidding to the grass. After the game, Keane told Neal Russo of the *Post-Dispatch*, "That was one of the greatest catches I've ever seen anywhere." On August 18, Russo told Flood that the catch he made the evening before, even if it did not match another two weeks earlier in terms of skill, more than equaled it in value for pitcher Larry Jackson, whose 2–0 victory it saved. Then there was the catch and hit on August 28 that the *Post-Dispatch* believed required a headline: "Flood's Glove and Bat Help Jackson Win 3-Hitter." When Russo saw Flood after the game and asked where he had found the strength to run down and spear Joe Amalfitano's drive on such a hot day, after a long, miserable summer, Flood admitted having some difficulty keeping his weight at 160 pounds, but added, "I feel strong now." And he may have; he was hitting .309, an average all but a very few play-

10. *St. Louis Post-Dispatch,* August 1, 1961.

ers would have envied. It carried the day with Keane; he agreed now that it was time to play Flood on a regular basis.[11]

It first appeared, however, that playing Flood every day was a mistake: his batting average fell over the next two days to .304. Then he benefited from what was either a stroke of luck, a bit of superstition, mere coincidence, or all three. On September 1, he inexplicably returned his own bat to the rack and picked up a model that had been designed for Bill White. That game saw him begin a hitting spree, getting 11 hits in 19 times at bat. By September 5 he was batting .325 and was the club's batting leader. It was then that Keane told the press what it had seen for itself: "We've finally impressed Flood on the idea of just meeting the ball instead of trying to drive everything out of the park." Flood ended the season at .322.[12]

Flood's newfound ability to hit consistently against pitchers every day meant that he had cemented his place in center field. He would play every day in part because of Hemus's departure, in larger part because of Keane's "small ball" style of play, but in the largest part due to Keane's nurturing support. Flood needed it. His nerves were as fragile as a violin's strings. Al Stump, after interviewing Flood for *Sport* magazine, reported that the young center fielder played regularly not only in the National League but also "in the midnight league": too often, Flood could not sleep after games. Indeed, the baseball fan, whether watching at the ballpark, listening to a game on the radio, or reading about it the next day in his newspaper, was treated to a masked man. Behind Flood's appearance as an easygoing, gentle, and gracious ballplayer lurked an insecure, extremely self-critical perfectionist who brooded nightly over the game just ended and that to be played the next day or the day after. Stump reported that Flood suffered from a stress-induced nervous stomach. He did not report, as he might have, or possibly because Flood did not tell him, that the young outfielder smoked while playing in the midnight league, an addiction that probably contributed to the acid in his stomach (and possibly contributed to his relatively early death from throat cancer). Flood did tell Stump—as did Gibson for the same article—that he paced his hotel room floor well into the wee hours and tormented himself because "I went two for four against [Sandy] Koufax . . . but I didn't have an RBI, and we lost the game." Of

11. Ibid., August 18, 29, 1961
12. Ibid., September 5, 1961.

course, there was no really good reason for Flood's harsh self-criticism; doubtless there was no better pitcher in baseball than the Dodgers' Koufax in the early and mid sixties. That, however, did not stop the extraordinarily sensitive Flood from worrying that he had let his team down, which he always thought the worst of sins for a ballplayer. And on the nights he thought he had, he worried endlessly over it and, after that, over the next day's game, for hours poring over the notebook that Harry the "Hat" Walker had advised him to keep on the tendencies of the pitcher he was about to face. He was waiting for a tranquilizer to do its "work" and trying not to worry about not getting his sleep. Gibson, his roommate, who suffered from various allergies, sinus trouble chief among them, was almost as high-strung as Flood and often had insomnia as well. He said of their sleep issues: "But at that, I'll bet I get more sack time than Curt does."[13]

What Gibson knew about Flood playing "in the midnight league," Keane quickly learned and dealt with quietly but well, as Flood would testify. Flood told *Sport* that his manager often dropped by his room to talk. "We always had a strange relationship. John could read any trouble I was hiding on my face. He knew me backwards. He was a wonderful uncle to me—and he gave me the break that made me a major-league ballplayer." That is how Flood spoke in 1965 of what his manager had done for him, coating Keane with praise that could not have been warmer or more appropriate. Unfortunately, Flood would subvert this gracious tribute six years later, gratuitously labeling Keane "a gentle person with a competent grasp of the game but no special prowess."[14]

Even if Keane had not been "a wonderful uncle," it was thanks to the new playing style he installed and his capacity for viewing players as individuals that Flood's career took off in the last five weeks of the 1961 season. Flood's "golden years" as a major-league star were launched. His new status was confirmed by Keane in a September 28 after-dinner speech to the Royal Vagabond Club, an occasion when an audience of black newspapermen was present to honor Flood. Keane told them that "the Cardinals in 1962 will go to spring training with center field in capable hands." He added, "If Flood can hit around .270 or .280 and keep fielding the way he has, we've got a center fielder for a long time." As for Flood, when accepting his award that evening, he could not resist

13. Stump, "Midnight League."
14. Flood, *The Way It Is,* 65.

tweaking Hemus. He blamed his former manager for failing to give him a serious shot in center, for his insomnia, and even for his being repelled by food. Flood's gratuitous mention of Hemus did not stop there. "Hemus," he added, "couldn't see me at all—maybe it was my size." He meant that Hemus did not want to see him because he was black. Even so, at the Royal Vagabond Club Flood did not attack Hemus as harshly as he did in his memoir a decade later.[15]

In February 1962, Flood received a contract that raised his salary from $12,500 to $16,000. It was a much-needed addition to his family's coffers, but no less to his ego: the pay raise recognized his commitment, persistence, and hard work as well as his prowess. Flood also greatly prized the public's recognition of his new status as the team's regular center fielder. Although he did not hit as well in 1962 as the previous year—he still hit a quite decent .296—he was asked to make appearances at various charitable events, and he did. One such appearance was at the suburban Westroads Center, where he did a benefit for the Nursery Foundation. And he was celebrity enough that the *Post-Dispatch* asked him to list the stadiums he as a center fielder preferred playing in, and to explain why. Tactfully, he preferred the sixty-year-old Sportsman's Park on North Grand Avenue where the Cardinals played—and would until Busch Stadium opened downtown four years later—stressing its "excellent background" and "some of the best lights around." Many fans would have disagreed because in some areas their view of the game was blocked by wood posts holding up the roof. On the other hand, while many fans in Chicago loved Wrigley Field, Flood said it was difficult to play in windblown parks like those of the Cubs and the San Francisco Giants. He did not like playing in the Houston Colts' ballpark either as the "sun makes white shirts in the stands even brighter."[16]

Flood made the Cardinals brighter, too, both off and on the field. At times he was the butt of good humor in the clubhouse on a team where, he said, humor was a must: it was essential for the relief of tension before a game. A sharp dresser, he looked the very picture of success in his continental clothes, but his teammates often barbed him because he was the only player who did not have cuffs on his trousers. Playing the game in the clubhouse, Flood said later that he faked defiance: "I'll change them before they change me." Whether Flood was faking is

15. *St. Louis Post-Dispatch,* September 29, 1961; Flood, *The Way It Is,* 65–73.
16. *St. Louis Post-Dispatch,* May 15, 1962.

questionable—often enough he was really defiant of the Cardinals' front office—but really faking or just joking served the purpose of enhancing or, at least, sustaining the team spirit that he believed essential to success on the field. Even silliness worked, as did almost anything that helped produce much-needed relaxation and, most important, bonding. The latter might lead to the readiness of a player to sacrifice his individual statistics for the greater good: winning. Flood stressed that this sense of unity, much like that of the Three Musketeers, should include the front office, which also meant the Anheuser-Busch brewery, and, as noted, that unity was enhanced in 1962 when the club leased two motels in St. Petersburg, seeking to end racial discrimination at its spring training camp. Black and white players sharing accommodations were more likely to view each other as the boon companions he thought teammates ought to be. But as important as Flood believed harmony in the clubhouse and out, racial and otherwise, was to winning, he was just as often moody as he was playful, and he was not, he admitted, quite as assertive or successful as Bob Gibson in endeavoring to close the racial rifts that at times threatened the team's cohesion. Gibson, Flood recalled in 1968, did not allow a gulf to develop between new, white players like the southern-born and raised Tim McCarver and the blacks on the team. He asked McCarver out for a drink, repeatedly if necessary, until, as happened, the gulf was bridged.[17]

Perhaps the fact that Flood was a bit of a celebrity by 1962 helps account for the fall-off in his batting average that season, but he thought, probably with more accuracy, that it was because he pulled the ball more often than not, still trying to hit for power, and infielders, watching him do it, played him to hit the ball through the left side. He thought the 1963 season also started badly for him, and for the same reason: he continued pulling inside pitches outside the foul line, and he tried to pull those on the outside as well, hoping, it seems, to reach the fences. By mid-May he was hitting a miserable .224. Fortunately for Flood's average, his career, and his peace of mind, in 1963 the Cardinals obtained Dick Groat, a great shortstop, from Pittsburgh, and Flood saw a real opportunity to learn from the former Pirate. "I got to learn to hit to the opposite field. You show me," he told Groat. And that season Groat tutored him. "He must have asked me 50 times for more instructions," Groat sighed to *Sport* two years later. Flood readily admitted the great debt he

17. Pepe, "How Flood Finally Made It," 45; Flood, *The Way It Is,* 86–90.

owed the shortstop, now his batting coach. "Groat and I would go out to the ball park for long periods of time, and he would help me to learn how to hit to right field. That Groat, he could hit .300 with a strand of barbed wire." After more practices than Flood could recall, Groat's tutelage took hold. Flood learned to hit inside pitches from the inside-out, sending the ball to right field and center, and at year's end he had a .302 average and 200 hits, along with a Gold Glove Award as center fielder of the year. Unfortunately for the Cardinals in 1963, it was not enough that Flood corrected his hitting problems. It was clear that the team lacked one essential piece—another outfielder with speed—if it was to win a pennant, even a World Championship.[18]

That missing piece was supplied in the middle of the 1964 season when the Cardinals sent pitcher Ernie Broglio to the Cubs for outfielder Louis "Lou" Brock. Flood fairly quickly pointed out how valuable Brock was, not only as an exceptionally gifted base stealer—soon to be one of the best of all time—but as a fast defensive outfielder. Flood reminded the *Post-Dispatch*'s Russo that during the previous season he was flanked by two of baseball's elders, George Altman and Stan Musial. Humorously but accurately he asserted, "Our outfield [had] Old Taylor and Ancient Age with a little Squirt for a chaser." Consequently, Flood asserted, he was forced to cover more ground than normal, certainly more than was desirable, and his legs and bat had tired. Now, Flood asserted, with the addition of the speedy Mike Shannon in right field and the even faster Brock in left, he had much less acreage to worry about. He could save his energy and concentration for hitting and focus on swinging only at pitches in the strike zone and hitting to all fields.

Flood insisted that most of the credit for his improvement should go to Groat's instruction and that of Harry "The Hat" Walker in 1963; but Cardinal pitcher Larry Jackson emphasized that Flood not only watched and listened carefully, but concentrated fiercely "in the batting cage." No wonder Flood's average improved in 1964, as he batted .311 and matched the Pittsburgh Pirates' famed Roberto Clemente in hits, the two tying for the league's lead with 211. At the same time, confounding Keane's assertion in 1961 that he would weaken in the summer's dogged heat and should be rested at various times, Flood played in every one of the season's 162 games. And that performance, coupled with the consistent hitting of third baseman Ken Boyer, the great pitching of "Hoot" Gibson,

18. Stump, "Midnight League," 79.

and the total collapse of the Philadelphia Phillies at the season's end, enabled the Cardinals to win the National League pennant at the last moment and, after that, the World Championship. Flood, however, batted a lowly .200 in the World Series against the New York Yankees. His average went unnoticed at the time, but it may be worth noting: his hitting would not improve much in the 1967 or 1968 World Series, suggesting once again that he did not hit well in the clutch and, by extension, did not handle pressure very well.

After the 1964 season, the Flood family—Curt, Beverly, and their four children, with a fifth soon to come—left for California as they always had in the off-season. In previous years they had headed for Pomona, to the house they first rented during Gary's surgery in 1961. But that autumn of 1964 they went to Oakland in northern California. They did so because of Flood's dinner with a very close friend two years earlier.

During the summer of 1962, while the Cardinals were in San Francisco playing the Giants, Flood met with Jim Chambers, the high school teacher he had bonded with at McClymonds. Since then, they had continued to be close, as indicated by the rather intimate letters Flood wrote Chambers during his lonesome summers playing ball in High Point (and, probably, in Savannah as well). Now, Chambers suggested during their dinner in San Francisco that they visit his cousin, Marian Jorgensen, and her husband, John, in Oakland's Montclair district. At first Flood said no, but Chambers argued, "They're great fans, Curt. They've been following your progress since the sandlot days. And they know all about your interest in painting. You'll love them." Flood was still reluctant. Fans could be well-meaning, but they were often troublesome. They asked the questions he heard too often, as if he were only a baseball player. He thought he should be able to "spend his leisure with people who think of him [first] as a person." However, he finally decided to trust Chambers's judgment and agreed to visit the Jorgensens.[19]

Chambers could not have been more prophetic in thinking that Flood and the Jorgensens would enjoy each other's company, and certainly he could not have imagined how important they, or Marian at least, would be in Flood's life for the next decade. They were two generations apart from him in age, but Flood felt after meeting them that he had made an "emotional discovery bordering on the spiritual." He felt at home right away. "Home from a long journey. Home from the wars. Home to the sta-

19. Flood, *The Way It Is,* chap. 7, "A Powerful Goodness."

bility and forgiveness of home. Home where I belonged." Flood may well have been influenced by his own messy marriage, but he was greatly impressed with how bonded the Jorgensens were: "What it boiled down to was that the Jorgensens and Flood loved each other on sight." He concluded that the Jorgensens as individuals and as a couple were what he and Beverly wished they were—but, unfortunately, were not. His marriage was "an armed truce"; the Jorgensens' was "a marriage of total congeniality." Meanwhile, although he once attributed his and Beverly's marital problems to a shared youthful immaturity, he now blamed her alone, and not just for the marriage's failure. She had undermined his innermost being. Flood meant that he now saw himself as a bundle of "delicately balanced, ruthlessly controlled raw nerves," the victim of the "stress of a discordant marriage."[20]

After the 1962 season, Flood took Beverly to visit the Jorgensens. Flood hoped that their warmth might help repair his troubled marriage, although he knew they were "not miracle workers." What most obviously intrigued him in 1962, however, was not how they could help his marriage but what he could learn from John Jorgensen's craftsmanship and business. Flood had heard from Chambers that Jorgensen was a genius in the art of designing and engraving dies for industrial use and that he made very good money in the business. Jorgensen in the interim found that what Chambers had told him of Flood's talents was true: Flood could sketch and paint, and he asked Flood if he would like to learn engraving as well. Flood answered that he would, and soon found himself carried away by the artistry, the infinite detail, and the absolute perfection that working with industrial dies required. He soon began to feel as if he were born for the craft. And Johnny Jorgensen soon reached the same conclusion, asking Flood to work in his engraving plant and eventually to become a partner in the business.[21]

Flood's growing interest in designing and engraving, and Jorgensen's interest in him as a partner, probably explain the Floods' "winter" move, in October 1964, from Pomona to Alamo, a small town fifteen miles east of Jorgensen's business in Oakland; but there is also good reason to believe that the timing reflected a resolution of problems in their marriage, one in particular—where they would live. The winter before Flood had gone by himself to Oakland and lived in the Jorgensens' recreation

20. Ibid.
21. Ibid.

room, which Marian had turned into an apartment. Beverly, who was left alone with four children, found her husband's decision to spend the winter in northern California without her the last straw in their difficult marriage, and in October 1963 she sued for divorce in a Los Angeles court. She claimed that her husband's criticism made her feel "inadequate and inferior," and that once he had struck her. Whether or to what extent Beverly was abused cannot be documented. Suffice to say that the court decreed on February 29, 1964, that "Mrs. Curt Flood [was] granted [a] divorce." Actually, she received only an interlocutory decree that would not be final for a year, and in fact never became final. For a few months during the winter of 1963–1964, the Floods lived (technically) apart, although whether in fact is questionable. Beverly became pregnant in May, though whether by Flood or, as rumored, "Shorty," is unknown. In any event the couple decided to make "another run at marriage." And they resolved at least one of their many issues: where to live during the winter. What better place than the small town of Alamo, just a few miles due east of San Francisco and Oakland? Apparently, Beverly had decided that for the sake of the children she would move there; possibly their marriage would stabilize if her husband was more relaxed because he was able to work with John Jorgensen and, after the shop closed for the night, both of them could enjoy the company of Marian as well as John. So they saw Alamo as a quiet sanctuary where they could regain their bearings. Neither of them gave sufficient thought to the possibility that this town, close to the Oakland which Flood had found to be racist, might itself harbor racists. Or perhaps a real need to be near the Jorgensens overwhelmed all else.[22]

In Alamo the Floods found a delightful ranch house with a swimming pool and a yard for their family's four—soon to be five—children. Happily, he and Beverly initialed the lease handed them by the realtor who showed them the house and gave her a check to cover their first and last months' rent at $290 a month. The realtor, in turn, was to have George Finn, representing the owner, sign the lease and give her the keys to the house so the Floods could move in the next day. But what began as a normal transaction quickly became complicated. Soon after Finn ini-

22. "Sports in Brief" clipping, source and date unknown, reflected a court case in Los Angeles County Superior Court, State of California, where Beverly's complaint for divorce asserts that they were married for six years by the time of their separation on November 23, 1965. Regarding the 1964 "divorce," see Summons, January 17, 1966, *Beverly Flood vs. Curtis Flood,* Alameda County Superior Court, case no. 356589.

tialed the lease, accepted the Floods' check, and gave the agent a key to the house, he learned that the Floods were black. Early the next day, Saturday, October 24, when the realtor went to the house to check it out, she found Finn and another man (his brother Charles) blocking the driveway with a car, both men holding shotguns, and George Finn demanding that she return the house key. The agent felt she faced grave danger in the situation—Finn, she said later, was "enraged"—and, as the lease did not officially go into effect until the following Monday, she hurriedly returned the key Finn had handed her the day before.[23]

When Flood learned later that day about the incident at the house, he played it down, at least publicly. He was, he told reporters three days later, "very upset, but no . . . not angry. I just want[ed] to move my family into this home." In fact, Flood was really angry—as he would say later—but, possibly because Beverly was four months pregnant, he tried to keep his anger under control. He did not quite succeed. He had no intention of surrendering what he believed his right to lease the house. He told the press on October 27, "It's not that I'm a professional athlete or a Negro, I'm a human being regardless of what I am." Bitterly, he went on—probably from a need he could not suppress—to speak frankly about his treatment in Alamo, so close to Oakland that he saw it as home: "I was born here, I graduated from Oakland Tech, all my friends are here, and my parents live here." Flood's words were few and quietly spoken, but the edge in them made their meaning unmistakable.[24]

However angry Flood actually felt about the racism implicit in the Finns' refusal to hand over the keys to the Alamo house, he acted coolly, turning to the law. On Monday, October 26, he went to nearby Martinez, the Contra Costa County seat, to engage a lawyer. He also called on the California Fair Employment Practices Commission (CFEPC) for aid. His mother had taught him when he was a five-year-old-boy in East Oakland not to back away from a righteous fight, and he did not intend to do so now. Accordingly, that Monday his lawyer, Robert Condon, obtained a restraining order against the Finns and the out-of-state owner of the house and filed a $10,000 lawsuit. And the next afternoon both Floods went to the house, despite troubling initial concerns about possible danger to the pregnant Beverly. They were accompanied by the Contra

23. *St. Louis Globe-Democrat* and *St. Louis Post-Dispatch*, October 27 and 28. Both papers carried reports supplied by an Associated Press reporter.

24. Associated Press story, October 24, 1964, in the *Oakland Tribune* and *St. Louis Post-Dispatch*,

Costa County sheriff, as well as eleven of his deputies, three members of the CFEPC, and a locksmith, who, because Finn did not appear, soon had to change the locks on the house. Meanwhile, the sheriff's deputies directed the heavy traffic from a fascinated neighborhood. Some of the onlookers brought food and drink, and when it was unloaded everyone sat near the swimming pool, picnicking. Later that afternoon two Presbyterian ministers welcomed the Floods to their Danville church. One young mother expressed great pleasure that Curt Flood, the baseball star, would be living there, telling reporters standing nearby, "My kids are thrilled. They hope he'll teach them to play baseball better."

Flood seemed very pleased at such indications of his family's welcome, even though the neighbors did not recognize him as a "human being," as he wished, but as a baseball player. Even so, he responded warmly to the crowd: "We hope to add something to your neighborhood. Bless you all. You're very, very wonderful."[25]

Flood's obviously warm interchange with his new home's visitors represented his effort to make a new start in Alamo by soothing troubled waters. Soon, however, he found that even his best efforts could not alter the reality that a few people opposed to a black family living in the area could make life at his new home unpleasant. In March 1965 he told a *Sport* reporter about several awful experiences following his family's Alamo move-in. He had received a death threat and had been called a "nigger" in front of his wife; with people all over the country looking in on their private life via newspapers, these incidents were "heartbreaking" and "humiliating." Comparing racism in Alamo as he had recently felt it to the racism he had long felt in St. Louis, Flood added, "I've never mentioned this before, but what helped make [moving into the house in Alamo] so hard to take is that when Beverly and I were living in St. Louis, we couldn't find a decent place to live. In Cardinalville!" He added bitterly, "We had to move to Los Angeles to get the house we wanted." And then they had moved to supposedly quiet Alamo seeking a decent home for their family. But Alamo was not quiet, he told Stump; not for a black family. "They call this [street] La Serena Avenue. That means a place of serenity, doesn't it? What's serene . . . about not being able to sleep . . . for fear some maniac with a gun will sneak in on your kids?"[26]

25. *St. Louis Globe-Democrat,* October 27, 1964.
26. Stump, "Midnight League," 78.

While there is no evidence that anyone threatened the Flood home, three-year-old Shelley was "tortured" by neighborhood children before Debbie came to her rescue with a bat, and other scuffles followed. Beverly soon found the children's situation and the attendant stress too much to handle, especially when she had little help from her husband, who was spending his time in Jorgensen's shop in Oakland. She left Alamo for a house she and her husband had bought in nearby Richmond, which had a large black population. As for her husband, when Stump interviewed him in March for *Sport*, Flood was training at the Cardinals camp in St. Petersburg, preparing for the 1965 season, and savoring a contract that raised his salary from $23,000 to $35,000. He was also relishing the financial and other benefits that would accrue from the prospective benefits of a commission handed him by a St. Louis radio station to provide it with drawings of sixty noted sports figures as wall decorations, at a price of $3,600.[27]

Flood's pleasure at the payoff for his and the Cardinals' achievements did not last beyond spring training. For the World Champions, the 1965 season was a dismal failure: they collapsed in their division's standings as precipitously as if they had fallen off a cliff top, ending the season in seventh place. Whatever the actual reasons, which were surely many and various, Flood made a scapegoat out of Bob Howsam, the Cardinals' new general manager. Howsam, he would later tell *Sports Illustrated*, had insulted him, Gibson, and a number of other Cardinals. After they won the World Championship in 1964, Howsam sent them contracts with miserably small raises. "The salary squabbles before the season started had a lot to do with [the team's disastrous season in the season just past]." Although Flood had somewhat disparaged the importance of money to a ballplayer in an interview with Neal Russo of the *St. Louis Post-Dispatch* the previous October, it now seemed to be a very important consideration. But in all probability it was not the amount itself that upset Flood, but rather the lack of respect that it signified. He had been offered a raise of only $1,500, surely too little respect for his contributions the year before. But Flood did not recall for *Sports Illustrated* that he and Howsam had finally agreed on what by almost any measure was a very excellent raise. Neither did he mention that, despite the salary squabbles, he had hit for just a single point less in 1965 than the year before, and Gibson, also supposedly angered over

27. Ibid.; Belth, *Stepping Up*, 93–94.

his raise, actually won a game more than in 1964. Flood seemed to be looking for someone to blame for the Cardinals' failure to win another pennant and World Championship. And Howsam was his target. The general manager needlessly annoyed and upset the team, Flood reported. He tried to police the players over the most picayune issues on the field and off. Memos flew around the clubhouse. The most egregious, Flood recalled, were silly, if not disgusting; among them were: "'Sit up straight in the bullpen. Don't run on the grass when you leave the plate. All socks [must be] cut the same way.' Hell," Flood told one reporter, "we are individuals, and we want to dress like individuals, and be treated like individuals should be." He meant it, too, as is at least suggested by his insistence on wearing trousers without cuffs, whatever other players did. Flood was not a man to toe the party line.[28]

However differently the other Cardinals dressed and however badly they may have played in 1965 compared to 1964, Flood continued to play with the same intensity that he had shown during the previous two and a half years, and with the same success. Although he did not get two hundred hits, as in the previous two years, it was not for lack of effort. On the contrary, he often played injured. Bob Bauman, the team's trainer, tagged him "the closest thing to a Stan Musial for playing despite physical handicaps." Flood was always that way, Bauman told the *Sporting News*. In 1958, his first year as a Cardinal, he played with a sprained thumb. In 1963 he pulled a leg muscle in spring training, but he took cortisone shots and begged—others said snarled at—Keane to put him back in the lineup. In 1964 he ran into a metal fence during spring training and tore muscles and ligaments; even so, he only missed a couple of games. Also that year he remained in a game despite a dislocated finger. He had the dislocated finger taped to a good finger, got a shot of cortisone, went back on the field, and later in the game hit a key home run. As for the season just past, he played with a foot gashed when spikes from one shoe went through another shoe after he landed very hard after a spectacular catch. Because of such injuries that year he had missed six games altogether, and in a number of games had been able to pinch-hit, but no more. So, it was marvelous, Bauman thought, that Flood managed 191 hits. And the trainer added more encomiums to his account for the *Sporting News:* "Like Musial, Flood never refuses a manager if he can possibly play."

28. Leggett, "Curt Flood of St. Louis," 21.

Bauman did not explore Flood's reasons for playing with the injuries he described. Of course, players in Flood's era had yearly contracts, so they played with injuries or, at least, pain more often than players in later eras with long, expensive, guaranteed contracts. But two issues were always on Flood's mind. Clearly, he feared losing his job, as poor Wally Pipp famously lost his to Lou Gehrig for sitting out just one day; and, equally, he feared letting the team down. Both factors, perhaps the latter more than the former, strengthened his commitment to play even when hurt. And he played well. True, he did not get as many hits in 1965 as in the previous two years, but he won a Gold Glove award for the third straight year, and on January 31, 1966, he received another honor, the J. G. Taylor Spink award as the *Sporting News*'s St. Louis Baseball Man of the Year.

Although Flood gushed extensively to Russo, and sometimes to other sportswriters, about his feats in the field, and sometimes about his learning to design dies and to paint portraits, he was either silent about his divorce in Oakland, or it was the type of personal story sportswriters of that era did not write about or even think of writing about, and hence did not inquire into or investigate. But if they had, they would have found much of later import to Flood's baseball career and, in time, his legal challenge to baseball's reserve system.

V

A Gold Glove Is Tarnished

It is understandable that sportswriters did not investigate and write candidly about Flood's personal life. Their expense accounts did not cover the former, and their job descriptions certainly did not cover the latter. Sportswriters and baseball announcers as well were "boosters" for, in order, the National Pastime, the club in the city where they worked, and that club's players. These men—for they were all men in that era—depended on the club's front office and players alike for access, but as fans they also wrote to protect the game they loved. Even were that not the case, they would have had no reason to start probing into Flood's personal life, at least not during his golden years in the sixties. But hindsight, although always tinged with the danger of fitting present clues to what is known only later, also sheds light where it seems desperately needed. In Flood's case, critical aspects of his personal life—his marriage and divorce, his court-ordered child support and alimony payments, his female amours and female friends, as well as his drinking and business activities—interacted closely with his baseball career. In time, several of these factors, if primarily those involving his ex-wife and children and an (allegedly) misplayed line drive, interacted. In so doing, they prompted Flood to unravel, leading to or exacerbating his feud with the Cardinals, his trade, and his decision to challenge Major League Baseball in court. In sum, Flood's personal life, his misjudgment on the field as he and others saw it, and his decisions thereafter cannot properly be separated. Indeed, they require the closest scrutiny.

In January 1966, a summons issued by the Alameda County Superior Court in Oakland advised Flood that his wife had sued for divorce. Among other complaints, Beverly said that her husband preferred painting in the garage to spending time with her and the children. It was a complaint her husband would not deny, and only later (in his memoir) would he try to explain it as a reflection of the stress he felt as he worried about losing his job, failing to score base runners, letting down the team, and not getting enough rest. Going to the garage was simply the lesser of two methods of handling his stress after a home game: he could either bark at his wife about her too-brief shorts, her failure to clean the house well, and her excessive spending—provoking a loud fight that hurt both them and the children—or he could leave the house. As he would tell a writer for *Sports Illustrated* in 1968, painting was "one of the few ways I've found to relax." And relaxation was a need a player's wife should accept as implicit in her marital contract.[1]

Obviously, Beverly did not accept her husband's view of the role of a woman married to a ballplayer. Neither did the Alameda County Superior Court judge. On March 22, 1966, Beverly received half of the Floods' community property—around $14,000 worth of cash, cars, and real estate. Beyond that, she gained custody of their children, leaving him with what the court called "reasonable visitation," court costs and attorney's fees, and a $1,400 monthly alimony and child support payment. If Flood objected, he did not say so even though his total monthly payments amounted to half his gross salary in 1965, a greater percentage after taxes; despite salary increases in 1966 and 1967, the payments would continue to take a large percentage of his income. Even so, he was able to leave behind the segregated neighborhoods in St. Louis that had been his lot, and that of Beverly, their children, and most if not all blacks for so long. Times had changed by 1966. He could move into an apartment in the Parkway House just a block from the very large, beautiful Forest Park, famous as the site of a World's Fair at the turn of the century and still featuring a notable zoo.[2]

Now that Flood was single and living in an upscale building in the newly renovated Central West End of St. Louis, he was able to build a more glamorous life, if also a more hectic one. He could eat and drink at the myriad new, excellent restaurants and bars along Euclid, the street that ran due north from his apartment. There, it seems, he overcame his normally quiet, introspective self; he talked endlessly with all comers, especially local businessmen and members of the St. Louis Blues National Hockey League team. He also spent much of his idle time in the evenings at the Playboy Club on Lindell, a few blocks from his

1. Summons, January 17, 1966, *Flood vs. Flood*, case no. 356589; Leggett, "Curt Flood of St. Louis," 21.

2. Property Settlement Agreement, February 18, 1966, *Flood vs. Flood*, case no. 356589.

apartment, where he flirted with the bunnies, gave ever-greater thought to owning such a club, and wondered how he could buy one given his heavy alimony and child-support payments. Although from time to time he took a bunny, those one-night stands began to dwindle and may have disappeared altogether in 1965. Some time previously he had met a blonde bartender at the Parkway House, and what began as casual dates with Jody Kramer evolved, according to her memory, into a four-year relationship of some depth, at least on her part. At the same time, Flood became involved in what would become a more memorable relationship with Judy Pace, a young black actress living in Los Angeles. A brief glance at Jody Kramer's relationship with Flood offers a little insight into his nature; a discussion of his relationship with Judy Pace suggests the character and influence of a woman he would one day marry.

What specific qualities about Jody Kramer stirred Flood's fancy he never said, possibly because of a discreet decency, possibly because their close relationship lasted just four years and did not affect his life afterward. She, on the other hand, recalls that she loved Flood, and not merely for the sexual gratification: he was sensitive, tender, and an excellent cook, and was always ready to discuss his interests openly—or so she thought at the time. He told her that he wanted to own a facsimile of the Playboy Club, and, perhaps indicative of the duration of their relationship, he singled out Copenhagen as its location, a city he surely knew nothing about until he visited the Danish capital in late 1968. Possibly further indicative of both the nature and duration of their relationship, she recalls that he asked her to marry him when he was about to make his legal challenge to baseball—which would have been late in 1969—but she "felt it would not be a good idea for him to have a white woman" with him while he was engaged in what could become a highly publicized court fight. Thus she decided to break off their relationship. Or so she said thirty years later. However, Jody Kramer could not explain why, if Flood was so open, he did not discuss with her his interest in challenging baseball's reserve system before he made his decision. Indeed, it may be that her explanation for the end of their relationship was a cover for another, possibly somewhat embarrassing reason: Flood was parading another woman.[3]

Jody Kramer may well have learned in December 1969 that her lover was, and had been, involved in a second, special affair with Judy Pace.

3. Jody Kramer, telephone interviews, summer 2001 and July 1, 2006.

Their relationship originated by coincidence just before Thanksgiving in 1965. Flood had learned that Willie Mays would be appearing on a television show, *The Dating Game,* and tuned in. While watching, his attention shifted from Mays to a coffee-cream-colored "bachelorette," one of the women who brought in the show's guests. Fascinated by her beauty, Flood somehow obtained her phone number, and every time the Cardinals played in Los Angeles during the 1966 season, he called her for a date. As Judy Pace tells the story, she answered "No" each time he asked; she, like her father, saw Flood as just another ballplayer seeking to take advantage of his celebrity status to obtain a one- or two-night stand while in town for a series. But Flood persisted. He had a plan, a new version of an old one. His father had often told the story of finding his mother in Oakland, so he developed a similar plan, based largely on where Judy lived—at home with her parents. Of course, he sent her flowers from time to time, especially when the Cardinals were about to play the Dodgers in Los Angeles. That was the usual thing to do when courting. But Flood was in a position to do the unusual as well. His father had just left Laura and Oakland and, fortuitously or not, bought a house in Los Angeles across the street from the Paces. Thus Herman was able to "accidentally run into" Judy's father at the mailbox and stress that his son was an honorable man.[4]

After some months of the Floods' combined efforts, both Paces decided that Flood might well be a decent, serious man, and one day she agreed to go out with him, with the proviso that he take her entire family to a Cardinals-Dodgers game at Chavez Ravine. Flood agreed, of course, and in the summer of 1966 he and the twenty-year-old Judy had their first date, chaperoned as it were. Other dates followed, and Flood and Pace began to develop a deep, loving relationship that probably would have led to marriage fairly soon but for the fact that Judy was already wedded to her acting career. In 1966 she had a small part in *The Fortune Cookie,* starring Jack Lemmon and Walter Matthau, and other, larger parts lay just over the horizon. Apparently she did not find the time to come east until December 1969, when she flew with Flood to the critical annual meeting of the representatives of the Major League Baseball Players Association in Puerto Rico, where the various teams' player representatives agreed to support his lawsuit against baseball. What

4. Judy Pace Flood, interview, Los Angeles, June 29, 1998; Rickie Riley, interviews, 1998–2006.

Judy and Flood said to each other while in San Juan or, later, on the way home, about his lawsuit or their future, is unknown. What is clear is that the following spring, Judy, then making the movie *Cotton Comes to Harlem* as well as several episodes of a TV series, was too busy or, possibly, reluctant because of a fear of bad publicity, to attend Flood's trial. Indeed, they did not see each other again for a quarter of a century when, his career behind him and hers largely so, they met almost by chance and quickly got married.[5]

For Flood his successful pursuit of two women, but most notably Judy Pace, was probably the only bright spot in his life in 1966. And just possibly it was one or both of those liaisons that contributed to the rather drastic decline in his batting average that year, forty-three points, to .267. Cardinals' field manager Red Schoendienst probably did not know about Flood's female liaisons, in particular that with Judy Pace. At least he did not see one or both women as the source of Flood's hitting problems. He thought that Flood again was trying too hard to hit the long ball. St. Louis sportswriters agreed. They suggested that Flood might be trying to compensate for the run production lost when power hitters Bill White and Ken Boyer were traded away. The fact is, however, that Flood's batting average and RBIs dropped off *only after the middle of the season*. This suggests, at least, that the distraction of pursuing two women, if most notably the pressure of handling the lovely Judy Pace at a continent's distance, was a factor impairing his hitting. However, it is very possible that his failure to pay alimony and child support and, possibly, his separation from his children weighed on him. Whichever of these factors, or possibly others, account for Flood's problems at bat in 1966, he continued to play center field with his usual great skill, finishing the year without an error and earning his fourth straight Gold Glove award.[6]

Flood was glad to see the 1966 season end, not only because his batting average had dropped so sharply, but also because he foresaw a great off-season. He expected to learn more about engraving from his mentor in Oakland, John Jorgensen. Curious though it might seem—engraving required truly great precision—Flood thought it was just what he needed to relax after a tough season. "Baseball makes me a bundle of nerves and wrecks my sleep," he said for a magazine article in *Sport*.

5. For Judy Pace's career, see http://www.thehistorymakers.com/biography/biography.asp?bioindex=1041&category=entertainmentMakers.

6. *St. Louis Post-Dispatch,* January 13, May 7, 1967; *Sporting News,* May 20, 1967.

"But one day I did an art engraving of The Lord's Prayer so tiny that it can be imprinted on the head of a pin. My hands didn't shake a bit. And I not only drew it, I memorized the prayer. Just might need it real badly some day. In this life you never know."[7]

While Flood looked forward to renewing his wonderful relationship with the Jorgensens, he first headed to Los Angeles to visit his father and, of course, Judy Pace. He was still there in December when he learned that John Jorgensen had been murdered. Immediately, he grabbed a flight to Oakland, thinking to console Marian—and be consoled in turn. It turned out, however, that speaking with Marian had to wait until after the police interrogated them and gave each a polygraph test, the law-enforcement detectives perhaps imagining a conspiracy by the two to have Jorgensen killed. After what Flood recalled as a curiously intense scrutiny (why the police might have suspected either or thought they might be helpful in solving the crime is information they will not disclose), he and Marian were able to commiserate with each other and try to make sense of what had happened. They could not. Robbery was not involved. It turned out that a psychotic adolescent with an axe had entered Jorgensen's plant while he was out for breakfast and killed him upon his return. Of course that made his murder no less devastating for Marian, and Flood insisted that she would feel better if she came to St. Louis. He was moving into a three-bedroom apartment on the nineteenth floor of a fairly new, prestigious building with a pretentious name—Executive House—in the Central West End, and she could have a room. Marian declined. She wanted to run the engraving business, at least for a while. She may have told Flood why, but he does not acknowledge her reason, just that he accepted her decision—what else could he do?—at least temporarily. However, he would learn the reason in a few months, and be sorry that he did.[8]

In 1967, during the Cardinals' last trip to the West Coast, Flood took Marian out to eat at their favorite haunt in Oakland—Diamond Jim's—and, as he tells it, persuaded her to visit St. Louis to watch the World Series, see his exclusive apartment, and consider moving in with him. He said later that he needed her desperately: "My apartment was a shambles. My finances were a shame. My personal life was scandalous. And furthermore, she was my dearest, closest friend. We were in each other's

7. Stump, "Midnight League," 79.
8. Flood, *The Way It Is*, 121–22.

blood." Such is Flood's account of their discussion. And Marian did come to St. Louis with his mother for the World Series, then went back to Oakland to settle her affairs, and soon moved into Flood's West Pine Avenue apartment on a visit it would seem both viewed as pretty much permanent. There, he wrote two years later, she "took command. She runs my house. She is my secretary and partner." These words of Flood's, as well as other of his comments about their unusual if not somewhat peculiar relationship, are doubtless true. However, it is almost certainly true that Marian came to St. Louis because at their luncheon she insisted that together they could deal with a much more significant problem than his finances and apartment: his oldest brother, Carl.

Marian had taken an intense personal interest in Carl, perhaps as early as Flood's visits in 1962. Carl, Marian must have thought then or soon after, was a painful victim of the "disasterville" that was West Oakland. Flood did not say how Carl had gotten in trouble; he merely stressed that his brother was brilliant and multitalented—a champion chess player in the federal prison system, a linguist, and an artist—as well as a good, sensitive, and personable man. Marian began corresponding with him. Soon (Flood's memoir does not say when) she decided that Carl was the basically decent man described by his brother, and that the prison holding him was corrupting and dangerous. First she managed to get Carl moved to a different, somehow better prison in Washington State. Then following the Miranda decision in 1966, she found out that if he pled guilty rather than demanding a new trial, the federal government would release him on probation, provided that he had a job and supervision. Such a plea on his part, coupled with the Jorgensens' agreement to see that Carl had a job and supervision, had brought his release. Then came Johnny's death. Not only was it a terrible loss for Marian, it also meant the end of the engraving business and Carl's job. Consequently, he might well be returned to prison. This was not something Marian could accept, and once she told Flood, they decided to bring him to St. Louis, where Curt would give him a job and Marian would see that he stayed out of trouble. Perhaps this arrangement, compassionate though it was, was unavoidable, but it was to have disastrous consequences for both Floods.[9]

However noble the reasons behind the decision for Marian to come to St. Louis to supervise Carl, what Flood desperately needed was

9. Ibid., 122–23. I based my version of Marian's coming to St. Louis on my analysis of Marian's obsession with Carl.

someone to supervise his finances. When he told Marian they were "a shame," he greatly understated. Baseballs stuck in Flood's glove, but dollars did not stick in his bank account. His 1967 gross salary of $50,000 did not cover his alimony and child-support payments, much less his lifestyle. His basic expenses at Executive House aside, he was seen many nights hanging out in St. Louis's bars, sometimes with broadcaster Harry Caray, even sometimes with Cardinals' owner Gussie Busch, and eventually with a promoter named Bill Jones. Whether it was from these expenditures or as a matter of choice, Flood had not fully paid the child support and alimony ordered by the Alameda County court in early 1966. By the spring of 1967, his twice-monthly payments were running from $100 to $550 below the court-required $700. He was delinquent to the tune of $3,800 since the previous November, and Beverly filed a lawsuit against him on April 18. She asked the court to make her former husband "show cause" as to why he should not be held in contempt for failing to honor the court's order of March 1966. A few days later Flood was ordered to appear before the court by May 31. He did not respond directly, but on June 16 his lawyer produced a letter from the assistant comptroller of the St. Louis National Baseball Club. It showed that Flood's income, $45,000 spread over twenty-six payments as was the norm in Major League Baseball, was in gross terms $1,562.50 every two weeks, and in net $854. The great disparity between the two numbers stemmed in part from the taxes Flood paid, and in part from the $300 deducted semi-monthly to repay an advance the Cardinals had given him the year before, money the assistant comptroller recalled him needing to cover expenses flowing from his divorce. Unfortunately for Flood, but unsurprisingly, the Alameda court was not interested in his financial problems. It ordered him to pay Beverly $1,700 on or before June 20 to reduce the delinquencies in his support payments, and also to have the Cardinals send her $500 semi-monthly from July 3 to December 18, 1967. Although the court, for some reason, reduced Beverly's alimony by $200 a month for the year's second half, two facts seem clear: it did not trust Flood to pay the alimony and child support himself, and his pocket was shrinking because of the Cardinals' deductions from his paycheck.[10]

10. John Siefert, assistant comptroller of the St. Louis National Baseball Club, to Leslie Kessler, June 13, 1967, *Flood v. Flood,* case no. 356589; also April 13, 21, May 31, June 16, 23, 1967.

Fortunately for Flood, he had found another promising source of income. He had learned to sketch and paint from his father, and he had been sketching and painting ever since. In 1959 and in 1960, he took special courses at Oakland's College of Art and Design. He continued to sketch, but by 1967 he was also painting portraits. All this and more he discussed with reporters from St. Petersburg to San Francisco and, of course, St. Louis, in 1967 and 1968. The *St. Louis Globe-Democrat* labeled him an "Artist of the Diamond," and the *Post-Dispatch* portrayed him as "Cards' Flood: A Rembrandt off Diamond." In several stories, Flood explained his work. He had combined what he knew about perspective, shadow, and light, and how to use brushes and oil with what he had learned about using a pantograph as an engraver in Jorgensen's shop. Placing a stylus on a photograph and connecting it using four rigid bars adjustably joined in a parallelogram to a pencil, it was possible to transfer a photograph at least an inch in size to paper. The paper drawing would be transferred to a canvas usually fifteen by nineteen inches in size. Only then would Flood turn to his brushes and oil paints to add texture and color, including light, shadow, and, if there had been an opportunity for a brief sitting, what he recalled of the subject's temperament. Curiously, he painted his two most notable portraits without sittings, the most famous being that of Cardinals' owner August Busch (the other was of Martin Luther King, painted after his death). Flood said that he did his boss's portrait "because Gussie's got such a classic face—wrinkles, good features, intelligent eyes." Completed in just two weeks early in 1967, Flood handed it to the Cardinals' owner that March. Busch said he was "tickled to death" and would hang it on his yacht. But first Flood had to repaint the braid on the cap. He had painted it gold, which was the correct color for a ship's captain, but Busch as the ship's owner required black. After Flood retouched the portrait, a brewery aide reportedly told his boss, "Flood just gave you a battlefield promotion, Mr. Busch." Busch was so pleased with what Flood had done that he gave him commissions to paint his entire family. And he was not alone in asking Flood to do one portrait or several. Gibson wanted him to paint his family; other Cardinals did as well, and there were surely others who took their cue from Busch's portrait. Consequently, Flood foresaw nearly endless commissions for portraits: "You can start in with a family and go right through it," he told a reporter. What Flood did not tell the reporter, perhaps because he failed to recognize the danger, is that his prospects for commissions and income were linked to Busch's patronage, and all that could disappear if he fell into disfavor with Busch.[11]

Flood said he made serious money painting portraits, the amount depending upon his time and temperament. He told Nell Gross of the *Globe-Democrat* that he worked on several portraits at a time: a portrait required layers of paint, and those paints smeared easily, so he would shift from one to another in order to give them the necessary drying time. But whatever his technique, Flood seemingly did very well from the publicity and the commissions Busch's portrait brought him. He said he made $1,000 every two weeks. He added, perhaps truthfully, perhaps because it sounded good, perhaps both, that getting paid for his portraits was of little import: painting was fun and helped him relax. "I can only paint when I feel like it . . . when it hits me—and that could be 4 a.m." Seemingly, that had to mean that when in St. Louis during the season he painted in his studio, but how he found the extra space in a three-bedroom apartment that was not very large, and with Carl and Marian living there, is an unanswered question. However, paint he did. Just how serious Flood was about painting he revealed in an interview with the *Christian Science Monitor:* "I'm having a special case made to carry my paints and brushes," he told its sportswriter. "I want it strong enough so it can be handled with the team's luggage." Always tense during the season, Flood added that he needed the equipment so he could work during the "time wasted in hotels [and] waiting for night games," and at other boring times. He denied that his painting interfered with baseball, but it must be wondered whether he could restrict his painting only to a few hours before a game and a few more when he could not fall asleep. Would he think about working on a portrait some day when he should have been focusing on a line drive hit in his direction or, perhaps, his ex-wife's demands, as he would a quarter century later admit to thinking during games about how wonderful a cold beer would taste while playing during the hot, humid St. Louis summer?[12]

With newspaper articles discussing Flood's portraits, his colleagues in the dugout began calling him "Rembrandt." It was a title that became

11. *St. Petersburg Times,* March 13, 1967; *St. Louis Post-Dispatch,* September 11, 1967; *St. Louis Globe-Democrat, Sunday Magazine,* March 31, April 20, 1968; *San Francisco Examiner,* September 29, 1968.

12. Ed Rumill, "An Artist—On Field or Off," *St. Louis Post-Dispatch,* May 26, 1967; Broeg interview, July 1998; Nell Gross, "Cards' Flood: A Rembrandt Off Diamond," *St. Louis Globe-Democrat,* April 20, 1968.

especially appropriate after his portraits were displayed at exhibitions in the St. Louis area. David Huntley, chairman of the art department at nearby Southern Illinois University–Edwardsville and host of one exhibition of Flood's paintings, recalls his work as more mechanical than creative in nature, which, given Flood's methodology, it was. Such criticism, however, was of no interest to the St. Louis parents of a child who died from leukemia, whose portrait Flood painted from her photograph. And possibly it was this very compassionate act that prompted St. Louis Mayor Alfonso J. Cervantes to appoint Flood honorary chairman of the Leukemia Fund's annual door-to-door solicitation, an addition to his solid image in the city. And the portrait of Dr. Martin Luther King that Flood sent to King's widow in the summer of 1968 did not hurt his image either. Neither did the time he spent working with the Missouri Department of Health and the St. Louis charity "Aunts and Uncles," which distributed shoes to needy black children. Presumably, these contributions, altruistic though they were, added to his stature and the number of his commissions, although the extent to which he could depend on this source of income remained to be seen. Flood gave one interviewer the impression that he had an inflated sense of his prospects to make a living only from painting after his baseball career ended. This writer warned at the end of his feature story: "Great artist Rembrandt Van Rijn died broke."[13]

Of course Flood was no Rembrandt. He did not claim that he was. He said he painted mechanically on canvases enlarged from photographs. But did he? Or did he farm the photographs out? In his Flood biography, *A Well-Paid Slave,* Brad Snyder argues that Flood outsourced his photos to a California artist. But Snyder's argument seems to rest on two questionable foundations. First, he writes that someone else signed the King portrait. But who? Snyder should be able to say. Second, in his research, Snyder found Karen Brecker in Alameda, who said Flood worked with her to restart his portrait business in the late 1970s. Brecker produced letters to and from the California artist from that time. It is undeniable that Flood exchanged such letters. But in one excerpt that Snyder cites as proof of this business relationship, the artist assures Flood that he will do very well with the portraits sent to him. This strongly suggests that Flood was not previously familiar with his work. Then, too, Snyder correctly stresses the depth of Flood's alcoholism during this period,

13. *St. Louis Globe-Democrat* cover story, March 31, 1968; David Huntley, e-mail, 2003.

which suggests an inability to paint. But while no doubt true in the seventies, it is less likely true of the sixties when Flood was playing baseball daily. Also, it is not likely that Flood would have outsourced Busch's portrait: he could hardly have foreseen a payoff. In any event, what counted for Flood in the late sixties is that everyone believed he did the portraits credited to him.[14]

Whatever the future of his art work, in 1967 Flood, by his own account at least, was able to keep his artistic talents and financial prospects in perspective, limiting his painting to a relaxing hobby. If possible, he was more than ever committed to baseball. He felt the Cardinals had an excellent chance to win the National League pennant and the World Series. Bob Howsam, whom he had so disliked for sending out low contracts and, even more, interfering with the players' lives, had left as the Cardinals' general manager, but during his tenure he had brought in two solid sluggers in Roger Maris and Orlando Cepeda. Flood recalled later that after the two power hitters arrived, he sensed a new vitality among the Cardinals. "When we got to spring training in '67, I took one look around the room and was amazed at the talent we had." And a few days later he had told a teammate, "You better find a place to spend $10,000, because we are going to win the pennant and the World Series." (Ten thousand dollars was the approximate financial bonus each player would receive if his team won the World Series.) Flood thought that the Cardinals had not only great individual talent but also the team chemistry he believed essential for a winner. He was reminded of the 1964 World Series championship team.[15]

In 1967 the Cardinals actually exceeded Flood's expectations. He had an exceptional year himself at the plate and in the field, although not without some major ups and downs during the season. In early May he played his 266th game without an error, breaking the National League record. He had handled 504 chances, exceeding by a hundred those of the previous record-holder. It was natural, then, that ringing praise came from his peers on the Cardinals and other teams, as well as from broadcasters and coaches. Joe Amalfitano, a Cubs coach, gushed how Flood had once leaped into the vine-covered Wrigley Field wall to rob him of an extra-base hit and how the Gold Glove center fielder had stolen a hit from him in the old St. Louis ballpark on Grand Avenue.

14. Snyder, *A Well-Paid Slave*, 9–10, 67, 325–26.
15. Leggett, "Curt Flood of St. Louis," 21.

"I was just a .240 hitter," Amalfitano joked. "Why didn't Flood pick on the .310 and .330 hitters?" Obviously, of course, Flood did not discriminate between an Amalfitano and a Willie Mays; he was an equal-opportunity no-ball-gets-by-me outfielder. Naturally, Cardinals pitchers thought him a great blessing. Larry Jackson appreciated his fielding so much that he told a writer, "I'm going to take Curt home to Idaho with me this winter to make sure nothing happens to him." In the same vein, Bob Gibson said, "Watching Curt's great catches is like watching pretty girls. Each one is the prettiest—until the next one comes along."[16]

It would be an understatement to say that Flood enjoyed his record-breaking achievement. He told a reporter, "It's really something when you think of all the outfielders in the long history of baseball. Even Willie Mays hasn't done it—and he's the greatest." As for himself, he added, "I'd never done anything really worthwhile record-wise, so that's why this was so enjoyable." Indeed, it was more than that; as will be seen, it constituted the core of his self-esteem. He credited former Cardinal outfielder Terry Moore with much of his success in making so many tough catches, but especially on how to get a good jump on the ball. Moore had shown him techniques essential to getting to balls slammed into the outfield gaps. Essentially, it required focus and anticipation, precisely the attributes for which Tim McCarver would later praise Flood. Both were essential assets for an outfielder. Nonetheless, Flood said, "Half the battle is keeping the legs in shape. Oh, I've had some pulled muscles, but I've been lucky."[17]

As of early May, Flood had been relatively fortunate with his leg muscles, but in April he had played in Chicago in very cold, windy weather— 38 or 39 degrees, he recalled—and suffered a muscle tear in his upper right arm. That hampered his ability to throw the ball back to the infield fast enough to prevent an extra-base hit on a line drive, or to throw out a runner trying to score from second base on a single, but he continued to play every day until July 6. Then he injured his arm running into the wall at Busch Stadium and had to be placed on the disabled list. He could not play for twenty-one days, but he continued to take batting practice, and when he returned to the lineup on July 28, he hit with a fury he had not shown earlier in the season. He batted at an exceptional .433 pace over the following two weeks, and the Cardinals won thirteen of seventeen

16. *Sporting News*, May 20, 1967; *St. Louis Post-Dispatch*, May 7, 1967.
17. *St. Louis Post-Dispatch*, May 7, 1967.

games. During the rest of the season he continued to hit well, finishing with a batting average of .335, the best during his entire career. But his arm did not recover fully for the remainder of the season. He had to throw the ball in from center field "submarine" style. Consequently, he continued to miss games in the hope that his arm would strengthen if it was rested, and more often than not when he did start a game, Keane had to replace him in the late innings for defensive purposes.[18]

Flood's weakness constituted a serious problem. Reporters heard him say he hoped a winter's rest and perhaps a day or two every week stretching his arms and legs in a gym would help his arm return to normal. But they also heard him admit that he had a major problem with working out in the off-season: "I've been so exhausted from playing that I've been taking it easy the last few winters," he advised one writer. This was true—indeed, it is unlikely that Flood worked out during any off-season—but it was also unfortunate; if his arm remained weak, then he would have to play shallower, limiting his ability to reach balls hit deep, especially those hit into the gaps in left and right center. Given Flood's pride in being arguably the best center fielder in baseball, it is difficult at first to understand his resistance to working out, if only for a day or two a week. But human nature is such that even the best of intentions arrived at during periods of stress often do not survive when that stress abates. And in Flood's case, exhaustion from playing ball was not the only or necessarily the most significant reason for his failure to work on regaining his arm strength during the winter; he was devoted to La Dolce Vita, and his good life consisted of carousing or painting into the wee hours, hardly the best means of resting, or of improving one's physique.[19]

Exhaustion at the 1967 season's end might account for Flood's weak batting average during the World Series—.179. So might worry about his weakened arm. But it is also likely that he was looking forward to expanding his sales of portraits and contemplating an investment strategy he had recently discussed with a newly met bar-hopper like himself, a man whose ideas and managerial skills he hoped would make him wealthy, or, at the very least, provide for his financial security after his baseball career ended.

Flood's opportunity to create wealth other than with his portraits and baseball seemingly came about by chance; only time, though, would

18. Ibid., July 28, August 31, 1967.
19. Ibid.

reveal whether fate had dealt him a great hand or was laughing at his ignorance of the real world's complexities. His opportunity arrived during one of his usual tours of Euclid Avenue's new, trendy bars and restaurants, talking as always with St. Louis Blues players, businessmen, and others interested in alcohol-laden conversations. One evening he met William "Bill" Jones, who some people called a "deal-maker," but who was widely regarded as a decent man. What Flood either did not know, or would not accept, was that Jones was better at promoting than producing. Flood thought that he would contribute his celebrity name, along with his knowledge of art, photography, and taking of portraits; thus he would attract customers to the partnership, and Jones, he expected, would supply the financial acumen and managerial skills.[20]

On November 1, just three weeks after the World Series, Flood and Jones incorporated Curt Flood Associates, Inc. The charter, although it contained a brief, almost incidental reference to real estate, offered no other clues to their intended investments. Seemingly unimportant, but in fact very significant, their corporate charter was notarized by Connie Reilly. She was romantically involved with Jones, but, more important, she was also a secretary in the suburban St. Louis law office of Allan Zerman. Earlier in 1967 she had introduced her boss to Flood, who soon did portraits of his children, inexplicably without a fee, as she recalled. Also, that October Flood, again seemingly inexplicably, offered Zerman World Series tickets. Zerman turned down the offer for reasons that Reilly did not remember, but in a different context she recalled his ever-deepening commitment to Judaism at this time, so it may well have been linked to the Sabbath or the High Holy Days, which took priority. Connie Reilly was not at all surprised that her boss filled in Flood's and Jones's corporate charter, meeting Missouri's documentary requirements, and that he did so without charging them a fee. She saw it in some part as a bit of reciprocity, in greater part as early signs of a bond blossoming between Zerman and Flood. If it seems strange that a close bond would develop between the lithe black Baptist ballplayer from Oakland and the chunky Jewish graduate of St. Louis's first-rate Washington University Law School, it should not. During the sixties, and for many years before and some after, the effects of discrimination against blacks and Jews led to an alliance between them. It is in that context that Zerman's bonding with Flood truly becomes understandable—and crucial. Only within that con-

20. Connie Reilly, interview, St. Louis, June 19, 2003.

text was Flood likely in 1969 to venture a challenge to what he and Zerman saw as an enslaving baseball establishment.[21]

Flood's relationship with Zerman was only in its formative stage as 1968 began. So was Curt Flood Associates, Inc. And his personal relationships with Jody and Judy were on track. As for his baseball career, with a new season about to open, he appeared to have the world at his feet. He was a true star with a contract for $72,500, a whopping 45 percent more than his $50,000 in 1967. His throwing arm, he told the *Post-Dispatch*'s Broeg, "feels great—100 per cent." As for the Cardinals, the club still boasted Maris, Cepeda, and Gibson, all coming off great seasons. All signs pointed to another great season in 1968.[22]

In fact, the 1968 season was to be quite different from the previous one. Flood's bat was fiery in the first month of the season, as he hit .414. With Cepeda doing his part by batting .396, the Cardinals soon vaulted into first place. However, both Flood's and Cepeda's averages slid sharply in May, and the club found itself in fourth place by Memorial Day. Although the team soon regained the top position, the credit belonged to Gibson and timely hitting off the bench, not to Flood's bat or even his fielding. As of June 26 he had missed five games because of a muscle tear in his right leg, and his batting average had slipped to .317. Both problems notwithstanding, Flood was picked to play center field in the All-Star game, the position previously held for many successive years by Willie Mays.

Honor though it was to have his center fielder picked ahead of Mays, the Cardinals' manager, "Red" Schoendienst, thought Flood should rest his leg during the All-Star break rather than play. Flood agreed, but he could not resist playing in the highly visible midseason classic. In all fairness to Flood's possibly selfish decision—failing to rest his leg could have cost the Cardinals his services and their opportunity for a National League pennant and a World Championship—it will always be immensely difficult to find any player able to resist the opportunity to play in the All-Star game. Just before and just after the game, however, Flood may have regretted his decision not to rest at home. First, Mays was picked to replace an injured player, and, in deference to his celebrity, was given center field to play. Although Flood was shifted to another outfield spot, not playing center field after so many Gold Glove awards had to hurt.

21. Ibid; Allan Zerman, e-mail correspondence.
22. *St. Louis Post-Dispatch*, February 27, 1968.

Then, too, the All-Star game was not really a team sport with victory as the goal; it was a showpiece for the best players to display their wares, catching the public's eye and boosting their egos; and the only one who did so, if in a limited manner, was Mays, who scored the game's only run. After that, Flood must have rued not taking Schoendienst's advice to rest rather than play.

The unusually low score of the All-Star game epitomized the 1968 season. It was "the year of the pitcher." No one knew why, but batting averages fell sharply everywhere, not least on the Cardinals. Cepeda, who had batted nearly .400 during the spring, ended the season at .248; Flood's average closed at .301; the team as a whole finished at a meager .249. Even so, the Cardinals won the National League by twelve and a half games. It was testimony to their splendid pitching, with Gibson leading every pitcher in the majors with a magical 1.12 earned-run average—still the lowest single-season ERA by far of any pitcher since the "dead-ball era" early in the twentieth century. But those records meant little as the Cardinals prepared to play the Detroit Tigers in the World Series. Detroit had good pitching too with Denny McClain, who had produced his own magic number by winning thirty-one games—the last major-league pitcher to win thirty or more games in a season—and Mickey Lolich. And while Detroit's team batting average was lower than the Cardinals', the Tigers easily compensated by hitting almost two and a half times more home runs than St. Louis during the 1968 season—and Mickey Lolich. A team built with more power hitters, Detroit could score more runs with fewer hits than St. Louis. Thus, the Cardinals, although slightly favored by odds-makers in Las Vegas, would need a solid performance to win the World Series.

Unhappily for the Cardinals, Flood performed well below the level St. Louis fans and the press had come to expect of him. After the second game, which the Tigers won easily, Broeg commented in the *Post-Dispatch*, "It was the kind of day yesterday when even Curt Flood, the finest center fielder in captivity, broke late on a low line drive and then, of all things for a performer of his credentials, couldn't hold the ball once he caught it." Why Flood "broke late," and why he might have dropped the ball once he reached it, the paper's exasperated sports editor did not say or even suggest. Even if he had seen Flood out partying the night before the game, he would not have dared attribute the misplay to a lack of sleep and consequent loss of concentration. Despite knowing about the young man's high living during the season, Broeg liked Flood for his varied talents, and probably personally. But even if that had not been the case, Broeg would not have mentioned his personal life as a problem. Not then at least. Doing so would undermine the Cardinals' spirit and their opportunity to win the World Series. Broeg's column, then, was remarkable solely for his obvious shock at Flood's failure to catch a line drive of the sort he usually handled with ease. But Flood's error, however shocking at the time, would not be worth mentioning now but for his two other lapses later in the series. In the sixth inning of the decisive seventh game, he and Lou Brock were both picked off first base. Their mistakes must be considered costly; possibly one or both could have scored and the Cardinals could have taken a lead and reduced the pressure on Gibson, who had shut out the Tigers for six innings. Of course, Lolich, also pitching a shutout, made two superb plays, and pick-offs are not unusual problems for a "running" team, which the Cardinals were. On the other hand, Flood's apparent misplay of a line drive in the next inning turned out to be a fatal problem for the team. The writer for the *Sporting News,* the magazine usually referred to respectfully as baseball's "Bible," could not understand how the "normally reliable—if not usually sensational—Flood, misjudged" the drive. As the writer recalled the play, at the sound of Jim Northrup's bat on the ball, Flood broke toward the infield, quickly realized that he had been fooled by the smash's "carry," and turned to run it down, only to have the ball sail over his head for a triple that scored two base runners. The game was not over—it was the seventh inning—but the Cardinals failed to mount a successful comeback and lost the game and the championship. Thereafter, most fans and sportswriters would claim, as did the *Sporting News,* that Flood's lapse had cost the Cardinals the World Series. Surely worse, he believed it himself.

Of course neither the *Sporting News* nor the two St. Louis daily newspapers mentioned that the series is a seven-game contest that is not won or lost in a single game, or that Brock, rightly famed for his base-stealing prowess, might have cost the Cardinals the fifth game when he was cut down at home plate because he failed to slide. Inevitably, perhaps, the focus was on Flood, who made the last, most obvious, and seemingly most costly misplay. In the next morning's *Globe-Democrat,* Jack Herman wrote a column headlined "I Messed It Up, Gallant Flood Admits." Herman, like the *Post-Dispatch's* Neal Russo, recited Flood's explanation of his failure to catch the ball: that he misjudged its distance because of the white shirts in the stands and haze on the field, so that he took two steps in before he recognized his error; then, turning around, he slipped on turf still wet from the previous day's rain, which made it impossible for him to reach the ball. Others among the Cardinals, including Gibson, excused him: "When the ball was hit I figured it would be caught, but it's a little different out there." However, Broeg was less charitable. He wrote that the Cardinals had lost because their best defensive performer couldn't make what for him should have been little more than a routine catch.[23]

What neither Broeg, nor Russo, nor Herman knew was that in mid-September Flood's ex-wife, Beverly, had asked the Alameda court to modify their divorce decree. Her lawyer said that Flood's salary had nearly doubled since 1966 when the payments for alimony and child support were established, and since then her expenses and the children's had grown substantially. Beverly felt compelled to ask for $300 more a month for herself and $110 more monthly for each child, as well as medical and dental expenses.

Only circumstantial evidence can be advanced that Beverly's newest demands distracted Flood during the series, and most critically just when Gibson was pitching to Northrup. But that evidence is powerful. Prior to that miscue, he had already dropped a ball in the outfield, and he had been picked off first base. Furthermore, recalling Northrup's drive in his memoir, he said angrily that he had missed a catch "that might have been easy for me if I had not been completely bushed." Why he was "bushed" he did not say. Neither did he say why he changed his first story about the sun shining on white shirts and blinding him. The two stories are not mutually exclusive, of course. But on that late October afternoon the sun was low in the west, behind the white shirts; it could not have caused him to misjudge the ball. Neither could his being "bushed"; that could have affected him after he started running back and to his right for the ball, but it could not have accounted for his initial misjudgment, if such there was. Arguably, then, Flood was distracted when Northrup was at bat. He may have been worrying about Beverly's recent demands and, if the Alameda court supported them, what that would mean for Curt Flood Associates and his lifestyle. It would not have been the first time his mind wandered during a game. It would have been one of many times. A quarter of a century later he would discuss rather vividly how often he thought of beer when he played. "It would start in

23. Jack Herman, *St. Louis Globe-Democrat*, October 11, 1968; Neal Russo, *Sporting News*, October 11, 1968; Bob Broeg, *St. Louis Post-Dispatch*, October 11, 1968.

the locker room after a game. You'd sit down with a beer and say: 'Boy, this really tastes good after a hard day.' Then in the ninth inning you'd start anticipating that beer. Then it would be the fifth inning, and you say, 'I wish this goddam game would be over so I can get in there and have a nice cold one.' Finally, you graduate, if that's the proper term, to wondering: 'Could I get away with having a couple of beers before we get out there and play this hot game? I wonder if anybody will know, I wonder how successful I will be.' And on occasion I did that. Not very successfully."[24]

Of course, October was not a hot summer month, and Flood surely was not drinking before and during a World Series game, but he could hardly have forgotten Beverly's demands. He was mailing her $1,400 a month for alimony and child support (of which she had to deposit $400 a month in a savings account for the children's future). This total represented slightly more than 23 percent of his salary, and not only was she demanding more, but also the total, if the court agreed to the medical and dental expenses she had asked for, would be almost unlimited. Unfortunately for the Cardinals, and for Flood personally, he had reason to lose his focus late in the seventh game of the World Series, although it cannot be said with absolute assurance that he did. It cannot be said, either, that he would have caught Northrup's drive if he had judged it properly and started for it immediately. What can be said, in any case, is that Flood always *thought* that he should have caught Northrup's drive. He thought so, and the press thought so. As he wrote in his memoir, "Attempts were made to brand me a 'goat.'" A quarter of a century later, shortly before his death, he told Ken Turan of the *Los Angeles Times* that he could see "every detail of that situation in my mind. It was unquestionably the dimmest, darkest day of my baseball career." But while the press would continue to remind the public of what had happened, even in his *New York Times* obituary in 1997, Flood was his own worst enemy. He was a "goat" because he branded himself one. Guilt smothered him as he blamed himself for the Cardinals losing the World Series, and, along with self-pity and anger, it shaped—and misshaped—his most critical decisions leading to his decision to sue baseball only fourteen months later.[25]

---

24. For Flood's alcoholism, see Flood and Turan, "Outside-Outside," 37.

25. Flood, *The Way It Is*, 73; Joseph Durso, *New York Times*, January 21, 1997; *St. Louis Post-Dispatch*, October 18, 1987; Flood and Turan, "Outside-Outside," 21.

Flood could not see then that his miscue on the field marked a turning point in his life—one does not see forward clearly very often, if at all—but a decision he made seven days after the game marked his descent into a vortex of terrible, often unreasoning, even seemingly irrational, decisions. On November 15 he gained a very good idea of the way the Alameda court was leaning: it told Beverly she could stop putting the $400 a month into the children's savings account. That meant it recognized that the children's needs, if not hers, had increased measurably, just as she had told the court. For Flood, that order, following hard upon his "dimmest, darkest day," was too much. He made a decision that would prove costly to all concerned, if especially to his children and his legacy: he would not write Beverly the $700 check due her on November 18. And he would not write her a check again until June 3, 1982, and then he would make payments only partially and intermittently until the year's end. Why Flood paid some in 1982 is a mystery not really clarified by the documents available; why he stopped on November 18, 1968, however, is another matter. Flood never said, of course. But his decision not to pay followed so close upon his failure to catch Northrup's line drive—one week—that it seems to be a direct consequence of the pressure Beverly put on him just prior to the World Series, coupled with the sportswriters' criticism of his performance and his own self-pity, guilt, and anger. He would punish her and her children, although they were his children too. Indeed, it seems fair to say that his decision to stop paying Beverly alimony and child support at that time signified that he was beginning to unravel, to make rash decisions that, only fourteen months later, would produce his notable challenge to Major League Baseball's reserve system. Other signs were about to follow.[26]

---

26. For Flood's failure to pay alimony and child support, see Judgment Debtor, March 21, October 19, 1983, *Flood vs. Flood,* case no. 356589. Curiously, and perhaps inexplicably, the judgments followed rather than preceded the payments.

VI

The Ultimatum

For Curt Flood the off-season following the 1968 World Series provided endless opportunities to escape what he later recalled, with a bit of exaggeration, as the efforts of the St. Louis press to brand him as the "goat" of the October classic. Fortunately, he had agreed to join the Cardinals in an eighteen-game exhibition tour of Japan; after that, he was escaping to Europe with Marian, his corporate partner Bill Jones, and Jones's new wife, Connie (Reilly). Unfortunately, he could not escape Beverly's most recent demands for more money. She now wanted $1,250 in child support and $1,000 in alimony each month, as well as medical and dental expenses. She asserted that her expenses had increased substantially since the Alameda court first ordered the payments in 1966, and her husband's income had almost doubled since then. She needed more money, especially for the children, and her former husband could well afford the additional payments.[1]

On January 7, 1969, Flood's lawyer responded. He not only questioned Beverly's expenses and asked that his client's monthly payments be reduced but also listed his expenses and aspirations. In so doing, he provided limited but fascinating insights into where Flood spent his money. The filing first listed $1,268 per month in "Personal Expenses." Apartment rent, which normally would have been anyone's major expense, was Flood's second-largest, because he fed three people: himself, Carl, and Marian. Otherwise, some of what he listed as personal expenses was deceptive. He did not include the operating costs for his cars (which he classified as business) or what he spent on entertainment, although it was probably a considerable amount given his visits to the Playboy Club and the many restaurants and bars on Euclid. "Business expenses,"

---

1. Beverly Flood, Schedule of Monthly Expenses, December 6, 1968, *Flood vs. Flood,* case no. 356589.

another major category, was also deceptive. While Flood rightly listed monthly gas and maintenance for a 1968 "Cad" and a 1964 Pontiac, the $6,000 he spent on their "purchases" was a capital expense, a nonrecurring expenditure and thus a distortion of his monthly expenses. Flood also paid Carl and Marian monthly salaries, the former $400, the latter $360. Carl's salary was actually an allowance: Flood told his brother that if he rambled through the restaurants and bars on Euclid flashing samples of his portraits and secured commissions, he would get half the proceeds. But there is no known correlation between Carl's allowance and what he might have sold. As for Marian, Flood paid her for supervising Carl and helping to establish an office and portrait studio for Curt Flood Associates, Inc. How much time Marian spent supervising Carl and how much time and effort she contributed to CFA cannot be determined, but the manager of the photo shop on Lindell thought any time was too much: she interfered in costly ways with the work there. It would seem, though, that Beverly's lawyer, as well as the IRS, might have questioned whether Carl's salary was essential, and whether Marian's salary was a legal business expense. They might also have questioned what Marian contributed to the household's cost, and thus to Flood's purse.[2]

Questionable as Flood's personal and business expenditures might have been—if only because some were wrongly categorized and some exaggerated—his "Additional Expenses" were much more significant. In several areas they foreshadow his future problems and those dilemmas he would leave behind for others to cope with. In the fall of 1968 Flood assumed responsibility for his mother's living expenses, as well as her life and medical insurance, a total of $332 a month. This package included a triplex in Oakland that he insisted she move into but which he purchased for her in his own name. In so doing, he paid $4,000 down plus $1,000 for unstipulated expenses. Despite his controlling approach to providing for his mother, all this was surely a very decent thing to do. Even the fact that her new home carried two mortgages does not mar his contribution to his mother's welfare. Flood expected his mother to rent out two apartments in the triplex for $100 each, so that the property would cost him only $132 per month in mortgage payments, plus $81 for insurance and taxes on the house. Altogether, assuming that Laura was

2. Curtis Flood, Comparison of Income and Expenses, January 7, 1969, ibid.; Ruth Sutterfield, interviews regarding the Lindell photo shop, July 1, 2002, and June 18, 2003.

able to rent two of the apartments consistently, Flood expected to pay about $450 per month for his mother's upkeep, including food and medical insurance, or about 7 percent of his salary from the Cardinals. At the same time he could probably look forward to a return on his investment one day. It was a good deal for mother and son if all went as planned—if both apartments were rented—but even if not, Flood would not have been unduly burdened had he only his recurring "Personal" and "Business" expenditures in addition to his mother's expenses. The total came to approximately $29,000 a year, about 40 percent of his salary of $72,500 from the Cardinals. This last amount, of course, did not include Flood's World Series share or his pay for the Japanese tour, although he could not count on either bonus in the future. Even so, Flood should have been able to pay his expenses, including the "salaries" of Carl and Marian, as long as he earned the same or more as a ballplayer, artist, and, possibly, entrepreneur. But adding alimony and child support at $16,800 per year sharply altered Flood's situation, and in a manner that he could only have considered disastrous. The payments to Beverly raised his total expenditures to nearly $46,000, or about 63 percent of his gross salary, and a greater percentage of his net after taxes, although what his taxes might total Flood either did not calculate, or did not communicate to his lawyer, and his lawyer to the court.[3]

Although Flood's lawyer did not say so, he must have been aware that there were major flaws in his client's financial accounting, and not just the absence, however justified, of any calculations for taxes. The most significant shortcoming was Flood's refusal to pay $3,500 in alimony and child support beginning with the payment due October 18, a week after the World Series ended. His arrears might well prove very costly when the Alameda court judge considered Beverly's request for more money. Furthermore, Flood's accounting of his income did not include portrait commissions. Flood did not mention any endorsements either, although these, if any, were probably small given the generally miserable number offered to blacks at that time. Probably, Flood hoped the judge would agree, as his lawyer argued, that his recurring income—his salary—was barely adequate for his expenses, including his very generous commitment to his mother. This was surely his implication. He was unselfish,

3. Curtis Flood, Comparison of Income and Expenses, January 7, 1969, *Flood vs. Flood,* case no. 356589. That Flood did not know his tax situation is understandable: essential tax information (such as W2s, 1099s, and 1098s) usually is not mailed out until later in January or even February.

whereas his lawyer would tell the Alameda court that Beverly's expenses were "puffed up" and her lifestyle extravagant.[4]

On January 13, 1969, the Alameda court decided that Beverly's expenses were not "puffed up," and ordered Flood's child support payments raised from $140 a month per child to $250. His alimony payments would be left at $700 if Flood agreed that Beverly no longer had to put $400 a month into a trust fund for their children; otherwise, he would have to pay $1,000 per month in alimony. The judge also ordered Flood to pay all reasonable medical and dental expenses for the children, a considerable if not easily calculated amount, because Gary, his adopted son, had just been put in a psychologist's care. Indeed, medical and dental expenses alone for his and Beverly's children had reached almost $2,000 in 1968, this despite only one bill from the psychologist. In sum, even if Flood agreed that Beverly would not have to place $400 a month in the account for the children—as he soon would—he would be liable for $1,950 per month in alimony and child support, or $23,400 yearly (an increase of $6,600 over what he had paid previously) as well as medical and dental expenses, and all this, of course, was to be retroactive to October 15, 1968. Obviously the numbers, which meant giving about 32 percent of his salary to Beverly, must have weighed on him during and after his two trips to Europe that winter as he heard bits and pieces about their reception from his lawyer and, finally, the decision of the Alameda court.[5]

Much of what Flood and his friends did in Europe must be imagined, although it can be imagined with some measure of certainty. Always the artist, he must have visited Paris and the Louvre, by most accounts the world's loveliest city and most famous museum. Then, too, he, Marian, and the Joneses probably stopped in Amsterdam and roamed through the Reichsmuseum with its "old masters." But Flood left no doubt that their tour reached its apex when they reached the Danish capital of Copenhagen. He was thrilled with this city on the Baltic. It captured his palate, his heart, his hopes for a new venture, and more. Later, in St. Louis, he told reporters that he loved Danish pastries, and that "the Danes ought to sue the people in our country for calling what we make

4. Curtis Flood, Memorandum in Opposition to Plaintiff's Motion and in Support of Defendant's Motion to Decrease Alimony payments, January 7, 1969, *Flood vs. Flood,* case no. 356589.

5. Ibid., January 13, 1969.

'Danish Pastries.'" He also told newsmen he had found a very special people who treated him as neither a black man nor an athlete, "just as a human being," however unlikely it was that he would know what the Danes were thinking. Then he also spoke in interesting terms about a cocktail lounge he saw there. The *Sporting News* quoted him as saying, "I bought a cocktail lounge in Copenhagen. It has to be remodeled." He did not say that he wanted to turn it into a facsimile of the Playboy Club; probably he feared that was too bold a step for the general public. But he did say he would rename the lounge Club 21, which was his uniform number—a somewhat curious decision if he did not want to be known as an athlete. More important, it is unclear whether Flood had actually purchased a lounge. Despite what he had told the *Sporting News,* he informed the *Post-Dispatch* that he had "all but closed a deal to purchase a night spot in the Danish capital." He said that the corporation he and his partners "in a real estate concern" that he had recently founded had taken on a Danish partner; at last, to cover all bases, "we sent some of our boys over there to make sure everything went smoothly." Why he went into such details about these matters is unclear. Perhaps he wanted to enhance his image as a budding entrepreneur; perhaps he wanted to show that he had partners to share the investment's expense; if not, then his ex-wife would demand even more money. But he might have had another reason for inventing the story.[6]

Flood's stories, at least partly contrived, about his financial adventures abroad may have been designed to distract reporters from bringing up his failure to catch Northrup's line drive. None seemed to have forgotten Flood's costly misjudgment in the 1968 World Series. None ever would. And then there was his holdout for a better contract. However, it is true that while in Copenhagen with his friends he had seen a lounge he liked and thought he might be able to remodel, possibly replicating the Playboy Club. Whether it could be profitable given the cost of the purchase and the remodeling was a question for which he needed a solid answer. Consequently, upon his return to St. Louis, he had asked his local lawyer and good friend Allan Zerman to go to Copenhagen with him and analyze the situation. Zerman agreed, inspected the lounge, spoke to its leaseholder (effectively its owner), and told Flood that the man wanted almost $200,000, far more than Flood should or

6. *Sporting News* and *St. Louis Post-Dispatch,* March 2, 1969.

could pay. Consequently, when Flood spoke to reporters again on March 2, 1969, he had bought and remodeled nothing.[7]

While Flood seems to have deceived reporters about buying a lounge in Copenhagen, he told them another story that was clearly true but that revealed his naïveté as a businessman. He said that Curt Flood Associates, Inc. had contracts for some thirty-eight thousand graduation pictures "for which we expect to charge $28.00 a package." And it was just one of several businesses he expected to bloom and to "make his eventual retirement from baseball more comfortable." Fortunately for him, none of the reporters asked him what the few sketchy numbers meant; he did not know. Two years later he would acknowledge that he had known nothing about CFA's business; he had sat, "celebrity fashion, on its outer fringes." Naive like many athletes then and since, Flood was blinded by his hope for big money to the great danger of gambling, and not just on the future of a settled business, but also on the integrity and skill of others in an entirely new enterprise. Giving him the benefit of the doubt, perhaps he thought that, if successful, he could honor his obligations to Beverly and their children, retain his present grand lifestyle, and continue to live well after retiring from baseball. Then, too, he may have suspected that, given his injury the previous season, his retirement was not too far off. But in March 1969, the corporation was little more than a work in progress.

CFA had opened a sales office at 8007 Clayton Road in St. Louis County. To organize and manage it, Flood's partner, Bill Jones, had hired Keith Collins, handing him the grand title of vice-president of sales. Collins, working with Ronald Mueller, an accountant and the company's bookkeeper, was to solicit portrait commissions and sell franchises for photography studios in St. Louis and elsewhere that would be blessed with the hopefully profit-enhancing sign in the window: "A Curt Flood Studio." He was also to obtain contracts for the high school prom and graduation pictures that Flood had told reporters about. It was a large assignment, and Collins might have obtained portrait commissions and orders for high school prom and graduation pictures, but he had sold no franchises. Of course it was early in CFA's corporate development—local Curt Flood studios were planned; one would open soon in suburban Kirkwood, another that summer in central St. Louis—but as of March 2

---

7. Allan Zerman to author, e-mail correspondence, October 16, 1999. Zerman does not recall the time frame of his trip with Flood to Copenhagen.

when Flood spoke to the press, he could only hope that CFA would make the big money he hoped for. He was spending, seemingly endlessly, for office furnishings, salaries, licenses, and everything else associated with opening an office and two studios. He owed Beverly and the children for back alimony and child support as well as medical and dental expenses. And in January he had received a contract from the Cardinals that offered only a paltry $5,000 raise.

Flood was aghast at the minimal increase in his salary, the more so as he weighed it against his growing expenses. He needed more than $77,500, a lot more. Adding support of his mother to his other expenses, including his new alimony and child-support payments, and spending the same amount as in 1968 on sustaining CFA, his expenses would exceed $52,000. Given that taxes would take a major bite out of the salary offered him, he would have little left to further develop CFA, much less any money for his personal entertainment. True, he was not sending Beverly a cent for alimony and child support at the moment, but how long could that last? In short order she would garnish part of his salary; she had done so before. No! The raise the Cardinals were offering was not nearly enough to meet his needs, much less repair his ego and image, shattered since the previous October. There was only one thing to do. On March 2, he rejected the Cardinals' contract offer. Instead, he sent the front office what amounted to an ultimatum, coupled with a promise: "If you people want a three hundred hitter who also happens to be the best center fielder in baseball, it will cost you ninety-thousand dollars, which is not seventy-seven five and its not eighty-nine thousand, nine hundred and ninety-nine." By Flood's own account, he wanted a nearly 25 percent raise, an increase of $18,000. Twenty-five years later, Broeg told *Post-Dispatch* readers that in a "banner-line story in the *Globe-Democrat*," Flood, after "demanding" $100,000, was quoted as saying: "And I don't mean $99,999.99 either."[8]

The discrepancy between what Flood said he asked for and, assuming Broeg to be correct, what the *Globe-Democrat* wrote that he demanded, is significant. If the number Flood wrote in his memoir was less than what he actually demanded, it suggests that in retrospect he knew that he had demanded more than the public would accept as fair. If they thought he had asked for too much, then they would not sympathize with his demand and support his case in the appellate courts—and

8. Flood, *The Way It Is,* 172; *St. Louis Post-Dispatch,* August 18, 1994.

the purpose of his book, other than to make money, was to raise sympathy and support. Indeed, it was not unlikely that the public would see even the lesser number as too much, given that the year before he had received a 45 percent increase over his 1967 salary, and that he had played so badly in the 1968 World Series. But whichever number is accurate, the amount demanded is less significant than his harsh, emotionally charged language. Why he employed language that constituted an ultimatum and was certain to raise Busch's hackles is not clear. Probably, he felt that more than money was at stake: a $5,000 raise was a slap in the face to a Gold Glove outfielder who had hit .301 in 1968, one of the best averages posted by any major-league hitter in the oft-called "year of the pitcher" of 1968. Then, too, among all athletes salaries were, as they remain, a phallic symbol, the yardstick by which they measure themselves and their value to their club, their peers, and their fans. Salaries were about respect, not least the public's respect, and, as the St. Louis press had not forgotten Flood's misplay of Northrup's line drive, even a raise of 25 percent would do much to relieve his distress over that damning issue and restore and possibly enhance the sense of being respected that he needed. Then, too, Carl was a distressing, stressful problem, if one his younger brother tried to avoid recognizing. He noticed "that Carl's efforts [in securing portrait commissions] were rather uneven," and he saw him at night "trembling in a cold sweat," but, encouraged by Marian, he accepted Carl's claim that he had a touch of the flu. Still, somehow Flood had to know that his brother was drug-addicted and to worry that the problem might explode publicly, hurting him as well as Carl. All this may help to explain not only Flood's ultimatum but also its potentially dangerous promise to hit three hundred, not a point less.[9]

Somewhat later, Flood learned that Gussie Busch "had a fit" when he heard of the ultimatum, that his "profanity rattled the windows and turned the air blue." How Flood heard he did not say. But Busch's proclivities were well known, not only in St. Louis but well beyond. He was viewed as one of the most paternalistic of the many often despotic, sometimes benevolent club owners John Helyar has labeled "Lords of the Realm" (in his story of the Major League Baseball Players Association's battles with the club owners). According to Helyar, the "Baron of Anheuser-Busch" viewed the Cardinals as his personal fiefdom and

9. *St. Louis Post-Dispatch,* August 18, 1994.

himself as their benevolent master. During the sixties he treated his players better than any other owner. When most teams traveled to the West Coast for games, they traveled in commercial jets, but Busch's team flew in chartered jets that not only allowed them to avoid crowds but also enabled them to arrive rested and better prepared to play. Furthermore, the Busch brewery provided free beer on its chartered plane and sent cases to the players' homes if asked, perhaps thinking it might breed a little gratitude, but also hoping it might help them relax and play better. In these measures, benevolent despotism equaled enlightened self-interest. At times, however, Busch's generosity extended to whatever served his fancy, although it could ultimately inspire greater efforts from others to follow. Thus he helped Stan Musial open a well-situated, upscale restaurant in St. Louis and become a Cardinals' vice-president; he handed home-run king Roger Maris a lucrative beer distributorship in Florida; and, according to Broeg, until March of 1969 Flood also had a special place in his heart.

According to Broeg, in 1961 Busch "asked" manager Johnny Keane to give Flood an opportunity to play regularly; at the same time he provided the Floods with financial help for their eldest son Gary's medical bills and found Beverly a job as a model with the brewery. Then, seven years later, he publicly expressed gratitude for Flood's portrait of him in a braided yachting cap, giving the young man new and significant credibility as an artist. In sum, Busch had done well by Flood. However, while the Baron enjoyed giving, he would not abide the slightest sign of disrespect. When he saw Flood's ultimatum as just that, Flood's special place in Busch's heart disappeared overnight. As Broeg wrote in several columns well after March 1969, Flood could no longer expect any favors or support from Busch. He was in the boss's doghouse.

But Flood was too concerned with his past, his present, and his forthcoming year to give much, if any, consideration to the impact his ultimatum could have on the Cardinals' decisions down the road. Possibly, given his injury the previous season, he recognized, as a doctor would soon enough, that his body was aging at an abnormal rate, and that his time in the majors might not last much longer. Carpe diem—seize the day—he must have thought. And he did seize it. At the time of his ultimatum, Busch was extremely angry at the Major League Baseball Players Association for marshaling a player holdout to improve pensions, the more so as it was the first time the MLBPA had been able to mount such an effort. But as the MLBPA also distracted Busch, it may have worked to secure acceptance of Flood's ultimatum. Bing Devine, whom Busch had fired as general manager of the Cardinals in 1964 but rehired in 1967, saw a rare opportunity for the club to win a third straight National League pennant and possibly a second World Championship in three years, especially with the newly acquired Vada Pinson joining Flood and Lou Brock in the outfield. So it was that, although the Baron fumed over Flood's ultimatum, he finally accepted the need to postpone taking action against the young man.[10]

On March 3, the second day of Flood's holdout, the Cardinals approved the $90,000 contract he said later he had demanded. However, it was a victory that he would rue, and perhaps the team also felt its pinch. Flood's victory exacerbated Busch's already heated anger and frustration over the club owners' loss to the union in the pension-fund battle. The Baron thought all major-leaguers were overpaid ingrates, and the Cardinals were the worst of the bunch. Not only did their total contracts run to more than a million dollars, the most of any team; not only did the club travel as well or better than a first-class commercial flyer; but they also complained that the club was taking advantage of them. Understandably, Busch stewed. Then on March 22, he called the Cardinals' players, manager "Red" Schoendienst, the directors of the Busch brewery and of the Cardinals, and local and St. Louis–based sportswriters to a meeting in the team's St. Petersburg clubhouse. There he opened up. He spoke at some length, stressing ownership's extensive financial commitments, what he saw as the players' responsibilities to help the club meet its obligations, where they were falling short, and what he expected them to do about it.[11]

Today, Busch's speech reads as paternalistic and tedious, but it seems threatening only if one had some reason to feel threatened. The boss began by describing the history of the brewery's ownership of the Cardinals, the club's investment of millions in Busch Memorial Stadium (opened in 1966); the great risks that inhered in a lease of thirty years; and the significant threat to attendance from other sports whose seasons overlapped, such as hockey, basketball, and football. Speaking apocalyptically, as if the club's franchise sat—and always would—on the edge of a financial precipice, Busch insisted that the language of the MLBPA and the tactics and behavior of some of the players were alien-

10. John Helyar, *Lords of the Realm: The* Real *History of Baseball,* 91.
11. Flood, *The Way It Is,* Appendix B, 228–36.

ating the fans on whom the club's survival depended. He warned the players that their "steady diet of strike talk and dollars," and their criticism of management, was suicidal, akin to killing the goose that lays the golden egg. No less dangerous was the players' failure to show up for appointments, their refusal to wait after games and sign autographs, and their reckless pushing of children who wanted to take pictures. The players were endangering the source of their incomes, and a source that could continue to benefit them long after their baseball careers ended, because as stars they could make "lasting and profitable business connections." They should see, Busch concluded, that the club and the players had a common interest in always exhibiting and sustaining good relations with one another and with the fans.[12]

While Busch's speech appears in retrospect as more of a prayer than a threat, or as an appeal for congeniality and cooperation after the harsh thrusts and counterthrusts of the pension-fund battle, Flood saw it very differently, or so he wrote almost two years later. He insisted that Busch unfairly attacked the players for alienating fans while he ignored the effects of the high prices management charged for food and beverages at the ballpark. And he cited other facets of Busch's speech that he deemed unfair. The boss talked about the players' flaws, but he did not recognize some of their contributions to the club and the game that went beyond duty, such as playing when sick and playing when injured. Flood's criticisms are, to this extent, true. And in this sense Busch's speech was a paternalistic lecture and unfair. But was it, as Flood alleges, "a spectacular tantrum . . . that demoralized the 1969 Cardinals," costing them another World Championship? Did Flood exaggerate? Was Busch's speech actually a lecture so harsh that it crippled the team spirit that he saw as critical to victory? And what, actually, is the relationship between a team's chemistry and its success? Which comes first? Does chemistry breed success, or does success lead to team spirit? Although there is no agreed-upon answer, at least in retrospect Flood argued that team chemistry came first. And he had a plausible argument. After all, the Cardinals were hardly less talented in 1969 than in 1968 or 1967. Unfortunately, the club's boss was telling the team, "Despite two successive pennants we were still livestock. . . . Busch's primary goal was to whip us into line and keep us there." And he succeeded in doing just that.[13]

12. Ibid.
13. Ibid., 86–87.

Reviewing the scene for the first time one year later, Flood insisted that Busch had bullied the team, and with what he felt were dire repercussions. "On that day millions of Americans learned in the newspapers that we had been publicly bawled out by our boss for being fat calves asking for too much money, that we were angering fans by not giving them autographs and annoying the press by refusing to be interviewed." Flood agreed that the boss had a right to chew out his employees, but in front of the press, which meant in public? Surely not. It was embarrassing. But there is more to the story. Slightly less than a year later, Flood said he would have responded vigorously had a stranger raised some of the issues publicly, for example in a bar, but in St. Petersburg, "the orator was the boss," and the boss was surrounded by his sycophants from the press, the brewery, and the Cardinals' front office. Had Flood spoken out, as he wished he had, Busch would have sent him packing within a week. This seems an unlikely rationalization, because the regular season was about to begin. But very near the end of his speech, Busch made remarks that Flood readily could have seen as directly threatening him. "Personally," Busch lectured, "I don't react well to ultimatums. I don't mind negotiations—that's how we get together—but ultimatums rub me the wrong way, and I think ultimatums rub the fans the wrong way."[14]

Given Busch's last remarks, one might understand why Flood felt himself in great danger and did not complain to Busch or the press about the speech. But if this was an obvious reason, Flood had still another, unstated reason for feeling threatened. A few days before, while he was in the clubhouse dressing after a game, Flood was told that he had a telephone call from the boss. Thirty years later he recalled, as clearly as if it were the day before, that the mere mention of Busch's name "stopped my heart right then, because Mr. Busch does not call anybody. He doesn't have to. What the fuck could he want with me?"[15]

Flood quickly found out what Busch wanted: Busch's voice on the line barked: "Goddamit, did you know that your brother has just been arrested here in town?" Busch was angry, and his words were a challenge to a fight, not a question to be answered. Even so, Flood responded quietly that he had no idea what Carl had done. What he heard back, he recalled later, was endless abuse heaped upon his head. "Busch ranted

14. Ibid.; John Devaney, "Why I Am Challenging Baseball by Curt Flood," 12.
15. Flood, *The Way It Is*, 130–32; Flood and Turan, "Outside-Outside," 23–24ff.

and raved about the great Cardinal tradition, about how never in the history of our great team had a player visited so much embarrassment upon the institution. Then he slammed the phone down."[16]

Busch's damning phone call and the details of Carl's arrest that followed shortly after threw Flood for a loop. Carl and a friend had botched a St. Louis jewelry store robbery, they had taken hostages and tried to escape in a car, and they had been caught in an alley after the police shot out the car's tires. But it was not those bare facts alone that had prompted Busch's lathered blasts. The shootout was captured on film by a KMOX television crew, and that evening's news featured Carl close up, with a St. Louis policeman's gun to his head, shouting, "Go ahead, pull the trigger; you'll be doing me a favor." Furthermore, unfortunately for Flood, KMOX noted that Carl was his older brother.[17]

Flood could have blamed Marian, his apartment mate and supposedly the protector of his interests and Carl's, for the trouble Carl had caused. She had persuaded him to help Carl, to take him into his apartment, and to find him a job. She had to know that Carl had gone back to drugs, but (apparently) said nothing to his brother. She had also assumed responsibility for Carl, yet failed to account for him on the day of the robbery. But Flood blamed himself and Carl, not Marian. Sentiment had clouded his judgment. His love for "Carl of my Blood," the older brother who had protected him on the dread streets of Oakland, had caused him to listen too easily to Marian's constant advocacy of their responsibilities and their hopes that what they believed to be Carl's better side—coupled with his brilliance and new sense of security—would guide him toward a productive life. But that had not happened. Curiously, it must be said, while Flood at first held both himself and Carl responsible, it was not long before he blamed Carl alone for not taking advantage of the opportunities offered him, and for a year he felt a bitterness toward his brother as great as his prior love. If he said anything to Marian about her responsibility in the matter, there is no sign of it.[18]

Such was Flood's presentation of Carl's theft and arrest, and Busch's phone blast, when two years later his memoir appeared. The incident was personal and unrelated to his ultimatum with his promise to hit

16. Flood and Turan, "Outside-Outside," 23–24ff.
17. Ibid.
18. Flood, *The Way It Is*, 132.

.300, his reaction to Busch's March 22 lecture, and his own difficulties with the Cardinals later in the season and after. Not so in his reminiscences a quarter of a century later. Then he said that he viewed his brother's robbery and the televised shootout, Busch's harshly charged phone call, and, soon after, Busch's lecture as dramatic early signs of the end of his career as a Cardinal. "I knew when I saw that [televised depiction of the shootout] that my days in St. Louis were numbered," Flood said. He failed to mention his ultimatum, his performance on the field, and his feuding with the front office during the season as factors.[19]

In these reminiscences from his last years, as in 1971, Flood was playing the innocent victim. He had done nothing to offend the boss. Even so, Busch had ordered a program of persecution. Before the 1969 season began, the front office relieved him as team co-captain, a position he had held for four years. The step was still another blow to his already gravely bruised ego, which had not yet recovered from his failure to catch Northrup's line drive in the 1968 World Series. His World Series failure, or what he believed was his failure, when coupled with gratuitous reminders from the press, did more than rub the open wound of his self-esteem: coupled with the loss of his co-captaincy and the televising of Carl's arrest, it threatened his commissions from portraits and the development of his fledgling CFA. So, he thought, did Busch's lecture of March 22. Just a bit more than a year later he would tell a federal court that Carl's arrest marked the beginning of his end as a Cardinal, but Busch's lecture at spring training marked a second, confirming milestone. Perhaps. But in fact Busch's lecture was just another in a series of milestones in Flood's burgeoning feud with the Cardinals' boss.[20]

After March 22 it seemed to Flood that whenever Busch even hinted about persecuting him, the Cardinals' front office quickly followed Busch's lead, and Flood sorely felt the impact of its decisions. Every issue that led to conflict he viewed as a threat to his job: "If I am not perfect, they will trade me." He was demoralized, but the team, as he saw it, was also demoralized. The whole complexion of the Cardinals began to change. A few days after Busch's speech, the club traded Orlando Cepeda, who Flood believed was still not only a star on the field but also, and perhaps more important, a spirited, essential leader in the

19. Flood and Turan, "Outside-Outside," 24.
20. Transcript, *Curtis C. Flood, Plaintiff, vs. Bowie K. Kuhn individually and as Commissioner of Baseball, et al., Defendants*, U.S. District Court for the Southern District of New York, New York, May 19, 1970.

clubhouse. In fact, whatever Cepeda's presence might have meant to the team's chemistry and optimism, he was no longer a star as a player; far from it. In 1968 he had slumped badly. Although admittedly it was a year dominated by pitching, he had batted only .248, with just 73 runs batted in. And after going to Atlanta in 1969, he batted a mediocre .257, although with 22 home runs and 88 RBIs. Meanwhile, the Cardinals obtained Joe Torre, who may not have been as lively as the now-departed Cepeda (who, it should be noted, was inducted into the Hall of Fame in 1999), but was a superb hitter with his best years yet to come—he would be the National League's batting champion, RBI leader, and MVP in 1971—as well as a smart, versatile player who could play first base and also catch. Furthermore, he was three years younger than Cepeda. The trade for Torre was one Flood should have praised, not faulted. A true professional would have done so. But much as in his businesses, where his factual knowledge was abysmal, Flood generally was now less than a model of reasoned judgment. In both areas he sounded like an amateur: as a baseball player, he surely placed undue stress on the importance of "joyful togetherness" for a team. Trading Cepeda for Torre was not the only front-office decision he faulted. Incredibly, given his obvious sentimentality, he was so blinded by his anger at Busch that he would not even give the Cardinals credit for bringing in Vada Pinson, a cherished friend, to play alongside him in the outfield.[21]

Flood's failure to mention, let alone praise, the Cardinals' acquisition of Pinson exemplifies the extent of his displeasure with the Cardinals' management in 1969. There can be no doubt, either, that he blamed Busch. The boss had followed his devastating March lecture with personal policies, other than the trade of Cepeda, which further undermined the team's morale. Two of the Cardinals' special perquisites disappeared: they no longer traveled in chartered planes, and the regulars found their names removed from the designated parking spaces at the ballpark. Although the latter deprivation, at least, might have been viewed as a gesture to equality, giving all the team's players equal treatment and strengthening team harmony much as integrating St. Petersburg had done, Flood saw it as undermining morale and a consequence of Busch's anger over the pension-fund holdout. The boss wanted retribution, even if it cost the team a pennant or, possibly, a World Championship.

21. Flood, *The Way It Is*, 175.

Obviously, what had been an apparently harmonious relationship between Flood and the Cardinals' front office collapsed during the 1969 season. The first sign after the season began was a skirmish that developed in late April when Flood missed a midday luncheon hosted by St. Louis's Advertising Club, the organization's annual salute to the Cardinals. The next day Bing Devine told a newsman that Flood's "unexcused absence was recognized by the club [and it was treated] accordingly." Devine did not say specifically how the club treated the incident and, perhaps, fearing even more retribution, Flood said nothing about it at the time. It was almost a year later, when he was out of baseball and had nothing to fear, that he spoke up. Then he told a writer from *Sport* that the day before the banquet, he had been spiked by the cleats of New York Mets shortstop Bud Harrelson on a slide into second base, cutting "a ten inch wound from my knee to my thigh." Somehow, Flood recalled, he finished the game, and afterward the team doctor stitched his wound and gave him a tetanus shot. That shot, he argued, was the central reason he did not make the banquet; it "knocked me loopy and all night long I was nauseous and dizzy, the leg still and painful. I finally got to sleep at six in the morning."[22]

The distortion of his sleeping caused by the tetanus shot, Flood said, should have explained to Devine's satisfaction why he slept through the scheduled midday banquet. It should have exonerated him. Somehow it did not. When he arrived at the ballpark, the general manager said, "Missing that banquet will cost you $250." At that, Flood showed Devine his stitched leg displaying clear evidence of his injury, and explained the tetanus shot and how it left him loopy. But Devine did not relent. "No excuses," he said. Flood had to pay the fine. It was just a little money, Flood explained to *Sport*'s reporter, but that was not the point of his complaint. By rejecting his justifiable excuse for missing the luncheon, the general manager had disrespected him, and the injustice left him very bitter.

If Flood's "unexcused absence" was mishandled—and Devine never seems to have contested his story—the penalty would seem as unfair as Flood said. Apart from his contract ultimatum, which was accepted, there is little or no apparent evidence of anything in Flood's behavior before that April issue that would justify fining him. On the contrary, he had often played hurt, and Devine knew that. Flood was being pun-

22. Devaney, "Why I Am Challenging Baseball by Curt Flood," 12.

ished, even though in every other respect he was more than toeing the club's line, actually, of course, the boss's line. Indeed, he was even responding favorably to Busch's March 22 lecture. He was not shouldering aside children who wanted autographs, he was working on behalf of the Aunts and Uncles charitable foundation that had recently elected him president, and he had handed out fifty passes to Cardinals' games. He was the kind of positive force in the community that reflected well on the Cardinals, very much in contrast with Busch's indictment. Of course, on the issue of the missed banquet, Flood knew, or at least felt, that the front office was looking for any excuse to punish him and that he should have phoned before midday. As for Devine, he might have known enough about Flood's late-night habits to believe that he missed the banquet not because of a tetanus shot but because he was out drinking into the wee hours the night before. But whatever Devine and Flood did or did not do, or thought or did not think, neither acted productively for themselves or the Cardinals.

Neither Flood nor the Cardinals began the 1969 regular season in a winning manner. From the outset a lack of hitting and runs was the rather obvious problem. By April 27, the day before the banquet, Flood was hitting a miserable .227, the Cardinals as a team were at a lowly .222, and the team was five and a half games behind the first-place Chicago Cubs. Flood's April average may have been affected by Carl's trial and sorrowful, cuffed departure for the Missouri State Penitentiary, the more so by reason of Marian's commiseration and plaintive insistence that he also commiserate—and feel as miserable as she did. Flood by his own admission did not; he could not handle Carl's situation as Marian insisted. For the time being, he was rightly bitter and angry at his brother's betrayal and tried to shut him out of his life. This upset Marian, and an ever-greater tension developed in the apartment. Flood would not have been human if those factors, along with the missed banquet and fine, had not had an adverse effect on his hitting, at least in the season's first month. Professionalism had its limits.

Throughout the rest of the 1969 season Flood's batting average and that of the team rose, but too little in a year when across the majors, batting averages and runs scored were rising sharply from the year before (aided by a decision to lower the pitching mound five inches, which reduced pitchers' effectiveness). In the last analysis, he and the team's other main hitters gave anemic support to the splendid pitching staff (led by Gibson and Steve Carlton, with earned-run averages of 2.18 and 2.17

respectively). The Cardinals closed the season with a team batting average of just .254 and managed only 87 home runs and 544 RBI. As for
Flood, after reaching .291 in mid-September, he closed the season at .285,
with only 4 home runs and 57 RBI. Thus he fell fifteen points below the
promise in his March 2 ultimatum that he would hit .300 for the season.[23]

Flood later blamed his mediocre season on Busch's "demoralizing"
March 22 speech and the various forms of harassment by management
that followed the boss's cue. High on Flood's list was management's
criticism of his and other Cardinals' off-field businesses—criticism that
he viewed as something new and highly distracting. Other Cardinals
were engaged in nonbaseball enterprises: Brock had his Dodge agency
and flower shop; Tim McCarver a Memphis restaurant; Gibson held
business interests in Omaha. But Flood emphasizes, "I was [consid-
ered] the worst offender of the lot." Flood says that his portrait work,
previously "tolerated, even encouraged," was now "deplored" as a distraction from his primary business, baseball. If this was the case, Flood
had a legitimate, if perhaps limited, criticism of the front office inas-
much as Busch had in a sense endorsed his painting. But Flood's criticism must be weighed against the number of hours and time of day or
night when he painted, as it might have worn him out, cost him sleep,
distracted him, and hampered his performance in center field. Unfortunately, it is impossible to know whether Flood painted too much or too
late into the night, or whether his painting in any way affected his work
on the field. However, it can be argued that the front office should have
worried more about what he might have been doing while out late
many nights, playing at Euclid's restaurants and bars or at the Playboy
Club. He and the club were probably better off if he was home painting,
however late at night. At least he would be near his bedroom, going
through an old and established if not always successful ritual of waiting
for sleep to kick in.

According to Flood, his portrait painting was not the only off-field
issue the Cardinals' front office castigated him about during the 1969
season. The front office, he said later, criticized his involvement in the
photography business. "How could I be expected to keep my mind on
baseball? The fact was," he said in his memoir, the club's "worry was
totally unfounded." Flood had told the sportswriters at spring training

---

23. These statistics are available on the Internet at www.baseball-reference.com/f/
Floodcu01.shtml.

camp that he played an extremely limited role in the photography business known as Curt Flood Associates, Inc. He was being honest. Bill Jones, Keith Collins, and, in one area, Marian, ran the corporation. He was only its public face. His name and picture ran in its advertisements for a new photography studio at 3543 Lindell Boulevard, but he was not present except for its grand opening on June 3, 1969. That noon he posed along with St. Louis Mayor Alfonso Cervantes, Cardinals' broadcaster Harry Caray, several Cardinals stars including pitchers Steve Carlton and Bob Gibson and speedy base-stealing artist Lou Brock, and two top-flight pitchers from the Oakland A's, Jim "Mudcat" Grant and Jim "Catfish" Hunter. But gathering endorsements from a variety of celebrities seems to have been the extent of Flood's contribution to CFA in 1969, at least directly. Again, at least according to the manager of CFA's photography studio, Marian acted in Flood's name, squabbling with Jones and Collins over buying too much equipment, spending too much for decorating, and ruining any chance that the studio might make a profit. Meanwhile, as Flood saw it, he dared not spend much time, if any, on the corporation. He was too busy working at baseball; he was always too "tense with athletic concentration," too worried that if he did not concentrate and play well, management would bring up a replacement from the minor leagues or find one via the trade route. He could not afford to give serious thought to any corporate activities Jones and Collins might wish to discuss with him. Furthermore, how could he, who was so often on the road, overrule executives who dealt with the corporation's problems on a daily basis; it would undermine them and impair morale. Finally, Flood would say, when he was at home he wanted to relax, and relaxation meant painting portraits whether because of commissions or a desire to help those in need. Consequently, he had neither the time nor the inclination to keep watch over CFA. He had to trust Jones, Collins, and his revered, highly trusted apartment mate, Marian, to run the corporation and its subsidiaries.[24]

Nominally, CFA's operations were divided into two parts: the midtown studio at Lindell and Grand (the Kirkwood studio apparently having fallen victim to racism when visitors saw Flood's name on the door), and a studio/office in suburban St. Louis that handled both the sales of high school graduation and prom pictures and the expected sales of

24. Ibid.; *St. Louis Globe-Democrat*, June 4, 1969; Ruth Sutterfield commented adversely on Marian's interference (interviews, July 1, 2002, and July 18, 2003).

"Curt Flood Studio" franchises. The first of these operations was supposedly supervised by Collins as vice-president for sales; but Collins
also handled the hoped-for sales of franchises, and he and Jones
worked together selling school pictures.

Such were the nominal position titles and assignments of authority at
CFA. They did not mean very much. Jones was the corporation's ubiquitous chief executive officer and strategist; Collins its ubiquitous chief
operating officer. Jones's office was wherever he chanced to be, at the
suburban St. Louis office/studio on Clayton Road or in a bar or restaurant;
but wherever he might be, he was trying to acquire the services of a professional photography company that would take the many thousands of
high school pictures which he and Flood hoped would be CFA's primary
source of revenue and profit. And by the summer of 1969, Jones had
found a St. Louis company he thought could handle the work: Howard
and Nancy Foster, Foster Photographers, located in the St. Louis area.[25]

On July 31, 1969, Flood and Jones signed a sales agreement with Foster Photographers. The photography company guaranteed nearly fifty-
six thousand pictures, and CFA promised payment according to the
wording of a promissory note signed August 12. Payment was due in
stages: the note for $22,607 at 4 percent interest called for payment of
$6,000 on June 1, 1970, half the balance as of January 1, 1971, and the
remainder on June 15, 1971. Penalties and attorney's fees would be
added to the balance if CFA did not pay its installments in a timely manner. Curiously, this business was not to be operated directly under the
CFA label but under the trade names of Foster Photographers and Midwest School Pictures, the latter a CFA subsidiary. Even more curiously,
it was neither Foster nor Midwest School Pictures, but CFA, that signed
an agreement on September 15, 1969, with the Delmar Printing Company of Charlotte, North Carolina, to "finish" the pictures. Finally, Flood,
despite accepting significant obligations in signing the promissory note,
took no part in the decision-making. He was involved, he testified later,
only at the last minute when he and Jones signed the note with Foster.
Indeed, Flood was so little engaged with CFA that he never attended a
board meeting. He was honest, then, when he claimed that the Cardi-

25. *Howard Foster and Nancy Foster vs. Curt Flood and William Jones; Delmar Printing Company vs. Curt Flood Associates, Inc.;* and *Delmar Printing Company vs. Curt
Flood Associates, et al.,* civil actions, respectively nos. 71C and 70C 209, U.S. District
Court for the Eastern District of Missouri, Eastern Division; documents in author's possession.

nals had no reason to worry about his involvement in the photography business, but he was very foolish in regards to his financial security.[26]

Apparently, Collins was much more active on a day-to-day basis than either Jones or, obviously, Flood in handling the nuts and bolts of CFA's operation. He had been trying to sell "Curt Flood Studio" franchises; to secure portrait commissions for Flood; to help Midwest School Pictures obtain contracts for high school pictures; and, not least, to acquire a manager, equipment, and photographers for the Lindell studio. To fill the manager position he hired Ruth Sutterfield, a genial, personable woman who had worked for twenty years in a photo studio at Famous Barr, one of St. Louis's better department stores. It was a wise choice. She seems to have been the only person in the entire CFA organization to have a clear sense of direction. And years later this redhead would have fascinating stories to tell of the "too many fingers in the pie" mismanagement of the photo studio. Meanwhile, she was not only eager to try to run the studio but also thrilled by the prospect of seeing herself standing next to Flood in a picture that would show a partial view of the studio in a St. Louis newspaper.[27]

That Flood may have paid too little heed to the activities and plans of CFA did not save him from his alleged critics in the Cardinals' front office, whom he does not actually name. However, he would not have found himself embroiled with the Cardinals' front office over his painting, his photography business, or anything else in his personal life if he and the rest of the team were playing at a pennant-winning pace. But they were not. For this Flood blamed Busch's various ill-conceived policies. The worst, he felt in retrospect, involved the appearance as early as spring training camp of men with movie cameras and tape recorders, who interfered with practices. They were not reporters; these men expected the players to provide them with unpaid interviews that they could use commercially. In short, management expected the players to make endorsements of a variety of products without getting paid for them. Flood insisted that the players should be paid, "rankling the front office even more profoundly than I realized," he later acknowledged.[28]

Whatever the merits of the battle over the interview-endorsements at spring training and the front office's irritation with his criticism, Flood

26. *Foster vs. Flood,* and *Delmar Printing Company vs. Curt Flood Associates, Inc.*
27. Ruth Sutterfield, interviews in St. Louis, July 1, 2002, and June 18, 2003.
28. Flood, *The Way It Is,* 182–83.

did not argue that either impaired his hitting. But he insisted that a decision by Devine near the season's end crippled his chances of reaching the .300 mark he had promised the previous March. As he interpreted the decision, Devine decided that the team was so far from first place that it had lost any real chance of winning its division title (both the American and National Leagues had divided into two divisions in 1969). Instead, it was time to rebuild for 1970. That meant giving new, untried men like catcher Ted Simmons and infielder Joe Hague opportunities to demonstrate their wares by playing every day, and Devine told Cardinals' manager Red Schoendienst to do just that.[29]

Flood steamed when he heard Devine's order. He said both men were "promising" but "raw," and their presence in the lineup would cost the Cardinals any chance of catching the first-place Mets. In fact, the team had no realistic chance of overtaking the Mets. On August 31 the Cardinals were five games out of first place; by mid-September they were ten behind; they ended the season thirteen and a half games out of first. While it might be argued that the results after August would have been different with the regulars in the lineup, there is no evidence to support that conclusion. September's results were as much or more a reflection of the Mets' surge than of any slippage by the Cardinals. Simmons, although he did not hit well—.214—played in only five games. As for Hague, he did not hit well enough for a major-leaguer—.170—but still played in forty games. But it is doubtful that Flood steamed because Hague played more. He was hot because Schoendienst installed Hague third in the lineup, just behind him and Brock. As Flood saw it, the opposition could pitch him on the very edge of the plate, hoping he would bite on a very difficult pitch and make an easy out; or opposing pitchers could walk him and pitch to Hague, which meant that he would have no chance to improve his average. But if Hague's place in the lineup was a real problem, it was a problem easily resolved. As soon as Flood complained to Schoendienst, the manager moved Hague to a lower spot in the batting order. Thus one is forced to conclude of this issue that Flood, who always visualized himself as a "team man," was, if understandably, trying to explain away his own very frustrating batting average, which was running several points below the .300 mark he had promised in March.[30]

29. Ibid., 183–84.
30. *Baseball Encyclopedia,* 10th ed., 1592 (Simmons), 1099 (Hague).

By September Flood's frustration was obvious to the *Post-Dispatch*'s Broeg. Recalling in two columns some years later what he saw and felt, Broeg wrote that he always liked Flood and wanted to help. He believed Flood was blaming management for problems of his own making and needed to wake up. Broeg would speak to Flood like a "Dutch Uncle." As a tactical matter, however, he would first butter him up. Approaching Flood in the batting cage one day, Broeg suggested that Flood was failing to get the singles he expected to get because Houston Astros Manager Harry Walker had noticed that Flood hit the ball most often up through the middle of the diamond, so Walker bunched his second baseman and shortstop to cover the area. The strategy worked, and other managers quickly followed Walker's lead, with similar results. But that was just the bad news. There was good news, which Flood possibly had not considered in terms of his own hitting: the Cardinals were replacing their grass field with artificial turf at the season's end. The faster field should mean that in 1970 balls that were now gobbled up by infielders would run through for hits. Flood's batting average should shoot up. In addition, Broeg encouraged him, "Just a couple or three more .300 years, Curt, and you can qualify for the Hall of Fame."[31]

That was Broeg's positive setup. Then, as he recalled, the "Dutch Uncle" in him turned it on. He knew Flood was "living as fast as he can." "Divorced and away from his family, he spent considerable time in other arms, including Bacchus and Morpheus"—and too much Bacchus, not enough Morpheus, Broeg wrote. He spared no words, warning Flood that he was hurting himself if not killing his career by "burning the candle at both ends and by pushing himself in an art hobby that had become a business." However, his warnings appeared to make little or no impression on Flood. "Curt," he recalled, "shrugged off my criticism of his life style, but smiled over the batting prospects."[32]

Flood's dismissal of Broeg's warning is understandable. His memoir reveals how locked-in he was in his belief that he was being persecuted by the Cardinals' front office. He was being victimized, as the team was being victimized that season. He attributed his performance and that of the rest of the team to the front office vendetta touched off by Busch's scolding the previous March 22. The club had failed to seize another pennant because "the front office was sabotaging us." Frustrated, Flood

31. *St. Louis Post-Dispatch,* August 18, 1994, January 27, 1997.
32. Ibid.

talked at length with *Globe-Democrat* sports reporter Jack Herman about how bitter he felt, for himself and for the team. Discussing part of this conversation later, Flood wrote, "Angrier than before, I confided . . . that the top management had tossed in the towel for 1969. I went on at some length."[33]

The next morning Herman reported that a Cardinal veteran had just told him that management no longer cared about the 1969 season, that the Cardinals had sold a million and a half tickets and saw a way to prevent the regulars from having good years and demanding large raises at contract time. He also reported that Devine exploded when informed of what the veteran—and it is almost certain that Devine knew it was Flood—had charged about the front office's policies then and earlier in the season: "The only reason the regulars are complaining is that they are afraid of losing their jobs." It was a response Flood recalled as especially ominous for his own future with the Cardinals.[34]

33. Flood, *The Way It Is*, 184.
34. Ibid.

VII

The Trade

Early in the morning of October 8—around 4 a.m., Flood recalled later that day when talking to his brother Herman—he was awakened by a phone call from a St. Louis reporter. It was an ungodly hour for anyone to hear the phone ring, but especially for Flood, who tended to party or paint late into the night. Thus he could not remember the reporter's name or newspaper, only that he said the Cardinals had just traded him to the Philadelphia Phillies. Despite what should have been news shocking him into full consciousness, Flood had ignored the message and gone back to his pillow. However, he could not slough off a second ring a few hours later. This time his caller was Jim Toomey, an assistant to Cardinals General Manager Bing Devine. He told Flood, in a toneless voice Flood would never forget, that the Cardinals had traded him to the Phillies along with catcher Tim McCarver, a relief pitcher, and an outfielder. He added, as if Flood might care, that the Cardinals were receiving three players from Philadelphia, the most notable, and obviously the key to the trade, being the versatile if at times troublesome slugger, Richie Allen.[1]

In his memoir, Flood says that he hung up the phone, weeping because the Cardinals no longer wanted him, and that he sat near it the rest of the day without answering its ring. He was shocked, but it was only the shock of finally hearing what he had feared for weeks if not longer. At the season's end, when he told a reporter that the Cardinals were giving up too early and Devine blasted that the "regulars . . . are afraid of losing their jobs," he had said to himself, "Brother Flood, you are going to be traded." And after the season's end, when he was cooling off and able to think more clearly, he returned to the issue, debating with himself. One voice said: "They would not dare," but another

1. *St. Louis Post-Dispatch,* October 8, 1969.

answered: "Wanna bet?" The team had performed miserably, and he had not hit .300 as promised in his ultimatum of the previous March. Flood knew he had fallen short but thought he could explain away his failure: "If only nine more hits had dropped," he would have hit the promised .300. Unfortunately, that explanation ignored the fact, obvious to all in baseball, that 1969, perhaps because of the lowered pitching mound, had been a much better year for major-league hitters than 1968 had been. Flood also argued that undue emphasis on batting averages prompted players to drink excessively. But if anyone heard, who cared? This was not only an insipid argument, but surely a curious one for a player with Flood's weakness for the bottle.

Flood's initial "reach" for answers to his trade reflected his inability to face hard truths. His failure to hit .300 had not been the only reason behind the trade, and probably it was not even the most important reason. During the past season, he had feuded endlessly with the front office; also, the Cardinals thought they needed more power in the lineup than he provided; and then his ultimatum the previous March had deeply offended Gussie Busch, his onetime patron and possible savior. Flood never totally accepted these factors as credible, but in the weeks and months following October 8 he found the trade itself less shocking. What did not diminish was his bitterness (for at least a decade) at the manner in which he was informed. He could not get over Toomey's phone call. As he saw it, after a dozen years of contributing to three league pennants and two World Championships, "All I got was a call from a middle-echelon coffee drinker in the front office. Was I not entitled to a gesture from the general manager himself?" Even were I "a foot-shuffling porter," he added, "they might have at least given me a pocket watch."[2]

If Flood had reason to be bitter at the crude, impersonal manner in which the Cardinals' front office informed him of his trade—Devine had personally called McCarver to inform him of the trade to Philadelphia—then he might have seen his treatment as a reflection of the Cardinals' anger at his behavior the previous year. But that would have meant thinking anew about his own behavior, which was out of the question, at least for the moment. Later, though, Flood would admit that he was of two minds. On the one hand, "the industry was merely doing its thing."

2. Flood, *The Way It Is,* 184, 187. The term "foot-shuffling porter" was an odd choice of words for a black man.

On the other hand, "I took it personally. I felt unjustly cast out. Days passed before I began to see the problem whole."[3]

Seeing the problem "whole" meant leaving St. Louis and going to Philadelphia, which, for the moment at least, Flood considered a dire prospect at best. In 1964 he had spoken bitterly of racism in "Cardinalville," but now many of the public barriers had come down, and for him specifically, St. Louis had changed dramatically for the better in the past five years. He was a celebrity who lived in a splendid apartment in one of the best and liveliest sections of St. Louis for a fun-loving man his age; he was served eagerly in the city's finest restaurants; he enjoyed a bit of status because of his philanthropic work with the Aunts and Uncles charity over which he now presided; and locally he was a well-known portrait painter as well as a prospering businessman. Then, too, he had good friends on the Cardinals—Gibson and Brock to be certain, but doubtless others—and he would be leaving them behind. Hardly less important, he would be leaving behind arguably the best fans in Major League Baseball. On the other hand, he saw Philadelphia, with good reason, as the nation's "northernmost southern city," Mayor Frank Rizzo's city, where a black man could hardly hope to be received with respect, much less warmth. And Philadelphia fans were known throughout baseball for their mean treatment of their players: as one wag put it, they would have booed Santa Claus. No wonder Flood wanted to remain in St. Louis; no wonder he told Marian, always his confidante, if not more, that "There ain't no way I'm going to pack up and move twelve years of my life away from here. No way at all."[4]

Angry and shocked though he was after Toomey's phone call, Flood explained his future intentions in a statement that an unnamed spokesman (no doubt Marian) gave the *Post-Dispatch* later that day. In the statement, Flood said that he had phoned General Manager Devine to tell him, "It has been increasingly difficult to stay in top shape. As you know, I'll soon be 32 years old." So he had decided to retire from organized baseball, effective immediately. But there was more. He intended to remain in St. Louis, where "I can devote full time to my business interests. I've had to think of my own and my children's future."

Of course Flood's claims did not ring true. By his own admission, he had not paid much if any attention to his business interests; he had told

3. Ibid., 188.
4. Ibid., 186.

reporters that in March. And he had paid no attention whatsoever to his children's present lives, much less to their future: he owed thousands of dollars in child support as well as alimony and medical coverage; precisely a year's worth of payments was past due. Possibly his talk of retiring was designed to give Devine a chance to abandon the trade, but surely Flood recognized that his words about remaining in St. Louis were essential to the well-being of Curt Flood Associates. In any event, he lost nothing by saying that he would retire and hoped the fans who supported him on the field "would understand my feelings and reasons for making this decision."[5]

In fact, Flood clearly was not as certain about retiring as he had advised Devine and the *Post-Dispatch*. Phillies General Manager John Quinn soon phoned and asked him to think it over, then told the Philadelphia newspapers that Flood said he would retire but sounded uncertain and agreed to meet with him after returning from Denmark later that month. Quinn was on the mark; Flood was about to reconsider retirement, although not necessarily to serve Quinn's needs.[6]

After the phone call from Toomey, Marian had suggested that Flood go ahead with his plans for the trip to Denmark. A change of scene would give him an opportunity to review whether to retire or play for the Phillies without constant pressure from the press or Quinn. Flood agreed. Then, by his account, Marian proposed a third option at the airport on Sunday, October 12. Tired of listening to him fume endlessly about the wrong done to him, his rights as a man shot down by his apparently limited options, "she asked: 'Why not sue?'" But it seems fair to ask whether Flood's account accurately represents what Marian actually said, the manner in which she said it, and perhaps even when she said it. Marian exercised a powerful influence on her apartment host. It may be recalled that in 1966 Flood asked Marian to come live in his new apartment, and she declined. However, when he returned in late 1967 and asked again, saying that his personal life ranged from "a shambles" to "scandalous," she agreed to come. Flood's needs may have played a part in her decision, but as asserted earlier, it more likely centered on her need to find Carl a job. And whatever the sorry consequences of her decision, Flood later acknowledged that she "took command. She

5. *St. Louis Post-Dispatch*, October 8, 1969.
6. Quinn's phone call noted in *St. Louis Post-Dispatch*, October 13, 1969; Flood, *The Way It Is*, 189.

runs my house." Furthermore, in late 1967 and after, Jody Kramer saw enough of Marian and Flood to conclude that her manner toward Flood was authoritarian and that he trusted her. In sum, given Marian's strength and apparent influence over Flood, it seems probable that, rather than *asking* him: "Why not sue?" she was prompting him. She wanted him to stop fuming and act, if only to think about a lawsuit while in Denmark. He did not answer her. However, although he thought the idea of a lawsuit crazy given the costs of pursuing it and the power of organized baseball, he found that he could only push it to the back of his mind, not out of it. Marian had planted a seed before his trip, and "there [in the back of his mind] it grew."[7]

Flood arrived in Copenhagen on the morning of October 13. He still hoped to buy or lease a facsimile of a Playboy Club; if not, then he would settle for "an American-style cocktail lounge, featuring the kind of rock music the Danes seldom heard except on records." However, he knew that he needed someone local to help him run anything he bought or leased. Looking around, haphazardly or otherwise, he soon found a congenial, olive-skinned, beautiful woman who was multilingual and knew something about the restaurant industry. Claire, whom he called his "black Dane," was quite willing to help him find a suitable location in Copenhagen and run the business when he was out of the country. Furthermore, she was prepared to come to the United States with him to learn to run a restaurant American-style. That she was married seemed not to be an obstacle: her husband gave Flood's plan his blessing, even though it included his wife traveling to the United States for what he was told would be a two-week visit. (As it turned out, she would stay in St. Louis until March, when Flood would take her to the airport.)[8]

Although Flood spent many hours with Claire during his seemingly two and a half weeks in Copenhagen, he also spent many hours alone, drinking and brooding in Copenhagen's nightspots or in his Sheraton hotel room. Late into the night he rummaged through the tattered sports pages he had brought from home. He wanted chapter and verse regarding the Cardinals' rationale for trading him for Richie Allen.

Statistics easily justified the trade. The Cardinals had not scored enough runs in 1969, and the problem had been a lack of power hitting.

---

7. Flood, *The Way It Is*, 189. For Jody Kramer's characterization of Marian and Flood, see phone call of summer 2001, confirmed in personal interview, July 1, 2006.

8. Flood, *The Way It Is*, 189; Zerman describes her "olive complexion" in e-mail correspondence with the author, October 18, 2000.

Richie Allen's numbers—more than 30 home runs a year in his six years with the Phillies, and 50 percent more runs batted in than Flood in 1969, though Allen played less often—suggested that he could help the Cardinals' offense. Then, too, Allen was twenty-seven, five years younger than Flood. All the statistics favored the trade. But Flood focused on negative factors that he thought outweighed Allen's numbers as a hitter. Allen was not a team player and he was egotistical and temperamental; in 1969 he was fined, then suspended for not paying the fine, and the suspension eventually stretched to twenty-six games. Consequently, that year he played in only 118 games, well short of Flood's 153. Furthermore, serious injuries to Allen's throwing hand had forced his manager to move him from third base to left field and, finally, to first base where he would do less damage as a fielder. Furthermore, he was a heavy drinker (as if Flood were not). Somehow, though, the Cardinals and the St. Louis press ignored Allen's patent liabilities. The *Post-Dispatch*'s Broeg lauded him as "the best available hitter of his type," who would very likely "hit even better in the friendlier confines of Busch stadium." Broeg, always a Cardinals booster, asserted that Allen might break the record for home runs by a Cardinal, that he had been unhappy in Philadelphia, and if his behavior had been troublesome at times, he also had told Philadelphia coach Elston Howard, "Don't worry, Ellie, when I get out of Philadelphia, I'll be a different man." Reflecting on Flood's remarks about retiring, Broeg, perhaps afraid that Flood would carry out his threat and ruin the trade, repeated what he had told him in the batting cage in September, but now about hitting in Philly's new artificial-turf stadium: he would have an opportunity to hit .300 for three more seasons and get into the Hall of Fame, a goal worth striving for even if he was doing well painting portraits and selling high school graduation pictures.[9]

Rereading Broeg's now-tattered column did not help Flood deal with his dilemma: to go to Philadelphia—or retire? Perhaps even to sue. Like Shakespeare's Dane of centuries past who brooded at Castle Elsinore, Flood pondered his options: going to Philadelphia would mean leaving behind his photography and portrait business, and if his first worry had no merit—he had never been active in Curt Flood Associates, Inc.—the portraits had been paying well, and he would lose them. On the other hand, the Phillies would pay him well, better in fact than many of the

9. See http://www.baseball-reference.com/a/allendi01.shtml>.

Cardinals, who in 1970 would find their salaries slashed. So dollars were not the vital issue. The real issue was pride. The trade hurt; it was unfair; and it hurt more sharply because of the insulting way in which he had been informed. Pride drove him into a fiercely burning desire for vengeance, not against Toomey of course—he was a nobody—but against the Cardinals, and Busch in particular. Marian had suggested that he sue, but on what basis he did not know. He knew only that Major League Baseball's reserve system gave the Cardinals the right to dispose of him as they wished, as if he were a slave on an antebellum southern plantation. That was morally wrong, obviously. No one should be able to treat his players as if they were "sheep or cattle or, if you will, slaves." But what to do about it was another matter.[10]

Walking the floor of his Sheraton hotel room into the wee hours, unable to sleep, Flood brooded. How could they have traded him for Richie Allen? Allen might be a better hitter, but he was more likely to lose games with his glove than win them with his bat, and even if Philly's missile-hurling fans and its press were the harshest in the majors, Allen had still earned his bad-boy reputation. Of course, Flood ignored the fact that he himself was not "ivory clean." He ignored his own total lack of responsibility to the Cardinals when he took his troubled brother into his home. He ignored his ultimatum the previous March when he promised to hit .300 if he received a $100,000 salary. He ignored his failure to appear at a banquet in April. And he ignored his feuding with the Cardinals throughout the past season. Like many people in such a situation, he refused to look in the mirror.

At root, Flood could not accept the fact that his trade to Philadelphia was a decision based on what the Cardinals' front office believed were the best interests of the team. "How could they not want me?" he asked himself again and again, as he had since Toomey called. "Have they lost their minds up there at the brewery?" Flood was close to losing his own mind. Unable to accept the reality that his skills had diminished, he flirted with the foolish and the impossible. "Maybe they don't want you because of what happened in the World Series. Maybe they think they've got too many black guys and don't want me because I'm black." Of course, his first insinuation made no sense: the Cardinals had surrendered to his salary demands as he portrayed them—a hefty 24 percent increase—after his apparently misplayed line drive in the World Series,

10. *St. Louis Post-Dispatch*, October 8, 1969.

and his second made no sense, because Allen too was black. It would appear, then, that the ever-sensitive Flood, blinded by loneliness, a crushing blow to his self-esteem, and perhaps his tendency to drink heavily in such circumstances, simply could not accept his trade as a valid baseball judgment by the front office, coupled with Busch's disinterest in protecting a man who had offended him. However, Flood's faults, including his self-inflicted wounds, did not detract from his right to question whether baseball's club owners had the legal right, let alone the moral right, to buy, sell, and trade players as if they were property or, to use his favored word at the time, "slaves." Of course, there was no answer to this question in Copenhagen.[11]

Flood probably flew back to St. Louis four days before October ended, his "black Dane" in tow. He was scheduled to display his portraits and be available to accept commissions at a bank in suburban Clayton on Friday, October 31. Meanwhile, he remained consumed by his trade, wondering if he had an option other than to go to Philadelphia or retire. After the weekend he went to the office of Allan Zerman, the lawyer who had filled out his corporation's papers two years before and defended his brother Carl in court the past April. A quarter of a century later the stocky Zerman, usually close-mouthed but passionate and loud when certain of his beliefs, would clearly recall Flood's appearance and demeanor when he entered the law office that day. Flood's eyes lacked the luster and his voice the confidence Zerman remembered from their previous meetings. Still, he listened quietly as his visitor first outlined what had happened to him on October 8, then asked: "How could they do this to me?" Zerman did not react to the part where Flood recalled for him that he had "business possibilities," apparently referring to Curt Flood Associates, seemingly aware that those possibilities were not what had brought him in. However, Zerman listened intently when Flood, "visibly angry . . . raised his voice" and detailed the lack of gratitude the Cardinals had displayed for his many years of service. Flood emphasized the impersonal, insulting phone call he had received from an inconsequential man in the front office and the scrap of paper with its formal notice from the front office that he had found in his mail the next day. Together, they had prompted his bitterness and anger: "Screw 'em. I'm quitting," he finished his venting.

Flood's tale of being dumped like a piece of garbage aroused Zerman, who said, "There's one other alternative." Flood responded

11. Flood and Turan, "Outside-Outside," 25–26.

quickly, as if he had been cued—which he had—"Are you talking about suing baseball?" Zerman parried: "Have you considered the idea?" Flood later said the idea had been "germinating in me for weeks," which was probably true, but even if it had not been, he still yelled, "LET'S DO IT" the moment Zerman asked him.[12]

Zerman had at least two critical reasons other than friendship for committing himself at the very least to examine the possibilities of Flood's case. As a boy he had suffered the sting of anti-Semitism, so he not only sympathized but also empathized with Flood as a black man and a probable victim of racism. In this connection, the fact that Zerman was then probing the meaning of his Jewish faith contributed to his sensitivity to Flood's plight and decision to help if he could. But Zerman had another, at least equally important, reason for his readiness to help Flood. He was the son of a shoe-store owner, and, like his father, held an abiding prejudice against the power of big business to bully small businessmen and others who crossed their shark's path. He saw the Cardinals and the Anheuser-Busch brewery as big businesses. This prejudice against them—some might prefer the softer word bias—not only strengthened his desire to help Flood but also helped to define the legal strategy that he soon decided was the key to ending or at least modifying Major League Baseball's reserve system.[13]

Once Zerman agreed to consider a lawsuit against baseball, he instructed Flood to bring to him a copy of Major League Baseball's Uniform Players Contract, which contained the various clauses that together constituted baseball's reserve system. He also told Flood that he would look up the law that supported the system. Probably he should have asked Flood if he could afford to sue—and probably lose. Although Zerman knew Flood well enough to know that he kept a camera in his bedroom aimed at the bed, he does not recall having any other knowledge of Flood's personal life other than that he, with Bill Jones, had founded CFA. He knew nothing of Flood's business in Oakland, his legal and moral obligations to his ex-wife and children, and his moral obligations to his mother. He did not ask about Flood's personal life then or later, despite the considerable amount of time the two spent

12. Flood, *The Way It Is*, 190; Zerman, e-mail correspondence with author, November 29, 2001, and July 23, 2000.

13. Various Zerman e-mail messages and personal interview, June 18, 2003; Connie Reilly interview, June 19, 2003.

together in the next eight months, in Zerman's office and, when traveling, in hotel rooms, in restaurants, and on planes. Or so he claims.

In the next two weeks Zerman studied Flood's contract, looking for any errors that might invalidate it. But he spent most of his time at the Washington University law library, reviewing the legal standing of the reserve system. He knew the reserve system involved collusion among the major-league clubs and a conspiracy in restraint of trade, almost certainly a violation of the Sherman Antitrust Act. Yet somehow Major League Baseball's reserve system had survived this apparently embracing legislation. Determining how required some time researching constitutional law, but eventually it led Zerman to two Supreme Court decisions. The 1922 case of *Federal Baseball Club of Baltimore v. National League et al.* established the precedent for all the legal battles thereafter involving antitrust law and organized baseball. The plaintiff, a club that had played in the since defunct Federal League, charged that the National League had conspired with other clubs to destroy its league and create a monopoly. That was a conspiracy in restraint of trade. More than that, because the National League's clubs traveled across state lines for games, they were businesses engaged in interstate commerce, and thus subject to federal regulation, meaning the Sherman Act. However, the Supreme Court rejected these arguments. The iconic Justice Oliver Wendell Holmes, writing for a unanimous court, asserted that baseball clubs competed in what he called "exhibitions" involving "personal effort," not "production," and therefore they were not involved in trade or commerce in the sense intended by the Sherman Act, and their crossing of state lines was "mere accident." A precedent-setting decision, *Federal Baseball Club* undergirded and preserved Major League Baseball's reserve system."[14]

This exemption was reaffirmed in 1953, in the *Toolson v. New York Yankees* case, involving a Yankee minor-league player "stored" in the minors until the major-league club might need him. Seven Supreme Court justices ignored the more expanded view of the Constitution since 1937 that would have recognized that baseball was involved in interstate commerce and on that basis was subject to federal antitrust laws. They relied in the main on the precedent established in the *Federal Baseball*

---

14. *Federal Baseball Club of Baltimore, Inc., v. National League of Professional Clubs,* 259 U.S. 200 (1922) can be found at http://www.baseball-reference.com/bullpen/ Federal_Baseball_Club_v._National_League.

case in 1922. Coincidentally, and perhaps more important, the majority's decision recognized the Supreme Court's commitment to the Holmesian doctrine of "judicial self-restraint," which usually required deference to the federal government's executive and legislative branches. The Court opined that if Congress had wanted to eliminate baseball's exemption from the antitrust laws, it had recently passed up an opportunity to do so. The House of Representatives Judiciary Committee Chairman Emanuel Cellar had held hearings two years before, and no action was taken. Those hearings, as well as the Court's *Toolson* decision, in 1953, almost certainly reflected the value that Americans with any interest in baseball placed on the game. It was the National Pastime, a game unrivaled in popularity by other sports; if just a game, it was at least a very special one. Baseball was still romance, legend, and myth. Club owners were often portrayed as philanthropists; players very often were seen as folk heroes. Parents watching games with their children would tell them stories about personalities that were larger than life, involving not only their home runs, batting averages, runs batted in, and strikeouts or steals, but in some cases—Babe Ruth being the most notable—their gargantuan appetites for food and drink, if not for women. Almost without exception these men fit into the "American mold," as most Americans wanted to visualize and preserve it: simple, rural and small-town men, virtuous, white, ambitious, and hardworking, but, like most men, always ready for some innocent relief from their duties. By and large these men came from the nation's heartland and, like baseball, confirmed its values. For these reasons, and more, baseball was still the National Pastime. Thus, it is hardly to be wondered that, like the highest court in the land, Congressman Cellar's Judiciary Committee did not tamper with the game's antitrust exemption.[15]

Zerman was well aware of the nation's identification with baseball, and he soon became familiar with baseball's exemption from the antitrust laws. Past legal precedents held little room for optimism. But it was the late sixties and the "times were a-changing" in the midst of the war in Vietnam, rock and roll, and the civil rights revolution. Although baseball alone of the major sports—which also included football and basketball—retained its antitrust exemption, it too was changing. No

---

15. *Toolson v. New York Yankees* can be found at http://www.businessofbaseball .com/toolsonvnyyankees.htm; Ken Burns, "When Baseball Was a Game," episode 7 of his baseball documentary; Helyar, *Lords of the Realm,* 8, 12; finally, personal recollections.

longer was St. Louis the westernmost city in the major leagues. No longer were big-league games available only to fans in attendance and listening on the radio. And there were now numerous new clubs in cities that spanned the continent, all of them serving food and souvenirs. As Zerman saw it, baseball games could no longer be seen in terms of "personal effort" as described in *Federal Baseball Club;* it was now a big business, it was obviously involved in interstate commerce, and it should be encompassed by the Sherman Act. The Supreme Court should, and could, be made to see that the *Federal Baseball Club* case was an anachronism that should be reversed, and that Flood should be liberated from the reserve system's constraints.

Zerman was not clawing wildly at hope in thinking that the courts might be ready to see baseball as a business. In their dissenting opinion in the *Toolson* case, Justices Harold Burton and Stanley Reed pointed to the multitude of ways in which baseball had become a big business. The clubs crossed state lines via their capital investments, their radio and television activities, and their competition that extended to Canada, even Cuba. Withal, Burton and Reed wrote, "It is a contradiction in terms to say that the defendants in the cases now before us are not engaged in interstate trade or commerce as those terms are used in the Constitution of the United States and in the Sherman Act." To Zerman, what the two justices wrote in 1951 about organized baseball being a business involved in interstate commerce and subject to the antitrust laws was even more apparent in the late sixties, such was the great amount of money made by the baseball clubs themselves but also by businesses that profited from the image they projected, as with the Cardinals and the Anheuser-Busch brewery. Zerman finally concluded that Flood could win a lawsuit by demonstrating very clearly to the courts, including the Supreme Court, that baseball was a business engaged in a conspiracy in restraint of trade as defined by the Sherman Act, and that it was wrongly restricting Flood's right to negotiate freely for his services with any club that was interested. More important, Zerman projected a scenario that might preclude taking the case as far as the Supreme Court. To demonstrate that baseball was truly a big business crossing state lines, it would be necessary to audit all the clubs' books and those of its owners, as well as the books of other companies that profited from association with those baseball clubs. Indeed, Zerman seems to have believed that just the threat of audits might prompt Major

League Baseball to modify its reserve system. And that alone was Flood's interest in a lawsuit for the moment, not the surely more difficult elimination of baseball's antitrust exemption. So in mid-November Zerman advised Flood that he might well win a lawsuit. But he also warned him that suing was always a very chancy proposition, that it required lengthy and expensive preparation, and that it would in all likelihood take at least a year, and probably longer, to reach a resolution. In the end, then, he had to tell Flood that he was not able to handle the case himself. He had a small office and lacked the staff and the financial resources required for a trial in New York, a hearing in an appeals court, and, if need be, a final trial in the Supreme Court. If Flood wanted to sue, then he must obtain the support of the Major League Baseball Players Association.[16]

Meanwhile, between sessions with Zerman, Flood heard once again from John Quinn, the Phillies' general manager. Quinn did not want to lose a player of Flood's caliber "for a [proverbial] player to be named later." So, on November 7, he flew to St. Louis after a business trip in Phoenix and lunched with Flood at the now-desegregated Chase Park Plaza hotel. There, he advised his guest that the Phillies were in the midst of a complete remodeling. They would soon have a new ballpark that would hold more fans and permit the club to pay good players more money and thus develop a better team. When Flood replied that he could not leave his various businesses, Quinn argued that in Philadelphia he would be in a position to expand. Seemingly, Flood came away impressed. According to his memoir, before leaving the dining room he told Quinn that he would keep an open mind and, as he admits, "agreed to see him again." He was no longer bothered about Philadelphia as such. However, when Quinn told the *Philadelphia Daily News* the next week that he was optimistic about signing Flood, Flood responded, "I don't know what he bases his optimism on. If I had to make a definite statement now, it would be that I will not play. Right now there's no story. I'll wait and see how I feel in March. I just wish everybody would give me a chance to make up my mind." He did not mention that he had

---

16. http://www.businessofbaseball.com/toolsonvnyyankees.htm; Zerman e-mail correspondence (especially November 18, 2001) relates his emphasis on baseball as a business as well as his failure to recognize that the "nine old men" of the Supreme Court might not be as full of a "youthful exuberance for justice" as he was; also, various interviews with Zerman.

just spoken to Marvin Miller, executive director of the Players Association, and was about to fly to New York to discuss with him the feasibility of a lawsuit.[17]

Earlier in the month Flood had phoned Miller, outlined his conversations with Zerman, and asked what he thought about the application of the antitrust laws to baseball's reserve clause. Briefly, Miller recounted the story of the *Federal Baseball* and *Toolson* cases. There were some indications that the present Supreme Court would rule differently. Miller did not specify his probable belief that the existing Court was more "activist" and concerned with individual rights than the Court of 1953; instead he warned Flood that it would be "foolhardy to bet on [the Court ruling differently than in 1953]." Flood had responded that he would not play in Philadelphia, after which Miller had invited him to New York to discuss a lawsuit; the issue was too complex to discuss on the phone. Flood agreed, and on Sunday, November 23, he and Zerman flew to New York.[18]

The next day Flood and Zerman discussed Flood's possible lawsuit over lunch and for four hours after with Miller and the Players Association's general counsel, Richard "Dick" Moss, at the Summit Hotel. Flood was definite: "I want to sue baseball on constitutional grounds. I want to give the courts a chance to outlaw the reserve system. I want to go out like a man instead of disappearing like a bottle cap." Miller could hardly contain his hope that the Players Association had found some means of challenging the reserve system and, in so doing, baseball's antitrust exemption, and he responded in an equally direct manner: "You are the answer to a maiden's prayers."

And so Flood was—if in the end he decided to sue. After some fifteen years since its founding, the Players Association could count few achievements. In 1954 it had worked out a pension-fund formula with the owners, and little more than a year later it had nudged the players' minimum salary to $6,000, but these gains had more to do with noblesse oblige and a desire to avoid bad publicity than threats of a strike or a holdout by frightened, passive players and a player's organi-

17. *Philadelphia Daily News*, November 18, 1969; also Allen Lewis, article in ibid., undated clipping.

18. Flood, *The Way It Is*, 190; for Miller's version of this discussion and his account of later meetings with Flood and/or Zerman, as well as his rise to power in the MLBPA, see Marvin Miller, *A Whole Different Ball Game: The Sport and Business of Baseball* (especially chap. 10).

zation lacking forceful, thoughtful leadership. Then, in early 1967, when the Players Association's pension plan was about to expire, the MLBPA's board of player representatives, recognizing that baseball's television income was about to multiply, searched for a strong, dynamic executive director who could help it secure its rightful share of the much-larger revenues it expected. Eventually, the board chose Miller. However, its choice was conditional. By its rules, Miller' candidacy required ratification by the Players Association's membership.

Miller was surely the best choice the Players Association could have made. Miller, who was born in 1918 and grew up in Brooklyn during the Great Depression, was not only a keen sports fan—of the local Dodgers naturally—but also an unpretentious intellectual with an excellent memory who worked his way through college, graduating with a degree in economics at nineteen. By the fifties he was working for the United Steel Workers Union. While his training first assigned him to technical tasks assembling data, his charismatic personality and pragmatic temperament, coupled with his factual knowledge, made him a superb bargainer. Although his strong personal talents enabled him to rise through the USW's ranks, he also had patrons who pushed him along. His talents as a negotiator were recognized and used quite early at the USW by its able general counsel, Arthur Goldberg, and then by the union's president, David McDonald. In this last connection, Miller became so powerful that he was known in some quarters as "assistant president." However, his power disappeared when McDonald lost the presidency. So Miller was ready for new opportunities, especially those that did not involve working within a large bureaucracy, and he readily accepted the Players Association's offer to campaign for the post of executive director.

Miller displayed precisely the kind of skills the Players Association needed. But he had to be ratified by the players, and many, especially those coming from nonunion or even strongly anti-union areas of the South and Southwest, were nervous about a man whom they saw, accurately enough, as a left-leaning New York Jew right out of the ranks of organized labor. In any case he was an alien figure to most players, and many feared that he was militant and would alienate the owners upon whom most of the players felt dependent, even grateful, for their jobs. This was the first impression of most players. It did not last. As Miller made the rounds of clubhouses during spring training, players saw a mild, understated man who spoke impressively but quietly about the benefits of a strong Players Association. He also advised them that better minimum salaries, improved working conditions, and other benefits would not come their way overnight. The MLBPA did not have the money or sense of purpose and unity. It was not the USW. It was not a union. Miller knew that he would have to be the patient technician-teacher, gathering and disseminating the facts about baseball's revenues and potential, about what players actually made, as opposed to what they were told and heard, so that they would no longer consent to be underpaid and otherwise abused by the clubs' general managers.[19]

After his ratification by the players, Miller pursued the patient, building-block methods he had advocated at spring training camps. He gathered facts that enabled players to see grievances they had not previously recognized. When Ron Fairly of the Los Angeles Dodgers told him that the club's general manager said he was the team's highest-paid player, Miller showed Fairly that he actually ranked eighth. In this manner, Miller raised the consciousness of the players. Gradually, he began transforming the Players Association into a union, always increasing its leverage against the club owners and their negotiating instrument, the Players Relations Committee. In 1968 the strengthened Players Association managed to get minimum salaries raised to $10,000; spring training allowances raised from $25 a day to $40; meal money on the road during the season increased to $15 a day; and the maximum salary cut allowed per year reduced from 25 percent to 20 percent. At the same time the PRC agreed to better working conditions: on planes and in their hotels the players would go first-class. Then early in spring training in 1969 Miller persuaded the players to hold out—for the first time—until the PRC agreed to a substantial increase in their pension fund. Meanwhile, he was giving serious thought to the reserve system and what could be done to modify it. Its heart was located in section 10A of the Uniform Players Contract. As the club owners argued, 10A gave them an automatic option on a player's services for another year whether or not the player signed a contract for any given season. Miller thought that interpretation was absurd and believed an independent arbitrator would agree. He believed that if a player did not sign a contract for any given season, then he was a free agent the year after, legally able to sign with any team that wanted his services. However, as late as November 1969, when Flood arrived in New York, there was no way Miller could expect to get his interpretation of 10A accepted: any appeal of its existing interpretation would go to the

19. Helyar, *Lords of the Realm*, 83–89.

commissioner of baseball, who was for all intents and purposes an agent of the owners who had appointed him, not an independent arbitrator. And a strike to force the club owners to modify the reserve system was impossible at the time: the Players Association was barely able to organize a holdout; it was not yet a union with the sense of purpose and solidarity required for a strike. Very few players were about to place their careers on the line to fight for modification of the reserve system. So it was that Flood's appearance at the Summit Hotel was, in Miller's words, "the answer to a maiden's prayer." Or, more precisely, to the MLBPA's prayer.[20]

While Miller was quite happy to talk with Flood and Zerman over an extended lunch, he recalled alerting them that he believed the lawsuit had a limited chance of succeeding, and also that he told Flood the dangers he would face in terms of his career and income. Perhaps the stern warning was a measure of Miller's worth, or perhaps he wanted to make certain that Flood would not change his mind about suing baseball after involving the Players Association. Probably it was both. Specifically, Miller pointed out that, although times had changed since *Toolson* in 1953, the Supreme Court almost always favored such property interests as the club owners held. It was unlikely that the Court would "discomfit the owners of the national pastime," and Flood should be aware of that. He should also know that he would surely lose at least a year's playing time and salary, probably somewhat more, and that he would "never manage or be employed in baseball again." The clubs would blackball him from the game, and the owners and their friends would make life difficult for him in other industries. In St. Louis, where Flood said he wished to continue living and working, he would have to deal with Busch's fury and great power. To this series of warnings, but seemingly to that about Busch's influence in particular, Flood responded very curiously considering his dozen years in St. Louis, "I hadn't thought about it, but that's the way it is, okay I'll live with that and deal with it somehow. You have not begun to scare me yet. Let's sue."[21]

Wanting to be certain that Flood truly understood what he would be getting into, Miller explained at great length the road ahead. First, Flood would have to get the support of the Players Association's board. That meant addressing its members at their December "winter meeting" in

---

20. Ibid., 35–36; Miller, *Different Ball Game*, 173.
21. Miller, *Different Ball Game*, 181, 183.

San Juan, Puerto Rico. Then there was the complicated issue of how to fight the case through the legal system and in the court of player and public opinion. As Miller evaluated these issues, he thought "Curt's attorney seemed competent but clearly did not have the experience or the stature to handle a case of the magnitude under consideration. He had never argued a case before the Supreme Court; he was not experienced in antitrust cases." On that basis, and presumably, one would think, with a measure of embarrassment, Miller told "Curt's lawyer I wasn't denigrating him in any way but that Flood's case required experience and expertise in antitrust cases," which Zerman did not have. More to the point, Miller believed that a first-rate, nationally renowned lawyer "could bring this case the kind of publicity it deserved." Flood's lawsuit, if he sued, should personify the inequities and iniquities of the reserve clause for all to see.[22]

Zerman did not take umbrage at this dismissal. He had known that he could not handle a lawsuit of the magnitude Flood was considering. However, one must wonder that as a personal friend he did not take Flood aside and explain that Miller intended to use him as a sacrificial lamb. Zerman had to know that if the MLBPA underwrote the legal costs and the hiring of a law firm, then it would control the case's strategy. His own strategic plan for winning the case—the one he seems to have sold Flood on in his office earlier that month—would focus hard on the business aspects of baseball, exposing its interstate character and, at least equally important, its obscene profits, and use the very threat of that exposure to secure modification of the reserve system. This strategy would almost certainly disappear if Miller hired the law firm. Miller wanted to rid baseball of the antitrust exemption that allowed the reserve system, at least as it was interpreted. If that effort failed, then he wanted to at least succeed in raising the consciousness of the Players Association's members and the public. Flood's freedom from the system was secondary. By necessity, then, Miller would hire a law firm with his objectives in mind, and Zerman almost certainly had to know this. If so, he should have warned Flood at the time. That he did not, however, is understandable. It is often difficult to make snap decisions in a situation where one comes cap in hand as Flood and Zerman did. This is especially true as Miller had the knowledge and charisma to dominate a room. Then, too, Zerman was fairly certain by this time that Flood was

22. Ibid., 175.

determined to sue, and for that he had to have the best legal support, which meant great expense. Flood himself seems to have recognized this when he told Miller, "You know I make a good salary, but I'm told by my lawyer that a case like this will take a fortune before we're through." So after his meeting with Miller, Flood seemed solidly committed to a lawsuit managed by and paid for by the Players Association. Even so, Miller told him to return to St. Louis and think very hard about whether he really wanted to sue. Could he afford it? Could he give up baseball, at least for a year, and perhaps for all time?[23]

That evening Flood dined with John Quinn. During the meeting a woman at an adjoining table leaned over and asked if he was Lou Brock, the Cardinals' star left fielder. Quinn in an affidavit later swore that Flood told the woman he had been with the Cardinals and now was with the Phillies. Flood later admitted telling the woman, "I'm Curt Flood and this is John Quinn, general manager of the Phillies. I'm with them now." Flood never explained why he told the woman this. And though the two men dined through the evening—four hours, according to Quinn—Flood did not mention either retiring from baseball or challenging the National Pastime in a lawsuit. Flood recalled Quinn offering him $100,000 to play for Philadelphia in 1970. Quinn recalled making the offer a few days later, and Flood responding that he would "think about it and be in touch with me." Whatever the timing, though, Flood's response suggests some hesitancy about suing. Although he sounded emphatic about it when in Miller's office, it seems that he had not made up his mind. Perhaps between his meeting with Miller and his meeting with Quinn, Zerman described the divergence in strategies, and that he should think again about suing. However, there is no evidence that he did so.[24]

For two weeks Flood deliberated. He phoned Miller in late November advising him that he wanted to proceed with a lawsuit. Miller recalls that even then his feelings about the lawsuit were mixed. "Realistically, we had little chance of overthrowing a reserve clause that had half a century of court precedents on its side, but at least in Curt Flood we had the right man . . . to mount a challenge. Since this could be a landmark case, it was absolutely essential that the man at the center of it be someone with great personal integrity," who would not back out of a lawsuit

23. Ibid.

24. Flood, *The Way It Is,* 191–92. John Quinn's sworn affidavit of January 28, 1970, in transcript of *Curtis C. Flood vs. Bowie Kuhn individually and as Commissioner of Baseball et al.* corroborates Flood's account.

if the owners cut him a deal or if the going got tough. Now Miller was persuaded that Flood was just such a man. Thus he did not question Flood's decision. Rather, he talked about the practical, financial aspects of the case they would fight. Flood would have to go to Puerto Rico in December and persuade the Players Association's board to support him. Miller added that he could not ask the association to cover Flood's general living expenses during the trial or, as would be the case, trials, only his legal expenses and his travel to and from New York, probably including his hotel and food (the last is not clear from Miller's memoir). Flood agreed, saying, "That's absolutely fair." Then, as he knew Zerman was not to be his attorney, he asked Miller, "Who did you have in mind as a lawyer?" It was a fair question, and Miller had decided who the lawyer would be, if he could get him, but he begged off answering. He did not say why, and Flood, who should have insisted on an answer and the exact strategy to be employed, did not press him.[25]

It would seem from Flood's conversation with Miller that he was determined to sue, end of story. A quarter of a century later Flood explained his decision more fully: "I had little money, but I was fortified by what I am not ashamed to call spiritual resources. I had spent good years with Johnny Jorgensen. I would do us both proud by trying to improve my corner of society before moving on. Win or lose, the baseball industry would never be the same. I would leave my mark." Flood's words are romantic, heroic, and self-sacrificing, but they were written in a very convenient time frame. Moreover, they are somewhat vitiated by a note he sent Quinn on December 4. Responding to a message relayed from the Phillies' general manager, who still hoped for an affirmative response to his offer of $100,000, Flood apologized for not returning his call, then wrote, "With regard to our conversations, I feel I must resolve a number of personal problems before I make a final decision. Therefore I intend to give the entire matter serious consideration during the next weeks and will be in touch with you during the week of December 22nd."[26]

Flood does not specify his "personal problems," but three can be suggested. One, he did not fully grasp the distinctions between a lawsuit with the limited goal and strategy Zerman had proposed and one with the far-reaching objectives and strategy of the MLBPA. Two, Flood was not certain that he wanted to sue. It may be that he had doubts in part

25. Miller, *Different Ball Game*, 184.
26. Quinn's affidavit, *Flood v. Kuhn*.

because Miller had withheld the name of the lawyer he wanted to handle the case. On the other hand, it must be presumed that Marian, who first suggested that Flood sue, continued to insist that it was the right course. Perhaps she reminded him of what her husband would have done. As Flood noted in his 1971 memoir, he had "little money" for living expenses; he was counting on his "spiritual resources . . . trying to improve his corner of society," and so he would do both himself and Johnny "proud." It was an argument, however idealistic it might sound today, that Marian might well have made, and Flood had always evinced an almost mystical faith in both her and Johnny. Third, Flood had to string Quinn along until he addressed the board of the MLBPA in San Juan. He had to know whether the Players Association would support him, because without its financing he could not afford a lawsuit.[27]

Unfortunately, Flood seems to have left a key moral and legal factor out of his decision: how could he sue, lose at least one year's baseball salary, and still meet his obligations to Beverly and his children? He was already a year in arrears in his alimony and child-support payments. Given Beverly's legal position, she was bound to come after him with a court order that would take most of his savings. But even if she did not, he surely had a moral obligation to his children, and it is difficult to see how he could ignore them yet claim that he was "trying to improve his corner of society." What was he thinking? Was he thinking? Had he truly been thinking since the seventh game of the 1968 World Series, when he failed to catch Northrup's line drive? Review the blatant facts: he had not paid child support since immediately after that failure; he had issued a relationship-destroying ultimatum to Busch and the Cardinals the following March; he had assumed full responsibility for his brother, Carl, a loving but suicidal act; he had reacted privately with hostility to Busch's March 22 speech, or, as he saw it, lecture; he had feuded with Cardinals' management and, according to Broeg, drank and partied to excess throughout the 1969 season. Finally, he became incensed that he was informed of his trade by a middle-echelon officer in the front office rather than by the general manager. Was he not getting what he deserved, and was he not now seeking revenge? Reason seems to have flown his mind. He blamed the Cardinals, Busch, Devine, and Toomey in particular, for his being traded, but there was no way he could strike at them directly. Thus, as his memoir reveals, he had morphed them

27. Flood, *The Way It Is,* 192–93.

into the baseball establishment and its reserve system. Like a poker player who raises his bets after a loss and, frustrated, loses more with every bad or weak bet, every error in judgment Flood had made led almost inevitably to the next. He compounded his mistakes as it were. At least that seems to be what happened—with possibly a single exception, his decision to string along Philadelphia's general manager. Contrary to what he had said publicly and privately about going to Philadelphia, apparently he would go if he could not sue. As he had told Miller, if in a different context, he did not want to "disappear like a bottle cap."[28]

Whatever Flood's reasoning, in early December he phoned Miller to tell him that he was going ahead with a lawsuit if he had the support of the Players Association, and Miller told him to be in San Juan by December 13. Apparently he also phoned Judy Pace, his Los Angeles amour, to ask if she would join him in St. Louis, after which they would fly to San Juan. So she recalls. And the two left for Puerto Rico together, soon to be joined by Tim McCarver, Dal Maxvill (the Cardinals' player representative), and Joe Torre, all of whom questioned him about his decision, saying he would be fighting his battle essentially alone.[29]

Flood did not change his mind. In San Juan, on December 13, after Miller and the player representatives discussed his case in some detail, Flood was sent for and provided a chance to address the "reps" on his own behalf. Some of them were skeptical of his motives and his constancy. Understandably, they did not want the Players Association to be left high and dry if he changed his mind for some reason, whether to pry more money out of the Phillies or because the owners bribed him. Jim Bunning, one of the player representatives, pointedly stated, "Suppose the owners do what they did with [Danny] Gardella [banned after playing in the Mexican League] and offer you a lot of money to drop the case [which Gardella did]?" Flood looked at Bunning, then said sharply, "I can't be bought. If the Players Association commits to help me in this lawsuit, I will . . . not withdraw the suit." He was committed. Of course, none of the players, or Miller for that matter, could know what Flood would do. They had to accept him on faith.

But Flood's constancy was not the only issue broached. Tom Haller, the San Francisco Giants catcher, spoke for many in the room when he brought up the delicate issue of race as a motive. "Are you doing

28. Ibid.
29. Ibid., 193; Judy Pace Flood, interview, June 29, 1998; Belth, *Stepping Up*, 152–53.

this simply because you're black and you feel that baseball has been discriminatory?" he asked Flood. The question surprised Miller, but it should not have. The late sixties was an extremely volatile period, the era not only of the war in Vietnam and its protest movements but also of the radical demands and methods of the Black Panthers in Flood's hometown. Conversely, this was also a period marked by a backlash among whites who feared the ends and means of this radicalism. Apparently, Haller wanted to know if Flood's desire to sue was linked in any way to this new black militancy, and if he would try to use his and their lawsuit, with its attendant publicity, to promote a militancy that would invite a backlash against the Players Association. Obviously, they had reason to fear just that.[30]

Flood looked squarely at Haller and said, according to Miller's notes, "I'd be lying if I told you that as a black man I hadn't gone through worse than my white teammates. I'll also say that, yes, I think the change in black consciousness in recent years has made me more sensitive to injustice in every area of my life. But I want you to know that what I'm doing here I'm doing as a ballplayer, a major league ballplayer, and I think it's absolutely terrible that we have stood by and watched this situation go on for so many years and never pulled together to do anything about it. It's improper, it shouldn't be allowed to go any further, and the circumstances are such that, well, I guess this is the time to do something about it."[31]

Flood's response to Haller seems to have satisfied the board, and he left the room. Miller returned to discuss some of the more practical aspects of the case, and to seek a vote. He told the board that the Players Association would have to hire a lawyer and cover the legal expenses and Flood's personal expenses related to the trial. He warned them that a trial could be expensive and that the association's coffers were not overflowing. But they might win, and in that case, Flood promised to pay back the Players Association from the proceeds. Otherwise, the association would have to satisfy itself with the beneficial publicity certain to develop as the public saw David facing Goliath in a battle for a player's right to negotiate with any club that might want his services. Those benefits should serve the association's interests, Miller asserted.

30. Flood, *The Way It Is,* 193; Belth, *Stepping Up,* 154; Miller, *Different Ball Game,* 185–86.

31. Miller, *Different Ball Game,* 185–86; Flood, *The Way It Is,* 193.

He then asked the board to vote whether or not to support Flood's case. This they did quickly and unanimously in support of Flood. As Flood noted one year later, the board also authorized Miller to retain "the best possible counsel for me."[32]

Miller had already found the lawyer he wanted. He had known Arthur J. Goldberg for twenty years, beginning when Goldberg was general counsel at the USW. And he had known him as secretary of labor in the administration of President Kennedy, later as a justice of the Supreme Court, and, after that, ambassador to the United Nations. Now he was a senior partner in the very prestigious New York law firm of Paul, Weiss, Rifkind, and Garrison. Quite naturally, given their twenty-year association and Goldberg's appointments, Miller thought highly of Goldberg's qualifications. He was skilled in the courtroom, but he also had a national stature that would draw much-needed attention to Flood's case, the more so in the likelihood that the Supreme Court ruled for the club owners: publicity and consciousness-raising would then be the only reward for their investment. No less important, Goldberg was fascinated with Flood's case, and he would serve pro bono, his free services a major plus for a Players Association that was very short of funds. Also, he could bring along a topflight partner, Jay Topkis, author of a *Yale Law Review* article on baseball's reserve system, and Max Gitter, a young and intelligent associate. Miller and his general counsel, Dick Moss, could see only one complication in this scenario: when they first spoke to Goldberg about taking Flood's case, he was considering a run for governor of New York.[33]

But the week before the Players Association's board met, Goldberg announced publicly that he would not run for governor. That accounts for the meeting that Miller, Moss, and Flood had with him on December 15, the day after their return from San Juan. Flood was nervous at the prospect, never having met a former Supreme Court justice. Later, he remarked that he liked what he saw: "a well-turned out man with unmussed white hair and an unmussed mind." And Goldberg's discussion of the facts and readiness to play devil's advocate quickly put him at ease. Indeed, he was so impressed with Goldberg that he thought to himself, "Ho-lee Cow! Curt Flood had him the most famous lawyer in the world." What Flood had no reason to suspect, but Miller, given his

32. Miller, *Different Ball Game,* 186–87; Flood, *The Way It Is,* 193.
33. Miller, *Different Ball Game,* 187–89.

long association with Goldberg, might have, is that this renowned lawyer, a very ambitious man, would change his mind about running for governor. In the end Goldberg would devote little time and attention to the case. However, in fairness it should be noted that Miller had little choice in picking Goldberg. The Players Association's funds were so low that it could barely meet the law firm's charges for in-house assistance in preparing the case (and, in fact, it was often in arrears). How could it have afforded the billing of a nationally renowned lawyer with the time and ability to handle Flood's case?[34]

On that Monday, December 15, the problems that might arise with Goldberg's handling of Flood's lawsuit lay ahead when Miller, Moss, Goldberg, Topkis, and Gitter met Flood and Zerman to discuss the best way to proceed. Quickly, they decided on a letter Flood would send to Baseball Commissioner Bowie Kuhn, with copies to Quinn, Miller, and the press. It would be the opening salvo in Flood's battle to modify baseball's reserve system, as opposed to eliminating it (which all agreed would create chaos). Zerman apparently thought this could be accomplished without eliminating baseball's antitrust exemption, but Miller and the Players Association had a larger, more far-reaching goal. It was a critical difference, but there was no sign of it in the letter they wrote the commissioner. None of the six men present thought it would bring a positive response from Kuhn. But filing notice on Kuhn et al. was a legal sine qua non for filing a claim against him and organized baseball.[35]

34. Flood, *The Way It Is,* 194.
35. Ibid., 194–95.

≡ VIII ≡

Trials and Tribulations

On December 24, 1970, Curt Flood mailed a brief letter to Bowie Kuhn, the commissioner of Major League Baseball. Nine days earlier he and Zerman had collaborated on its drafting with Miller and Moss of the MLBPA as well as the Players Association's lawyers, Goldberg, Topkis, and Gitter. During the discussion of its wording, Goldberg, Miller, and Moss, seeking a catchy phrase, had first suggested that Flood begin the letter with: "I'm free, black, and thirty-one." However, this play on an old standard was later cut as "corny." The letter, a legal necessity, required sober, straightforward language. What emerged was a brief, plaintive statement that went directly to Flood's grievance. Its character is captured in the first sentence: "Dear Mr. Kuhn: After twelve years in the major leagues I do not feel that I am a piece of property to be bought and sold irrespective of my wishes." Flood's letter added that any system which produced such results violated "his basic rights as a citizen" and was "inconsistent with the laws of the United States and the several states." Thus, although he desired to play in 1970, and had received a contract offer from the Philadelphia club, he believed he had the right to "consider offers from other clubs." And he asked Kuhn to "make known to all Major League clubs my feelings in this matter, and advise them of my availability for the 1970 season."[1]

Kuhn responded six days later. Just as Flood's brief letter should be seen as a plea and not as the opening "shot" that Flood as well as Miller conceived it, Kuhn's answer, December 30, should be seen as a brief, disingenuous rejection. Kuhn agreed that Flood was "a human being, not a piece of property to be bought and sold. That is fundamental in our society. . . . However, I cannot see its applicability to the situation at hand." He reminded Flood, as if it were not the reason for his letter, that

1. Flood, *The Way It Is,* 195; Miller, *Different Ball Game,* 190–91.

160

he had a current contract with the St. Louis Cardinals, "which has the same assignment provisions [giving one club the right to buy, sell, or trade a player's contract to another club] as those in your annual major league contracts since 1956. Your present contract has been assigned in accordance with its provisions by the St. Louis Club to the Philadelphia Club." Kuhn added, again as if he had not read what Flood wrote him, "If you have any specific objection to the propriety of the assignment, I would appreciate your specifying the objection. Under the circumstances . . . I cannot comply with the request contained in the second paragraph of your letter."[2]

Kuhn's letter, along with Flood's, produced flat, neutral reports from the *St. Louis Post-Dispatch* and *Globe-Democrat* on December 31 as well as on January 1, both papers noting that the Major League Players Association had hired Arthur Goldberg to represent Flood. At the same time, Leonard Koppett of the *New York Times* produced a commentary in favor of the plaintiff. On December 30 and 31 he rebuked Kuhn for saying that Flood had refused to live up to his contract, pointing out that the player had not refused to negotiate with Philadelphia; he had asked a court to prevent all clubs . . . from refusing to negotiate with him. He also revealed the "damned if you do, damned if you don't" nature of the reserve system, Paragraph 10A of the Uniform Players Contract. Entitled "Renewal," it gave a club the option of extending a contract to a player on or before January 15; if the player did not sign the contract by March 1, then the club had the right to renew his previous contract. In effect, "Renewal," as then interpreted, was automatic. Finally, Koppett noted that "the exchange [with Kuhn] will enable Flood to show that he did request his 'freedom,' exhausting the procedures available to him within baseball, and the Commissioner did not grant it." Now Flood and Goldberg could go to court and challenge baseball contracts that tied all players to a club forever and made such trades as Flood's permissible.[3]

Koppett was on the mark with regard to Flood's intentions. Miller told the *Post-Dispatch* that Flood "intends to exercise his legal rights." And his affirmation was quickly endorsed by Cardinals catcher Joe Torre

2. Miller, *Different Ball Game*, 191–92; Flood, *The Way It Is*, 194–95.

3. *St. Louis Post-Dispatch,* December 30, 1969, January 1, 1970; *St. Louis Globe-Democrat,* December 31, 1969; *New York Times,* December 30, 31, 1969; also Exhibit A, Uniform Players Contract, National League of Professional Baseball Clubs, in "Complaint," January 16, 1970, *Curtis C. Flood, Plaintiff, against Bowie Kuhn et al.,* 70-Civ. 202, U.S. District Court for the Southern District of New York.

and Houston Astros pitcher Jim Bouton, the player representatives for their clubs. Both pointed out that the Players Association meeting in Puerto Rico had voted to provide Flood with legal counsel and some financial assistance. However, both made it clear that the Players Association did not seek to eliminate the reserve clause but only to modify it. The MLBPA hoped the threat of a lawsuit would produce immediate negotiations to that end. If not, Bouton said, "drastic action is needed. The owners have brought this on themselves. There will be no buying off here, not with the Players Association involved." Unfortunately, Bouton and Torre did not stop there. They muddied the issue, saying that the Players Association sought only modification of the reserve system, not its elimination; thus they undermined the lawsuit's stated purpose: to have "the reserve system, and defendants' conspiracy against plaintiff . . . [declared] unlawful under the Sherman Anti-Trust Act." If Bouton and Torre were speaking for the Players Association, and it is virtually certain that they were, then the reserve clause appeared much less ripe for a court's broad axe—it looked more like a tangled dispute requiring labor-management negotiations.[4]

There would be no "buying off." But for obvious reasons the MLBPA wanted to avoid what might well be a lengthy, expensive court battle or, more likely, battles as Flood's case was appealed through the judicial system. That such was the union's preference is reinforced by events after Flood and Zerman flew to New York on Thursday, January 3. Flood, along with Miller and Joe Cronin, the president of the American League and a spokesman for Major League Baseball, were to advocate their respective cases on ABC-TV's *Wide World of Sports* that evening. Flood and Zerman were also supposed to meet with Goldberg that day to discuss strategy. However, Goldberg shunted them to an associate. He was too busy, he said, preparing a request for a temporary injunction that, if approved, would allow Flood to play that year for the club that offered him the best deal. This may have been true, but Goldberg's offhanded manner angered Zerman, leaving him in no doubt that he and Flood would be left on the periphery of the litigation, little more than bystanders. Such qualms as he had had earlier when the letter to Kuhn was drafted were magnified. With the best of intentions, it was possible that he had led Flood down the garden path. First, he had suggested that Flood might sue; then he had advised him on what he believed would be

4. *St. Louis Post-Dispatch,* December 30, 1969.

a successful strategy; finally, and perhaps there was no other way, he had sent him to Miller, which in the end meant Goldberg and his firm, for them to strategize as they saw fit. If so, Zerman had to bear a certain measure of responsibility for his friend's plight if the case turned out badly.[5]

Later that month, Goldberg told Flood that he had met with Kuhn and Paul Porter, the prominent Washington lawyer who represented the baseball commissioner's office, in one last effort to resolve Flood's case short of litigation. Goldberg said he had told the two men that the reserve system issue might be resolved either by arbitration or by negotiation with the Players Association. Porter had replied for both men that neither approach was "practical." He was right in the sense that the club owners would not budge. For two years a joint study group of the MLBPA and the PRC (Player Relations Committee, the negotiating arm of the owners) had met, their agreed purpose to somehow modify the reserve clause, and every proposal by the Players Association had been rejected out of hand. At the same time, the PRC had never offered an alternative. As Miller saw it, the owners did not want to compromise in the slightest way. As he recalled their position, "If you want to change one comma, they say Yankee Stadium will fall." Yet circumstances differed to some extent in January of 1970, at least in Goldberg's view. He believed that he had powerful new leverage in Flood's decision to bring a lawsuit; furthermore, he knew from Miller's briefings that in somewhat similar cases baseball's owners had settled either with cash or in some other way when seriously threatened. Unfortunately for Goldberg's hopeful prospects, it seemed that the owners wanted a showdown, and that Kuhn was upset because he believed Goldberg had imposed on Flood a decision not to play baseball until the antitrust issue was satisfactorily resolved.[6]

---

5. Nell Flynn, e-mail, October 5, 2004; Zerman, e-mail, August 13, 2000; for some evidence of Zerman's sense of responsibility, note his pro bono work for Flood on lawsuits in 1970–1971 (see chapter 9) after which he saw Flood only once more, at an autographing.

6. Flood, *The Way It Is*, 107; Miller, *Different Ball Game*, 177–80; Helyar, *Lords of the Realm*, 110, 112. Three cases gave Goldberg cause for optimism. In 1949 the owners paid off Danny Gardella rather than spend money on a court battle they might lose (although Gardella was barred because he played in the Mexican League; he had never signed a contract containing the now-challenged reserve clause). But more recently two players, Donn Clendenon and Ken Harrelson, had let it be known that they would retire rather than accept their trades, and they had been appeased. Also, Maury Wills, who had expressed great displeasure at being traded from the Los Angeles Dodgers to the Montreal Expos, was allowed to return to the Dodgers.

The latter, surely, was not the case. Goldberg had merely reminded Flood that he must forget about playing while suing; if he continued to play, then a court would find his suit hypothetical, lacking in legitimacy, and no longer worthy of consideration. Zerman had told him that, too, on more than one occasion. However, Flood did not need reminding. Since the trade in October he had stated, if with a bit of equivocation at times, that he would not play for Philadelphia. Now, when told that Philadelphia general manager John Quinn was sending him a contract for $90,000, he said that he would send it back: he "wouldn't play until this thing is completely resolved." And Zerman echoed his friend and, now in a quite limited sense, his client: "Flood is a man with a cause, and now after considerable thought, has set his course. I don't see Curt backing down, or reneging."[7]

During the first week of 1970, nationally syndicated writers weighed in on Flood's battle against baseball's reserve system, reporting, judging, and commenting. On January 4 the eminent Red Smith chimed in with a satirical column, "Ye Olde Tale of the Count and His Portrait Painter." An abridged version of the mocking piece goes like this: Once upon a time, young Kurt, the finest portrait painter in the kingdom, was in the service of Count Augustus. And the Count was greatly pleased, arraying young Kurt in rich garments and supplying him with strawberries in winter time and egg for his beer. At the same time, however, he owned renewable articles of indenture on young Kurt. They were necessary, he said, to protect his investment against wealthier lords. There came a day twelve years later, however, when all the portraits were painted, and the Count told Kurt he had been traded to Duke Roberto. To this, Kurt replied: "Sire, I'm sorry to have to say this, but I can't go." When Count Augustus insisted on the trade, Kurt said, "I'll have to appeal to the king." And so he did, explaining that he was only eighteen years old when the indentures were signed and "didn't know alizarin crimson from cadmium red," only to have King Boo respond, sadly, "You seem to have no understanding of the sanctity of contracts. Under the circumstances, I do not see what action I can take."[8]

Smith's satire, doubtless unknowingly, portrayed Flood as more innocent than his behavior vis-à-vis Busch and the Cardinals the past year warranted; otherwise it was an accurate, devastating indictment of

7. *St. Louis Post-Dispatch*, January 9, 1970.
8. Ibid., January 4, 1970.

Kuhn as representative of baseball's almost medieval indifference to human rights. It was, Smith insisted in a more sober column, an indifference comparable to that of slaveholders to the rights of their slaves. Not every columnist agreed, however. Milt Richman, a veteran sportswriter for the United Press, parried in an equally sober story. "I don't believe Curt Flood, in all conscience, can argue that he was treated like cattle since he's been in baseball. . . . I know we're in the middle of a paralyzing inflation, but $90,000 for one head . . . still staggers the imagination." Of course, Richman missed the point, or so Smith thought: "You mean at these prices, they want human rights, too?" Still, Flood's very large salary (for that era) would be a very weak link in his lawsuit for damages and surely the weakest in his prospects for public favor, as sportswriters, baseball's owners, and the Players Association awaited the filing of his suit for a temporary injunction that would allow him to play for the club that offered him the best deal.[9]

Flood was in New York, staying at the Hotel Warwick, when on Friday, January 16, his co-counsels, Goldberg and (nominally) Zerman, filed his suit in the city's federal district court. Legalistically, it argued that Kuhn, the presidents of the National and American Leagues, and the twenty-four individual Major League Baseball clubs were violating the Sherman Antitrust Act of 1890 and the Clayton Anti-Trust Act of 1914. The petition argued that the reserve system constituted an *unreasonable* conspiracy in restraint of trade, unreasonable being the key word from a legal point of view. It also claimed, in more personal and colorful language, that this system subjected Flood, as it did every other player, "to peonage and involuntary servitude." Finally, it asked for an immediate hearing to secure an injunction that would enable Flood to bargain with other teams to play during the season without prejudice to his case. In addition, should the court grant the injunction, the petition requested $25,000 for damages Flood had already suffered. The petition went on to claim that if the court did not grant the injunction sought and Flood could not play in the 1970 season or even after while his case wound its way through the reaches of the whole judicial system, he would suffer "irreparable damages"; it requested $1 million in compensation.[10]

9. The exchange between Smith and Richman is to be found in *St. Louis Post-Dispatch*, January 4, 1970.

10. "Plaintiff's Memorandum in Support of Motion for Preliminary Injunction," in *Flood against Kuhn et al.*, U.S. District Court for the Southern District of New York, 70 C 202, January 16, 1970.

This was the essence of Flood's lawsuit. Of course there was more lengthy and detailed language that attempted to set Flood's lawsuit apart from those that since 1922 the Supreme Court had rejected as inconsistent with Congress's intent in the Sherman Act. Flood's suit alleged that because the St. Louis Cardinals restricted beer sales in Busch Stadium to its parent company, Anheuser-Busch, the beer company increased its earnings at the baseball club's expense, thus slicing the team's revenue available for player salaries. In the same vein, the Columbia Broadcasting System, because it owned the Yankees, had refrained from bidding for national baseball broadcasts, the absence of competition again reducing the revenues available for player salaries. Both cases represented plaintiffs' efforts to bolster their central premise, that the court should treat baseball as a monopolistic business engaged in "an unreasonable restraint of trade" in interstate commerce, therefore violating the Sherman Antitrust Act.

Whether or not these new arguments added to the previous arguments connecting the reserve system to the Sherman Act, they sufficed for Judge Dudley Bonsal to tell plaintiffs he needed time to study them, and that the defendants rightfully needed time to prepare a response. He scheduled a hearing for Tuesday, January 20, and told the defendants to appear and "show cause" why an injunction should not be granted.[11]

Over the weekend spokesmen for Major League Baseball responded with appeals to public opinion. They argued that free agency would create "chaos" in their industry. It would kill baseball. Clubs had to protect their investment in players through their minor-league years and sometimes after. Free agency would not allow for that. Operating in a "free market," the wealthier clubs would wind up with all the best players: competition off the field would eliminate competition on it. Also, the integrity of the game would be threatened if players could negotiate with one club while playing for another. Altogether, Joe Cronin, president of the American League, and Chub Feeney, his National League counterpart, posited seven such objections to free agency.[12]

The Players Association quickly responded. On the one hand, it accepted organized baseball's view that free agency, if unrestricted, could very well lead to chaos, ruining baseball for owners and players

11. *New York Times*, January 17, 1970.
12. *St. Louis Post-Dispatch*, January 18, 1970; *New York Times*, January 18, 1970.

alike. On the other hand, the reserve system as it stood constituted "an unreasonable restraint of trade." It deprived players of the freedom to secure a "fair market value" for their services and to choose where they wanted to play and live. Furthermore, it undermined a player's "dignity": the player was forced to accept the restrictions, abuses, and fines of the club that owned his contract because he was not free to negotiate a better relationship with another club. But the Players Association argued that there was a reasonable way to solve this conflict between the needs of baseball's owners and those of the players: negotiations could be held to modify the reserve system. This was the actual goal of the Players Association. Again, probably to strengthen public support, the MLBPA's response undermined its stated legal position, which called for eliminating the reserve system by eliminating baseball's antitrust exemption.[13]

Although the conflicting arguments and proposals were not new, baseball's chieftains advised Judge Bonsal that they would not be ready to respond to his "show-cause" order by Tuesday, January 20. They asked for more time to prepare, and Judge Bonsal reset the hearing for February 3.[14]

The judge's decision left Flood with little choice but to fly back to St. Louis. There he opened his door to an interview with Jack Herman of the *St. Louis Post-Dispatch*. He told the sportswriter that he had returned to find hundreds of letters, some praising his vision and courage, others vilifying him as a jerk or a "Benedict Arnold," and he lay awake at night tossing and turning, evaluating what he had done. Though it was now fairly clear that an injunction, if granted, would not come down in time for him to play in the coming season and that his case might drag on for perhaps two years in the courts, he was sure that he was "doing the right thing." He also praised Goldberg and his firm. He told Herman, "There are five people in his office working on our case night and day. Three stayed up all night to prepare for last week's filing." As for his lead counsel, Flood said he had been greatly impressed with Goldberg from the moment he first met him: "When he talks about legal ideas and his business he becomes 6-feet-8. His office on Park Avenue looks like Busch stadium." That Flood was greatly impressed by what he saw and heard of Goldberg and his firm is certain, but he may have been unduly

13. *New York Times,* January 18, 1970.
14. *St. Louis Post-Dispatch,* January 21, 1970.

swayed. There is no reason to believe he saw people working day and night on his lawsuit; indeed, he did not know that a significant amount of the preparation of the case was handed to a young associate just out of law school. However, it is understandable that as a layman Flood was overwhelmed by Goldberg: his legal jargon, his firm's upscale address, and its elegant interior made a statement of its own, real or inconsequential. Consequently, Flood conveyed to Herman his strong optimism for the future of major-league ballplayers and even his own chances of playing again. But the sportswriter thought he was too optimistic and concluded his story by questioning whether "the impact of his action [had] hit him yet, or will he feel it opening day."[15]

On Sunday, January 25, the day after his interview with Herman appeared, Flood found himself the butt of a stinging commentary by *Post-Dispatch* sports editor Bob Broeg. Broeg, who had advised Flood the previous September to stop partying and start playing, reproached him in a column titled "Does 'Principle' or 'Principal' motivate Flood?" The column might more accurately have been titled "You Ungrateful Wretch," as it pointed out how decently the Cardinals, and Gussie Busch in particular, had treated the young man. In 1961, Busch as "club president asked [manager Johnny Keane] that the in-and-out young ball hawk be given a regular chance in center field." Busch's order, for that is what it really was, had given Flood his first real opportunity to display his wares. To be sure, Flood rewarded the Cardinals with several brilliant seasons, but the Cardinals also rewarded him very handsomely: they sent him a $90,000 contract for the 1969 season, "probably the highest in history for a singles hitter." Of course, Flood, like most of the regulars, would have been "asked" to take a 20 percent pay cut after their slippage in 1969. But that was a small slice compared to losses stars had taken before negotiations between the Players Association and the Player Relations Committee had reduced the maximum pay cut allowable for any one year. And, Broeg wrote, that was "just one of the many financial improvements that had accrued to—careful you don't gag on this one—the poor victims of peonage and servitude. . . . So it is difficult to be sympathetic to the little man, particularly when the issue really is not a matter of principle, but of principal." If it had been otherwise, Broeg contended, then Flood would have sued for $1, not for $75,000 if he were able to play during the coming season and $3 million

15. Ibid., January 24, 1970.

if his case was not resolved. In sum, Flood's avaricious numbers told the story. Or so the *Post-Dispatch* sportswriter argued.[16]

Broeg ignored the fact that Flood, if avaricious, could have gone to the Phillies for a salary in excess of $90,000, not only escaping the pay cut other Cardinals players would take for the coming season but instead ratcheting up his income, perhaps by as much as 10 percent. Broeg also ignored the fact that antitrust laws automatically tripled the damages asked. Furthermore, he either did not know or did not explain that Flood had nothing to do with the preparation of the lawsuit, including the amount of damages or, as Broeg put it, "principal," asked. Flood and Zerman had flown to New York the evening before the scheduled January 16 hearing, quietly read the petition set before them and, after a few questions and answers, signed what was a *fait accompli*. The exchanges did, however explain the rationale behind the damages Flood as plaintiff was asking. The Players Association hoped the potential $3 million in damages if the case lazed its way through the judicial hierarchy might prompt the baseball owners to undertake serious negotiations to modify the reserve clause, or at the very least to substitute an independent arbitrator for the commissioner in the Second Basic Agreement then being discussed. (The first collective bargaining agreement in 1968 dealt with minimum wages and working conditions, among other matters.) Then, too, the numbers were large enough to catch the public's attention. Finally, although Goldberg was serving pro bono, the expenses at Goldberg's law firm would probably take a significant bite. As for Flood, he was battling the enslaving effects of the reserve system, to paraphrase his petition for an injunction. As stated, then, he was fighting for a principle, if one a bit muddied by the probability that he had sued only because of an unusually sensitive and insecure temperament that prompted him to react bitterly to what was, after all, a commonplace trade. The cynic might add that Flood was not only putting his career and life on the line in fighting for a principle, but also he was more dubiously undermining the lives of others, his children and his mother in particular.

Flood's battle for a principle, however cloudy his motives and worrisome his values, did not conflict with his right to seek monetary damages, or principal, as well. As Zerman put it, "he did not need to be a martyr to the extent of winning the battle, then starving to death. If he

16. Ibid, January 25, 1970.

won, he deserved compensation." However, Zerman did not agree with the Players Association's request for a specific amount of damages. Thirty years later, he argued vociferously, and repeatedly, that the association made a fundamental mistake by establishing an amount for damages and getting baseball to stipulate to that number. Zerman believed that the amount of damages should have been based, at least in some part, on the aggregate club owners' ability to pay. That would have given Goldberg a reasonable argument in court for prying open their books, and that might have brought to light what Zerman suspected were the huge profits that resulted from their monopolistic practices. That approach, stressing monopoly, would have provided Flood and the Players Association with a powerful weapon in its battle to end baseball's exemption from the antitrust acts or at least to modify the reserve system. Presumably, Zerman advised Flood of his differences with the Players Association, as well as his fears regarding Goldberg's strategy. But by this time Flood had become greatly enamored of Goldberg and his firm; Flood was, on his own terms, a man of honor, and as his eldest sister put it, he always wanted to be liked, not least, it should be said, by prominent people. And he was committed. After the letter to Kuhn, there was no turning back.[17]

Zerman had to console himself with the hope that if the hearing seeking an injunction was not the place to seek entry to the owners' books, then the Players Association and Goldberg might consider the subsequent trial the place to do so. Perhaps Zerman encouraged Flood by suggesting this. In any event, his friend needed encouragement. Some of the country's most prestigious newspapers, magazines, and sportswriters endorsed his challenge, as did well-known sportscaster Howard Cosell, but in St. Louis their endorsement did not match the impact of a sportswriter like Broeg. Broeg was a heavyweight in the local media, and Flood felt dismayed and even betrayed when the *Post-Dispatch* columnist labeled his lawsuit a battle for money by an ingrate. It made little difference that Zerman insisted Broeg was a "bootlicker for the Busch family, especially Augie." But Broeg's words were not the only ones that stung Flood. Although the Players Association board and many ballplayers endorsed his lawsuit—if too often quietly—he was deeply hurt by the criticisms of former Phillies' pitcher and later Hall of Famer Robin Roberts,

17. Zerman, e-mail, August 14, 2000.

who thought a lawsuit was the wrong answer to the reserve problem, and of Boston Red Sox star Carl Yastrzemski, who portrayed him as a dangerous wrecker. Flood was also hurt by the letters he received from baseball fans who saw him endangering their National Pastime. And some went beyond criticism to threats. No wonder he felt a desperate need to tell his story in full, to let the country hear that the Cardinals had traded him, as other clubs had done with their players, in a way that treated him like property to be handled as the club owner wished, much as slaves were once traded. Fortunately, an opportunity to tell his story had presented itself; whether he could pull himself together to create or help write it was another matter. Depressed, he could not even paint; the Playboy Club, booze, and women were his only solace. He still hoped that somehow he would be able to play in the 1970 season. But for the moment, he lived helplessly, haplessly in limbo, his future dependent on the decisions of others.[18]

Any serious hopes Flood might have had of playing in 1970 all but expired after the hearing on February 3. Judge Irving Ben Cooper, who, for reasons unknown, had replaced Bonsal, listened to Goldberg's request for a preliminary injunction and the responses of baseball's lawyers—Paul Porter for Bowie Kuhn, and Mark Hughes for the National League—then heard the rebuttals and re-rebuttals that followed. The first arguments boiled down to the applicability of the two Supreme Court decisions exempting baseball from the antitrust laws. Goldberg argued that the *Federal Baseball Club* case in 1922 and the *Toolson* case in 1953 were no longer applicable because so many factors had changed in the years since. Baseball was now obviously a real business involved in interstate commerce, much as professional football, boxing, and basketball; like those sports, it should not be exempt from the antitrust laws. That baseball had become a big business was true, but this was already well known, and Goldberg failed to produce evidence that something so significant had changed in the decade and a half since *Toolson* that the Supreme Court would be likely to eliminate baseball's special exemption. Unlike Flood, who focused on the hearing as his only door to playing that year, Goldberg seemed focused on the future. The hearing itself turned into what can only be described as a charade. This may

18. For Flood's reflections on Roberts's and Yastrzemski's criticism, and the support and criticism of others, see Flood, *The Way It Is,* 196, 198.

help explain why, after Goldberg finished his opening statement, and the hour being appropriate, Judge Cooper in ordering a recess used baseball jargon, calling it time for a "seventh-inning stretch."[19]

After this time-out, Hughes, speaking technically for the National League but effectively for all of baseball, expectedly argued the opposite of Goldberg's position; he insisted that the Supreme Court had spoken and its precedents still held. At last, after many exchanges, Goldberg insisting that Flood would suffer "irreparable damages" if he could not play and Hughes arguing that "irreparable damages" would accrue to baseball if he did, Cooper congratulated the counsels for both sides: "You are certainly saturated with the merits of your cases. Now you have thrown the ball to me and I hope I don't muff it."[20]

One month to the day later, Judge Cooper handed down his ruling. The crucial part denied Flood's bid for a temporary injunction. According to the judge, baseball was more likely to suffer "irreparable damage" from a preliminary injunction than Flood would if he did not get it: he could play for the Phillies if he chose. Second, the plaintiff's counsel had failed to demonstrate that Flood's case was likely to be winnable at a trial, the second justification for an injunction. Indeed, Judge Cooper added that although he was impressed with Flood's argument that baseball, like other sports, should be included under the federal antitrust law, the Supreme Court had twice ruled otherwise. And that fact was controlling.[21]

The decision came down as Flood, Goldberg, Zerman, and Miller expected. Flood admitted that he had been forewarned by Goldberg to expect no less than a battle through the judicial system, a battle that would take time and, he hoped, be decided differently in a full-scale trial or, if need be, by the Supreme Court. Even so, until the judge ruled, Flood had some hope that he could play in the 1970 season. Now even that slim hope was dashed. Asked his reaction to Cooper's decision, Flood told the press that he would not play for the Phillies—"I just can't be bought; I won't be bought"—then added, obviously sadly, "In my own mind, I don't think I'll ever play again." When pressed by a reporter who wanted to know how he could afford to give up the $100,000 salary the Phillies were still offering, Flood said, for the first time publicly, and

19. *New York Times,* February 4, 1970.
20. Ibid.
21. *New York Times,* March 5, 1970.

somewhat mysteriously: "I can't really afford to lay out for one season." Then, seemingly in contradiction, he spoke vaguely of the small business deals that would sustain him. "The salary I'm going to lose isn't my biggest concern," he said. And he would not just lie around waiting for the trial of his antitrust suit. He would promote the franchising of his photographic studios, and he would work on his life's story, which Simon and Schuster earlier in the winter had agreed to publish.[22]

For the most part Flood was blowing smoke. He had little money, and what he had was flowing either into his photography studio or into the cash register of the Playboy Club. According to the manager of his studio on Lindell at Grand, Marian had spent an exorbitant, essentially useless, amount of money for equipment, renovations, and repairs: the money went for too many cameras, grandiose decorating in a quickly declining section of St. Louis, and fixtures that had to be replaced on several occasions after roaming toughs threw rocks through the plateglass windows. Although Flood's status as a Cardinals star had at first brought the studio a solid clientele, such was no longer the case, and more cash was flowing out of the business than was coming in. Meanwhile, another studio in Kirkwood, in St. Louis County, had collapsed with severe losses, rumor had it because the community discovered that a black man owned it.[23]

So much for the business deals Flood had often mentioned to reporters. The investments that he must have counted on after baseball were collapsing. But he was putting his life's story together. Thanks to a sympathetic businessman and former ballplayer who lived in Connecticut, he would have a serious opportunity to tell baseball fans in St. Louis and throughout the country how his upbringing, adolescence, and life in baseball, but especially with the Cardinals, had influenced his righteous decision to challenge Major League Baseball's hallowed but enslaving reserve clause.

Flood's good fortune can only be labeled serendipitous. In early January, David Oliphant, a Connecticut entrepreneur with connections in New York City's publishing world, received a bulletin from the Players Association briefly outlining the purposes and merits of Flood's lawsuit. Oliphant quickly became interested: Flood's problem with the reserve clause reminded him of his own frustrations and anger with the clause's

22. *St. Louis Post-Dispatch,* March 6, 1970.
23. Ruth Sutterfield interviews, July 1, 2001, and June 18, 2002.

restrictions during his short career as a pitcher in two minor-league systems. A New York City high school "phenom," Oliphant at age seventeen had signed with the New York Yankees organization in 1953 for a $3,000 bonus and $200 a month. During the next two and a half seasons he was shuttled from one Yankee farm club to another, five all told. By 1955 he lost patience with the Yankees; he believed he had pitched well enough to be playing in the park that Ruth built. They should have called him up. But they did not, in part, he thought, because the anti-Semitic manager of one minor-league team had bad-mouthed the "Jewboy's" capabilities, and also in part because of the desire of the Yankees to "park" him in their minor-league system so he would be available if a series of injuries struck their first-line pitching staff. "Parking" was common practice for major-league teams, made possible by the existence of the reserve clause. Oliphant could do nothing about his apparently permanent consignment to the minor leagues. He could not negotiate with another team unless the Yankees released him from the contract he had originally signed, even though he had signed it before he became an adult. The Yankees insisted that they could not release him; they had to protect their investment. Happily for young Oliphant, a series of hectoring letters from his determined father, Morris, finally prompted the Yankees to negotiate his release, for a price that, however negligible it might appear today, gave notice that the reserve system remained intact. In September 1955, Morris and his wife borrowed $2,000, and the couple bought their son's contract and freedom. Later, the Yankees returned $1,000.[24]

After a botched tryout with the Cleveland Indians, David Oliphant signed with the Brooklyn Dodgers in 1957 and, technically at least, spent three years in their minor-league system (he did not play in 1959). Again he thought he pitched very well, but the Dodgers had a superb pitching staff, and he did not make it to the majors. Eventually, in 1960, at twenty-

24. Flood, *The Way It Is,* 199–200; Morris Oliphant to Nick Ward, sports columnist, *New York Daily News,* August 20, 1964, complaining about the two thousand dollars he sent the Yankees on September 16, 1955. However, a letter to Michael Burke, president of the Yankees, possibly of October 12, 1969 (date is partially clipped at top of letter) acknowledges the return of one thousand dollars. For Morris Oliphant's lengthy complaints about the treatment of his son, see his letters to Daniel Topping, co-owner of the New York Yankees, ranging from November 23, 1960, to October 15, 1961, the most important undated, but probably from Topping's (noted) response of August 17, 1961, explaining at length how his son was held captive in the minors by the Yankees because of the reserve system. In the last letter Morris Oliphant continues to complain about the money he and his wife paid for their son's release.

five, Oliphant left baseball and, after two years, established a company, Academic Industries. Although successful at this venture, he could not forget the years he had suffered because of the reserve clause—it was a form of slavery—or the financial pain it had caused his mother.[25]

Oliphant's resentment smoldered through the sixties, and it burst into a flaming rage when he read the Players Association's bulletin about Flood's forthcoming lawsuit. Oliphant also recalled that as a pitcher for the Macon Dodgers in 1957 he and Flood, then playing for the Savannah Reds, had become friends. Playing for teams miles apart, they had not known each very well. However, Oliphant recognized that they had much in common once he read the Players Association's bulletin. He, like Flood, had been a slave to the reserve clause, but he had been a slave as well to anti-Semitism, and now he believed Flood was a victim of racism. No wonder he identified with Flood's battle and thought about what he might do to help him. And with Oliphant's solid connections in the publishing world, a book quickly came to mind, one that would not only present Flood's case but also provide a financial opportunity for both of them.[26]

That meant finding the right publisher and writer. Fortuitously, Oliphant knew Herbert Alexander, the publisher of the Trident Press, and found him greatly interested in a book about Flood. So on January 12, after watching Green Bay and Minnesota battle in the Super Bowl in New Orleans, Oliphant stopped over in St. Louis on his way back to Connecticut. Flood knew when he was coming and his purpose. Nevertheless, when Marian welcomed him into Flood's apartment, Oliphant discovered his man asleep and, when awakened, still "hung over" from his previous night's frolics. Except for days when he was to talk to the press (and even then Zerman spoke for him), escapism was by all accounts, including Flood's own, typical of his behavior during that long winter: thinking about the end of his baseball career, he could not

25. David Oliphant to E. J. "Buzzie" Bavasi, as vice president of the Los Angeles Dodgers, five letters from December 29, 1959, to March 9, 1960; and "Hank" Greenberg, general manager of the Cleveland Indians to Morris Oliphant, February 24, 1956, promising to "personally look at your son" at spring training.
26. Telephone interview with David Oliphant, December 12, 1998; fax to David Oliphant of November 5, 1999, followed by his response to the questions as of November 7, 1999, written up in a memo of that date. But David Oliphant and I had many other conversations by phone, fax, and letter until June 2002. All were the result of my phoning his mother, Claire, whose address was on letters from her husband, Morris, for his phone number in September 1998. He first replied to "Stewart Whitess," October 1, 1998.

paint and he could not sleep; obviously he was depressed and also deep into the bottle. Still, after a few coffees, Oliphant was able to discuss the prospect of a book with Flood and Marian. Both were more than receptive, but the former obviously had the most at stake. Flood, who was still living as if he had a salary of $90,000, desperately needed the sizable advance on royalties that Oliphant thought he could promise. Perhaps as important, Flood believed that he could inform fans of baseball in St. Louis and across the country what had prompted him to fight Major League Baseball's enslaving reserve clause.

After getting Flood's approval and promise to curb his drinking and carousing—for whatever his promise was worth—Oliphant flew back to New York. There he informed Alexander of Flood's readiness to have his story told. Clearly, though, Flood could not write the book himself; he would have to provide the details, but he would need a professional to organize and polish the story in a manner that would attract readers. Alexander had a writer in mind: Richard Carter, who resided in Ossining, a few miles north of New York City. He only needed to find out if Carter was sympathetic to Flood and, if so, whether he would do the book. A phone call answered both questions. Carter was sympathetic, and the money sounded about right: he would receive $40,000 when he produced an "acceptable" manuscript. Even so, he wanted to meet Flood before he actually agreed to take on the job. This was fine with Alexander: his reputation and significant advance payments were at stake. So, too, Oliphant, deeply committed to the book, wanted to ensure that he, Carter, and Flood could work together harmoniously. Consequently, he wanted to dine with everyone concerned. He would be there to make the introductions and grease the gears as needed. That meant coordinating a meeting of four busy men, including Alexander, but primarily it meant waiting for Flood to visit New York, which he would not be doing until after the presentation of his request for injunctive relief before Judge Bonsal.

It was mid-January before the four men dined together at the Warwick Hotel. There it quickly became apparent to Oliphant that he had worried for naught. Before dinner ended they agreed on the book's general contents and tenor. And, Oliphant would recall, they easily moved on, after coffee and brandy, to sign the necessary contracts. Alexander then gave Flood his advance of $15,000. The money was a much-needed windfall for Flood. For the moment, though, Flood knew only that with a little effort he would not starve; indeed he could still attend the Playboy Club. He was in fairly good shape financially unless his ex-wife came after him with a court order stripping him of his advance, or he failed to manage his corporate activities more closely, leading to major financial and legal difficulties, or, worst of all, both problems struck him at the same time regardless of what he did or did not do.[27]

Carter arrived in St. Louis in late February. Although he registered at the city's Holiday Inn downtown, he spent so much time with Flood that he might as well have bunked at Flood's Executive House apartment. Quickly he bonded with his subject. Most nights they drank and flirted at the Playboy Club. Flood, always charming, and still very much a celebrity, captivated many of the bunnies and, according to Carter's conversations with Oliphant, brought one or two of them home with him. But Flood and Carter did little work on the book, and Oliphant, who was monitoring them, began to worry. He warned Alexander, "I think we are losing the book. The boys are drinking all the time. I better fly out there."[28]

In St. Louis, Oliphant found himself no more successful than Carter in getting Flood to work on his life's story. They got along famously, as former players tossing baseballs on warm afternoons, but when Oliphant tried to persuade Flood to cut down on his drinking and nightlife and work daily with Carter, he found himself drawn instead into Flood's alcoholic web. Listening over a bottle of Vodka to Flood's tale of his ill-treatment at the hands of Gussie Busch, Oliphant was brought to tears and almost forgot the purpose of his trip. He returned to Connecticut having achieved nothing. He could only hope that Flood stayed sober and out of the Playboy Club long enough to give Carter the details of his life. He told Alexander that Flood had fifty thousand reasons to do so, apparently referring to his potential royalties. He had seen, though, with his own eyes how miserable Flood was that March: spring training had started in Florida, and for the first time in fourteen years Flood would miss it.[29]

Neither Oliphant nor Carter, perhaps not even Marian, could have fully grasped the pain that drove Flood to carouse so desperately. They could sympathize; they could abandon themselves to it, as Carter did for a while; but they could not really understand, much less empathize.

27. Ibid., Dec. 12, 1998.
28. Ibid.
29. Ibid.

Flood had long since discounted the likelihood that, should Judge Cooper grant him a preliminary injunction, a major-league club other than the Phillies would negotiate for his services. Even so, he retained a bit of hope until March 4, when Judge Cooper ruled against him.[30]

Flood, who recalled throwing up twice that day while waiting for Cooper's ruling, at last felt its full import: losing a season's salary was painful, but a sharper, deeper problem stemmed from the fact that "his body was aching for the exertions of baseball." Naturally he was depressed, so much so that he could not speak with reporters about the decision's impact. When the various media requested interviews, he sent Marian to stall them. He told Carter, "I don't want to see those guys. I don't want to see them and put on a brave front." He did not want to discuss his options in business as he had on other occasions. "It's a lot of bullshit. I'm a baseball player and I'm supposed to play out my string. . . . I'm supposed to be in Florida now, romping around and hitting the ball and cussing with Gibson and banging chicks." Those words spoke to the heart of his depressed state: he could not do his thing that year, on the field and off. And there was no relief in sight. Rumor had it that an angry Gussie Busch had "deep-sixed" Flood's portrait commissions, but it hardly mattered, since he had not been able to pick up a paint brush for weeks, even for his own enjoyment. But he had other reasons to be depressed that March. Claire, his "black Dane," was going back to Denmark (why is unknown). And Marian, sickened by the winter's stress while waiting for Judge Cooper's decision, as well as by her knowledge of problems in Flood's photography business, could not offer him any comfort. Consequently, Flood was feeling such strain and pain by early March that it was with the greatest reluctance that he finally agreed to meet with the press in Zerman's office. As he told Carter soon after, he knew that television cameras would be there, so he put on his largest, darkest glasses, "hoping that nobody could see the despair in my face."[31]

That afternoon, after taking Claire to the airport and priming himself with a couple of drinks, Flood appeared at the press conference. What little he had to say, however, was gloomy: "Let's face it. I'm 32 now and if the case does drag on for two years, I'd be 34. It would be difficult to come back." Judge Cooper's decision had effectively ended his base-

30. *Los Angeles Times*, *New York Times*, and *St. Louis Post-Dispatch*, March 5, 1970.

31. Excerpts from Judge Cooper's opinion cited in *St. Louis Post-Dispatch*, March 4, 1970; Flood, *The Way It Is*, 200–202.

ball career. He had nothing more noteworthy to add. Neither did Zerman in the statement he released later that afternoon, advising only that Flood expected vindication after a full hearing.[32]

Goldberg and Miller had warned Flood that the wheels of justice usually ground very slowly, but Judge Cooper set the trial date for May 18. By then Flood faced what seemed at the time to be a serious problem. Goldberg, upon whose legal expertise and stature as a former justice he and Marvin Miller had counted, rediscovered his desire to be governor of New York. In late March, with the Democratic primary in New York three months away, he announced his candidacy. Thus he would be unable to devote all his attention to the forthcoming trial. Miller insists that he was stunned and embarrassed. And undoubtedly he was. But Goldberg's decision probably made little difference at the time. He would make at least one appearance in federal district court, and the case would not suffer thereafter by his absence. It would be tried by Jay Topkis, an extremely competent partner in Goldberg's firm who was not only steeped in the reserve system's legal history but also deeply committed to Flood's cause. Besides, it made little difference who represented Flood in New York's district court. His personal fight had ended in March when Judge Cooper refused to grant an injunction allowing him to play that year. After that only the MLBPA's determination to eliminate baseball's exemption from the Sherman Act remained to be fought, and that would be resolved eventually in the Supreme Court. By then Goldberg might be available.[33]

Even then, however, the MLBPA had achieved a major goal. In negotiations with the Players Relations Committee, it had put the finishing touches on a Second Basic Agreement that replaced the commissioner as arbitrator of disputes with an independent judge. It was a crucial reform. In a few years it would produce immeasurably successful results (in 1975 an independent arbitrator would rule that Section 10A, which gave a club the right to renew a player's contract for a year, and to do that in perpetuity, was invalid). It is quite possible that Miller used

32. *St. Louis Post-Dispatch*, March 5, 1970; *Sporting News*, March 6, 1970.

33. Miller, *Different Ball Game*, 188–89. Years later, Topkis wrote, "I took the case to heart. I thought that the reserve clause was just another classic matter of exploitation— the fat cat owners . . . built a cozy system that precluded competition." Also, Topkis had written a paper in law school on the Gardella case that sportswriter Red Smith thought significant enough to turn into a column. See Topkis to B. Keith Murphy, Purdue University, Fort Wayne, Indiana, May 16, 1990 (Topkis Papers, Paul Weiss, Rifkind, Wharton, and Garrison, 1285 Avenue of the Americas, New York, N.Y., 10019).

Flood's lawsuit to help pry this concession from the PRC. "Help" is the key word. The Players Association had been bringing pressure to bear on the PRC to change the arbitrator, and that pressure alone might have produced the desired result. But the change may have been more than incidental, a reflection of the publicity produced by Flood's lawsuit. How could club owners insist that Flood was wrong about the merits of the reserve system if he could not get a fair hearing, if his only forum to appeal a grievance was in front of a commissioner the owners named? Kuhn's all-too-blithe dismissal of Flood's appeal in his response of December 30 might have sharpened the point. However, thirty-five years later, all Miller could say was that he believed Flood's lawsuit might have helped secure the Second Basic Agreement; he could not say so with assurance. In any event, if the agreement signed on May 1 is traceable in any way to Flood's lawsuit, it served up a major victory for the MLBPA, and for that Flood should be credited. Unfortunately, the benefits of having an independent arbitrator did not bear fruit for five years, so that no one, it appears, noticed the connection. Flood himself, while claiming free agency as his legacy, never tried to connect the dots and assert specifically what he contributed.[34]

It is understandable that Flood did not see a possible connection between his lawsuit and the Second Basic Agreement during his trial or soon after. Vodka aside, he had other issues, much more immediate and dangerous to worry about. Beginning in early April he had been distracted by serious financial and legal problems that involved not only firms doing business with Curt Flood Associates, Inc. but also the Internal Revenue Service. And some of those embarrassing problems were already in the public domain.

In early April a squib in the *Sporting News* noted that the St. Louis County sheriff padlocked the doors of Flood's photography studio and, if that was not woeful enough, on April 19 the Delmar Printing Company of Charlotte, North Carolina, filed a lawsuit against CFA in federal district court in St. Louis. Delmar alleged that commencing in September 1969, CFA had delivered to its photo-finishing plant film negatives, to be developed by Delmar in accordance with enclosed directions and then mailed to such addresses as designated. As of April 17, 1970, Delmar's charge continued, it had provided goods and services in the sum of

---

34. Helyar, *Lords of the Realm,* 109–14; Miller, *Different Ball Game,* 214; Marvin Miller, telephone interview, October 10, 2004.

$85,464 but had been paid only $17,489, leaving CFA owing it $67,975. Consequently, Delmar not only demanded payment of the money owed plus interest but also alleged diversion of funds and asked for punitive damages amounting to an additional $150,000.[35]

Whether CFA had diverted funds from Delmar is not clear, but CFA's arrearages had been piling up since February 15. At that time Delmar had demanded payment and been informed by Collins and Jones, speaking for CFA, that if it sued, CFA would "file for bankruptcy." Somehow, Flood learned of the problem and acted. Why he suddenly decided to take a hand in the problems of his company he did not say. However, he wrote CFA a $20,000 check, part of which seems to have gone to Delmar, satisfying the company temporarily throughout the winter and into the early spring. The problem remained, though; Delmar was not being paid in full for its finishing work. Why not was disputed at the time and remains unclear. On April 20 Jones told Delmar that CFA had a man "working full time out collecting the receivables." He also said that Collins was using some of the receivables for other purposes. Two days later, however, Collins and Jones advised Delmar that CFA had enough receivables to cover its bills, but (curiously) it could not assign them to it; it owed other creditors nearly $30,000. And it had no other assets.[36]

Understandably, Delmar was dissatisfied with CFA's responses and on May 1 asked the court to appoint a receiver to collect the receivables. Zerman, when informed of Delmar's claim, appeared in St. Louis's federal district court to refute its allegations and ask for a jury trial. Judge James Meredith then set the case for trial in October.[37]

Thus Flood was relieved of immediate concern about problems stemming from his investment in CFA. But long gone was any likelihood that CFA might produce a reasonable income. No wonder Flood quietly

---

35. *Sporting News*, April 5, 1970; "Summons," *Delmar Printing Company v. Curt Flood Associates, Inc.*, April 19, 1970, Civil Action 70 C, 209, U.S. District Court for the Eastern Division of Missouri, St. Louis.

36. "Affidavit of May 1, 1970," Civil Action 70 C, 209; other defendants included Rebecca Collins, Ronald Mueller, and Foster Photographers. For Flood's check to CFA, see "Memorandum of August 27, 1971," Civil Action 70 C, 209, the opinion of Judge James Meredith settling *Delmar vs. Curt Flood Associates, Inc., et al.*

37. "Affidavit of May 1, 1970"; Zerman, "Memorandum of May 1, 1970"; Judge Meredith, "Memorandum of May 6, 1970"; Zerman, "Memorandum of May 29, 1970"; response to Delmar's complaint, June 3, 1970, all in Civil Action 70 C, 209, *Delmar vs. Curt Flood Associates, Inc. et al.*

agreed to follow Carter to his home outside New York City. He desperately needed the advance on his life story, which he would receive when the manuscript was submitted. Then, too, living on Carter's small estate outside Ossining, he was in easy commuting distance of New York City and able to drive down for daily preparation for his trial, which opened on May 19.

Meanwhile, Flood was offered an opportunity to perhaps regain his financial footing, even to resume his baseball career, and to regain the high life he loved so much. According to intermediaries, Bowie Kuhn said Flood could "play for the National League team of his choice without jeopardizing the litigation." Flood knew this was not true; acceptance would render his case—and that of the MLBPA—moot, and that he could not do. The question is, why not? If honoring commitments was the issue, Flood had failed to pay alimony and child support, and now he would not be able to pay the mortgage on his mother's house if her rents fell short. The answer, it would seem, is that his commitment to the MLBPA fell into a different category. It went to the very heart of his being, including his alcoholism, his intense desire to achieve and be liked, and his great, omnipresent fear that he would let the "team" down. In the past his team had been the Cardinals; now it meant the MLBPA. Unfortunately for Flood, this fear of letting the team down had become a reality that fateful day in the 1968 World Series when he thought he misjudged a line drive that alone cost the Cardinals the World Series. From that point forward, he had lost his bearings. He failed to pay child support; he issued the Cardinals an ultimatum; he fought with the Cardinals' general manager over a fine; he otherwise feuded with the front office during the season; and he publicly criticized management near the season's end. Then, too, throughout the 1969 season—and almost certainly in seasons before—he drank and partied late into the wee hours despite a warning from the *Post-Dispatch*'s Broeg that he was endangering a possible Hall of Fame career.

Given Flood's year-long descent into victimhood and the bottle, it is not surprising that after being traded he would challenge baseball's reserve clause. What is surprising, at first sight, is that he would he let himself become a puppet of the MLBPA's interest and strategy in eliminating baseball's antitrust exemption. But the same compulsive, self-destructive nature that had driven him for a year bore him blindly down that path as if he were a bobsled on an Olympic course. In the autumn of 1970 he would blame his disastrous decisions on exhaustion.

He would tell Merrill Whittlesey of the *Sporting News* that "his refusal to sign with the Phils and his slavery charges against baseball came at a time when he was mentally tired and disgusted. I was fatigued mentally and physically." No doubt he was fatigued, given his carousing and his expressed fears that he would be traded. But whatever the reasons, he was "bent out of shape" from the day he thought he alone "lost" the 1968 World Series. And now, a year and a half after that decisive mishap, he found himself committed to the MLBPA and its mid-May trial.[38]

The opening day of *Flood v. Kuhn et al.* witnessed Flood testify but say nothing useful for his or the MLBPA's case. If anything, he undermined his case: he admitted that he would have played for Philadelphia if the Players Association had not agreed to support his case, which was belatedly realistic, but opened the door to an argument that his hostility to the reserve system was essentially pragmatic. Significantly, he testified at cross-purposes about the system itself. When asked if he would drop his lawsuit if the MLBPA secured modification of the reserve system, Flood answered, "Yes, I would." However, a few minutes later, he said, "I would like the whole system to be struck down and declared illegal." He seemed not to recognize these conflicting points then or later on the witness stand. Very possibly he was confused because he was mentally fatigued, just as he admitted was true the previous autumn.[39]

Flood's testimony was followed by that of Miller and various witnesses, some former players and owners, who favored modifying the reserve system, but in an orderly fashion. Such testimony did not help the Flood/MLBPA case: as on other occasions, it sounded like a solution should be found through negotiation, not through the courts. Even an appearance for the plaintiffs by economist Robert Nathan, who asserted that the reserve system depressed players' salaries, did not help: it was merely intuitive. Yet in a "crazy," roundabout way it might have, by provoking a response that opened the door to the strategy Zerman had advocated. When the defense presented its case, John Clark offered statistics on baseball's revenues, expenses, and profits. He suggested that the players received their fair share of baseball's revenues. Clark stressed the amount clubs spent on player development, arguing that without the reserve system a club could not protect its

38. *Sporting News*, October 1970.
39. *Curtis C. Flood, Plaintiff, v. Bowie Kuhn individually and as Commissioner of Baseball, et al., Defendants*, May 19, 1970, 70, Civil Action 202, 55–78, 1–2–107; and 116 and 118.

costly minor-league investments. Players would sign with the highest bidder, the wealthiest clubs would acquire all the best talent, competition would disappear, and the game's fans would lose interest. In sum, the reserve system was essential if the game was to survive.[40]

At that point Topkis, now in Goldberg's absence Flood's lead counsel, might have challenged Clark's detailed percentages of club revenues and the players' shares. Certainly, Zerman thought that he should have. At least he would claim years later that he thought Clark had "opened the door" to an investigation of the various clubs' books, and that Topkis should have asked the judge for a broadly based audit. An inquiry, if granted, would almost certainly have demonstrated conclusively that Clark's numbers did not truly reveal the totality of baseball's profits, that many of those profits were hidden, one example being "upstream" in the Anheuser-Busch brewery's sales to the baseball club. Zerman still believed that if it could be demonstrated that the club owners were much more interested in holding onto baseball as a monopoly for its profits than because of a commitment to the game as a sport, it would be difficult for the Supreme Court to reject Flood's and the MLBPA's case. Indeed, Zerman remained convinced that a legal strategy which threatened to exposed the financial records of all the baseball clubs might well prompt the clubs to cave in on the reserve system, winning Flood's case. Unfortunately for Flood's hopes, Zerman was not in charge of the case; he could only make suggestions. He was outside the loop.[41]

Topkis's memory, unlike Zerman's, has dimmed in the many years since he worked on Flood's case. For Zerman, Flood's case was a singular matter of the heart; for Topkis, despite his real commitment to the battle, it was just one among many significant cases he litigated over more than three decades. However, Topkis insists even today that prying into the finances of the major-league clubs, even if Judge Cooper had agreed to such a request, "would have been incredibly expensive," more expensive than the MLBPA could afford. And he may have been right. So it was that Zerman's suggestion remained hardly more than a minor *frisson* in

---

40. For Clark's testimony, see *New York Times,* June 9, 1970; Zerman e-mail, August 10, 13, 2000.

41. Zerman to author, e-mails November 28, 29, 2001, and discussions in his Clayton, Missouri, office afterward state that Goldberg stipulated before the trial that the plaintiff would not ask for Major League Baseball's financial records. Topkis (to author, January 15, 2003) was "very skeptical that such a stipulation was made." But his memory was, by his own account, dim.

a trial that was otherwise painfully dull. Neither Topkis nor Goldberg pursued any course of action that might have embarrassed baseball's barons. Years later Zerman recalled that when he argued the evidence presented was "weak, sparse, and off the point," both Goldberg and Topkis told him "the issue was a legal one not a factual one, and the trial decision was not important." Indeed, the manner in which the trial was conducted by not only Goldberg and Topkis but the other side as well suggests a *pas de deux,* a dance of gentlemanly adversaries well aware that the result in a federal district court meant little if anything. The decisive battle would be fought in the Supreme Court.[42]

Flood did not need Zerman to tell him that the trial was a farce, interesting if only because of one witness who showed—Jackie Robinson, retired—and the many who did not: no active ballplayer attended, not even Lou Brock or Bob Gibson. In his memoir Flood says that "the trial was dull. The points at issue were matters of constitutional and legal scholarship. Testimony was less significant than the arguments contained in the briefs. . . . The proceedings held little interest for me after I caught their drift." Even so, he reports that when he left the courthouse on June 10, the day the trial ended, he expected that the Supreme Court would rule the reserve system specifically and baseball generally to be in violation of the antitrust laws. In the interim, though, how would he "live" without baseball? How would he pay his bills? How would he deal with the complaint from Delmar Printing? How would he handle the public embarrassment stemming from his financial and legal problems? How would he pay the thousands in arrearages and continuing support for his ex-wife and children? And how would he take care of his mother? Those questions remained to be answered.

42. Topkis to author, January 15, 2003; and Zerman e-mail, August 10, 2000.

IX

Second Chance

After his trial in New York City's federal district court ended in mid-June, Flood found himself at loose ends. By his own admission he spent the rest of the month, along with July and the first weeks of August, in his St. Louis penthouse, "bedding and boozing and waiting for Judge Irving Ben Cooper to shunt my case toward the U.S. Supreme Court where it belonged." He did nothing useful, he told Carter that fall when they were putting the finishing touches on the memoir he would call his "life story." He was too depressed and had been for several months, not just since the trial's end. Since Judge Cooper's ruling against him in early March, he had known with virtual certainty that he would never play baseball again. Even if the judge had ruled in his favor, no major-league club would have broken ranks and negotiated for his services; and even if one had, he could not respond affirmatively—he must honor the commitment he had made to the Players Association in Puerto Rico the previous December to fight for elimination of the reserve system and of baseball's antitrust exemption. No wonder he felt useless. It is no wonder that, devoid of even the public's attention since the trial, he drank day after day; all he could do was drink and idly sulk. His world had collapsed.[1]

Flood told Carter in the autumn that after the trial, as before, he lacked the patience to paint or to involve himself with his photography studios or any other gainful pursuits. He told Carter that he had a folder just outside his bedroom door, "pregnant with overdue portrait commissions," but vodka martinis had killed the mood he required to put brush to canvas. He also confessed that after lengthy nights at the Playboy Club, he awakened in midmorning, "bleary-eyed," and made numerous trips to the refrigerator from which he took endless "restorative" beers. Some days he considered looking at his various baseball awards, but he usually

---

1. Flood, *The Way It Is,* 207.

decided against opening the drawer and viewing them. He did not want to be reminded of what he had been and surely never would be again.[2]

The only responsibility Flood accepted that summer of 1970 revolved around his association over the years with the philanthropic organization Aunts and Uncles. However, his responsibilities to Aunts and Uncles were limited. He signed letters delivered from the Missouri Department of Health and Welfare that asked probable donors to send money to buy shoes for the children whose names and ages he listed. Apparently, his endorsement still carried some weight. Other than that, he did nothing until early in August. Then, Marian—dear Babe, as he still fondly called her—somehow forced him to focus on unpleasant facts. "The Curt Flood corporations are on the rocks," he recalled her saying. "They're about to go under. You simply can't go on like this." Flood reports that he responded lightly, "Don't curdle my vodka. It's a great big beautiful world. Love conquers all." But Marian would not let go: "Things are past the joking stage, dear. Try to listen to me."[3]

Eventually, after more vodka and sharper words from Marian, Flood says that he recognized he had serious problems. Referring to what he called the "Flood Corporations" as being in very "serious trouble" (they were, in fact, already bankrupt), he reported telling Marian, "I'll be ashamed to show my goddamned face in St. Louis after playing bigshot all this time. I might as well clear out now, before the stuff hits the fan. I'm through in St. Louis baseball and I'm through in the town itself. Time to go, baby." But fear of embarrassment was not the only reason Flood felt it was time to leave St. Louis. Soon after his trial's end and his return to the city, he was hit with another "show-cause" order from his former wife's attorney. Beverly wanted her spousal and child-support arrearages, totaling about $25,000 since his failure to pay in mid-November 1968, and she wanted her monthly payments, altogether $1,950 per month. Flood's San Francisco attorney responded with a request for modification of his monthly payments to $100 per child and $100 for his ex-wife. But there was no way Flood could handle even that reduced monthly number, assuming that the judge agreed, which was at the very least questionable. Flood casually outlined his monthly expenses at $4,342 and explained why he could not pay the amounts asked: "I do not have any regular income since I am not presently working. I have only

2. Ibid, 11–12.
3. Ibid, 208.

the advance on the book I am writing, which is not yet finished." How much of that $15,000 he had left is unknown, but he had not received a salary since the end of the Cardinals' 1969 season, and he had spent many evenings partying at the Playboy Club, so it could not have been much. Circumstances being what they were, with his ex-wife's demands adding to the embarrassment of his bankrupt corporation, he decided that the time had come to leave the city, even to go abroad. "I'll go to Copenhagen," Flood informed Marian. "Nobody knows me. I can stretch a dollar further there. Maybe I can find a bar or restaurant to buy into. Best of all, I can sweat out the federal courts without having to worry about my image all the time. It will be a real vacation." With real sorrow (Flood would dedicate his memoir to her) the two said their good-byes, probably hoping the separation would only be temporary.[4]

Flood's "real vacation" began splendidly enough. Before mid-August he was in Denmark's capital. He had always loved Copenhagen's wonderful pastries and its color-blind society, although with a bit of irony he especially loved the city's beautiful blondes. As for his expenses, despite what he had told Marian about needing to "stretch a dollar further," he stayed at the expensive, four-star Marina Hotel about a dozen miles from Copenhagen. There, looking out, he had a superb view of the yacht basin in Vedbaek harbor, and now, an ocean away from the pressures that had stifled his brush in St. Louis, he could paint again—compositions featuring the basin, the many sailboats anchored there, and those coming and going. With plentiful leisure and relative anonymity (excluding, of course, some of the many young Americans, some of them fans, who went to Denmark to avoid the military draft), he could take a thirty-five-minute train ride into Copenhagen without bother from a nagging press. There he set up his easel near the city's famous Tivoli Gardens or its lovely old "New Harbor" and was free to sketch the city scenes he loved. Although it might seem that he wanted to avoid recognition, as he wore a goatee, he chatted with some visiting American tourists and expatriate servicemen so long as their chats did not center on his ongoing challenge to baseball's reserve system. These chats, even when brief, kept him in touch with the fortunes of his good friend Bob Gibson, who was doing "great" as usual, and of his former team,

4. Ibid, 208–9. Final Judgment, Dissolution of Marriage, April 17, 1970; Show-Cause order of June 23, 1970; and Flood's Response of June 18, 1970, *Flood v. Flood,* case no. 356589. Why Flood's response precedes the show-cause order is an unresolved question. A document may be missing from the Alameda court files.

the Cardinals, who were doing "terrible." When he could restrict the conversation's subject matter, he was generally happy, but on occasion these chats reminded him that he was no longer a ballplayer, but rather an anonymous tourist with a slightly bohemian twist—and that could be depressing. On the other hand, some of his much-cherished blondes may have stopped to talk, as he wrote later: "Little do these beautiful Danish pastries realize that the aesthetic black in the beret and goatee is actually Curt Flood, the famous St. Louis business tycoon and athlete, vacationing between [his] triumphs." These words might be read either as facetious, an indulgence in self-pity, or both. However, Flood really wanted readers of his "life story" to know that he was creating a new, serious life; that he was negotiating to buy a restaurant. As usual, he wanted to project an image. But this time he may have been serious.[5]

Even if Flood enjoyed himself in renewing his acquaintance with Copenhagen and its Danes, any happiness he felt must have been very brief. A few days after his arrival—probably on August 13—he read in the *International Herald Tribune* an article noting that Judge Cooper had ruled against his challenge to baseball's reserve system. Shortly after, it would seem that Flood might have been able to read Cooper's opinion in its entirety. Goldberg's associate, Max Gitter, sent a copy of the opinion to Zerman on August 12, the day it came down. Gitter seemingly assumed that Flood was still living in St. Louis and that Zerman, being his personal attorney, would "tell Curt," possibly explaining its major points as necessary. And Zerman presumably forwarded the opinion to Flood, although this can only be surmised. Flood says only that he "learned by mail that Judge Cooper had ruled, as expected," not from whom he received the opinion or whether his correspondent explained any aspect of it. In truth, Cooper's opinion did not require an explanation. It was not a weighty document. The judge was well aware that his ruling was only a temporary stop on a case that was almost certain to end up in the Supreme Court. As Gitter wrote to a colleague in early September, "The Federal District Judge did not make any findings on the reasonableness of the reserve clause," acknowledging that he lacked the capacity to do so because the Supreme Court had exempted baseball from antitrust regulation. Cooper ruled negatively on other ancillary complaints lodged by Flood. He threw out charges of baseball's illegal labor practices, of involuntary servitude, of peonage, and of blatant disregard

5. Flood, *The Way It Is*, 209, 215; Shelby Whitfield, *Kiss It Goodbye*, 155.

for players' interests. He called these charges in the lawsuit noisy win-dow-dressing, lacking serious supporting evidence, and he was proba-bly right. In any case, what mattered to the MLBPA above all else was baseball's age-old exemption from antitrust regulation, and this was the issue Goldberg's firm was now preparing to appeal to a circuit court.[6]

Flood, by his own admission, was neither upset nor surprised by Cooper's decision. He had expected his claims to be rejected, just as he now expected that they would be appealed. Neither was he affected by his ex-wife's refusal to accept a modification of his spousal and child support and the order from the Alameda County Court that he appear for a hearing on September 30. What did upset him, he told Carter in the fall, was news that he was the subject of "a lawsuit or two." In fact, one of those lawsuits was not news at all. Flood had known before he went to Copenhagen about the Delmar Printing Company's lawsuit: it was filed in mid-April. Obviously, he wanted to convey the impression that he had just learned of this and that it made him feel "downright awful." CFA's failure "hurt some people badly." That was embarrassing. Worse, "Technically, but entirely without design, I was on the lam." It would look as if he had flown the country to escape embarrassment when the story became public: "Was the black champion of Players' rights sup-posed to end like this—hiding from creditors in a Danish hotel room? And what a splendid combination of lawsuits to be involved in! One case [was] majestically on its way to the Supreme Court and history. The other before some lowly tribunal concerned with unpaid bills."[7]

As if the Delmar case were not enough, Flood faced another, possi-bly more serious problem stemming from his failure to supervise the administration of his photography studios. Flood learned about it just a few days before leaving St. Louis and, given its timing, it may well have figured more prominently in his decision to go to Europe than the Del-mar suit. In late July, the Internal Revenue Service announced publicly that it was auctioning a camera and a camera stand from Flood's photo studio on Lindell to recover funds CFA had failed to send on its FICA

---

6. See reference to the *International Herald Tribune* in the *Globe-Democrat,* April 20, 1981; also Gitter to Zerman, August 12, 1970, and Gitter to Stafford, September 3, 1970, in Topkis Papers; U.S. Supreme Court Justice Harry Blackmun's opinion for the majority in http://www.ripon.edu/faculty/bowenj/antitrust/fldvkuhn.htm.

7. Flood, *The Way It Is,* 209–10; *Howard and Nancy M. Foster, Plaintiffs, vs. Curt Flood and William M. Jones, Defendants,* filed January 7, 1971, in U.S. District Court for the Eastern Division of Missouri, Eastern Division, St. Louis.

(social security tax) obligations, and it was holding Flood responsible. He would have to pay the Internal Revenue Service, or else his mother's home in Oakland—the only property he owned, and which was already saddled with two mortgages—would be hit with an IRS lien.[8]

As summer gave way to autumn, Flood, weighed down by what he said were his newfound legal problems, worried increasingly about his diminished funds. How long would they last? What would he do when his money gave out? Then, on October 14, he learned via transatlantic telephone that his financial worries might soon be much diminished and possibly even eliminated. He listened as William Gildea, a *Washington Post* staff writer, asked, "What do you think of the deal?" "Deal?" Flood questioned. Gildea explained that Robert "Bob" Short, who owned the Washington Senators, had just acquired Flood's contract and the right to negotiate with him in a trade with the Philadelphia Phillies, and Short would be phoning him shortly. Flood did not believe Gildea at first. "Are you really calling from America? . . . I have a lot of flakey friends in Denmark," he continued. After Gildea reassured him, he went on to mumble in a wandering fashion about the problems of being "on stage 24 hours a day." Flood said that was very "hard for a very high-strung athlete," which he, always playing the victim, acknowledged being, and he enjoyed relaxing with his paint brush in hand. Then, too, he wondered to Gildea if he were in shape to play, although he immediately mused that a few weeks in the Florida sun might renew him; and, after all, like riding a bicycle, "you don't forget something you did for 14 years."[9]

Flood's backing and filling did not give Gildea a clear picture of whether Flood would play for the Senators, but the sportswriter did note that the former Cardinals star could use the money Short would offer him. At the very least Flood owed the IRS for nonpayment of taxes.

In fact, Short was even then stoking the interest of the Senators' fans. Of course both the fans and the owner wanted a winner; however, Short desperately needed to sell tickets, even if it meant acquiring a few players primarily for their celebrity. No wonder he told the fans that he would go the extra mile—even across the Atlantic Ocean—to get them the seven-time Gold Glove winner. "I am now ready to talk directly to Flood. He is in Copenhagen, and I will go there directly myself to do it."

8. IRS auction of August 1, mentioned in *Sporting News,* July 29, 1970, also *Washington Post,* October 15, 1970.
9. *Washington Post,* October 15, 1970.

Perhaps Short was prepared to go to Copenhagen, perhaps not, but publicly saying so cost nothing, and it could help fill the many usually empty seats in RFK Stadium, helping him to deal with the Senators' truly serious financial problems. He had already hired as manager Ted Williams, the great Boston Red Sox slugger and, since 1966, a Hall of Famer, and he was looking for players with big names, hoping they would not turn out to be has-beens. In those circumstances, just phoning Flood was a no-brainer. But Short knew from Gildea, if not from other sources, that Flood was worried about his capacity to still play well. So while Flood, answering the phone in his hotel, heard Short ask him for a meeting, the next thing Flood heard was a gruff voice saying, "Curt, this is Ted Williams." Flood, in disbelief, responded, "Get out of here. Who is this?" After which he heard, "No, this is Ted. You know what? I am managing the Washington Senators and I've got some fucking guys on this team. I am not sure they can play. . . . But I know you can. And I really want you to play for me." Flood was thrilled at Williams's words, saying years later, "You have to be a baseball player to know what that means." Even so, there was an obstacle to his playing again. He reminded Williams that he was involved in a lawsuit against baseball. However, he was told (apparently by Williams) that the Senators' owner had discussed the matter with Goldberg and his other attorneys and they had said his playing would not make any difference in the outcome of his case. Then Short got back on the line, and Flood questioned him about salary. Short suggested that they discuss that and other matters at his office in Minneapolis, but Flood said that he must discuss with his lawyers in New York whether or not he could play "before I can even consider talking to you." Short tried to persuade Flood that he had made his point in federal district court and by staying out of baseball for a year. But he made no headway. Flood responded warily, "Maybe so, maybe not. The last I heard, I could not play without harming our case. If anything has changed, I'd love to know it."[10]

Short finally proposed a solution to their place of meeting, one that should have been obvious from the outset of their conversation: "Come to New York as my guest," he pleaded. "Talk to your lawyers. Then let's get together. I'm sure we can work something out that won't hurt your case but will put a lot of money into your pocket and help my ball club."

10. Flood and Turan, "Outside-Outside," 31–32; Flood, *The Way It Is*, 210.

Flood thought Short's proposition "sounded unrealistic," but he could not resist a free trip to New York. Neither could he afford to forgo the opportunity to join the Senators. In a second talk with Gildea he said that what he would do depended on the contract offered: "If I signed a contract with that [reserve] clause I'd be making a big farce of my case. . . . If I could sign a contract without that clause in it, then I'd do it. I'd say: 'Beautiful, let's go. I've been in Denmark too long.' But I don't see how it's possible." This was Flood's story when his case was in the judicial system and in the public eye. Years later, though, he would acknowledge, "I was running out of money. I was in Copenhagen, drinking too much, feeling sorry for myself, and that's just not me." Furthermore, his body felt out of sorts; it desperately needed to play baseball again. So it was that Flood, poised, as it were, between what he wanted desperately to do and what he feared he could not do, headed for New York and discussions that would determine his immediate future.[11]

Once in New York, Flood went to Marvin Miller for advice. He wanted to know if he should negotiate with Short. Specifically, he needed to ask "would my playing in 1971 hurt our chances in the higher courts? Can a suit be dismissed as moot *after* it has been tried and has entered the appeals process?" Was the situation not "different now that the actual trial is over?" Miller suggested that Flood discuss it with Goldberg. Flood found Goldberg ready to help him even though it meant taking time off from his gubernatorial campaign; and he liked what he heard from the lawyer: "By remaining out of baseball and giving up more than a hundred thousand dollars in income last year, you suffered real damages which go to the heart of your dispute with the reserve system. I therefore think that you could play in 1971 without hurting the case in the higher courts."[12]

On October 29, Flood, Goldberg, Gitter, Miller, and Dick Moss handed Short a list of written proposals for a contract. Flood was to have a no-cut contract for $110,000 for the 1971 season, half of it up front; he was not to be traded without his consent; he was to be released unconditionally if he and Short were unable to agree on terms for the 1972 season; and the (other) owners were to agree not to argue in court that his presence on the playing field invalidated his suit. Short agreed to all the proposals "without turning a hair," after which Goldberg and

11. Flood and Turan, "Outside-Outside," 31–32.
12. Flood, *The Way It Is*, 211.

Gitter returned to their offices to draw up a memorandum embodying the agreement. For three hours Flood thought he had secured the "first equitable player's contract in the history of major-league baseball." But when the men met later, a sheepish, subdued Short said that he had spoken to Kuhn, and the commissioner would not approve a contract that did not include the standard reserve clause without reservations.[13]

Flood thought Kuhn had intervened on the orders of "Short's fellow owners," in the interest of maintaining the sanctity of the reserve clause. He was right. The next day Kuhn would tell sports reporters that he "would not approve a contract without the reserve clause and if there were a modification of the reserve provision it would not be approved." If Flood wanted to play, then he must sign the Uniform Players Contract. Kuhn added that he hoped Flood "has ability left. If he does, it would be a misfortune not to utilize that ability." However, whatever the commissioner might hope, there was an obvious problem: Flood's appeal of his case to the Second Circuit Court of Appeals and, almost certainly, to the Supreme Court, could be prejudiced. Kuhn advised newsmen, "Flood is concerned that if he signs, he prejudices his case, and the defendants are concerned that if he signs he prejudices their case." Kuhn then told the press what he had already told Short: the Washington Senators' owner could include in a contract with Flood a covenant that both plaintiffs and defendants would write and sign. It would stipulate that Flood's playing for the Senators would not prejudice the issues under dispute.[14]

All this Flood had known the previous day. Within the limitations imposed by Kuhn, he and his lawyers had continued their discussions with Short. The Senators' owner had offered what Flood recalled as two contracts, one written, the other oral. Short would pay Flood $110,000 for the 1971 season, handing him half of his salary up front, or so it was reported, although, significantly, as will become apparent, this was not literally true—Flood actually would receive bimonthly checks beginning that November rather than at the beginning of the season. Short also agreed to give him a job in the off-season; agreed (vaguely) to help him straighten out his seriously deteriorated finances; and, finally, agreed to stand on his commitment (the one he had made before Kuhn intervened), effectively eliminating the reserve clause's operation. Referring

13. Ibid, 212–13.
14. Ibid.; *New York Times*, October 30, 1970; *St. Louis Post-Dispatch*, October 30, 1970.

to his readiness to release Flood unconditionally if they could not agree on a contract for 1972, Short said, "I made good-faith assurances, and I'll keep them."[15]

By the next morning, October 30, Flood was prepared to sign the Uniform Players Contract. He had little choice, he told the press: "Like everybody else I've had some business reverses and I need the money. But I still think the reserve clause stinks." Responding to questions, Flood spoke about his problems and his aspirations. "I'm paying alimony and I've got five children to support. That's enough to drive any man back into the game." Fortunately for Flood, no sportswriter or editor knew, or thought it desirable, to write that he had not paid spousal and child support for two years. As always, there was a disconnect between Flood's personal life, including his business enterprises, and his baseball career. The *New York Post*'s Maury Allen filed a much-copied column filled with Flood's positive, at times colorful, comments. After pointing out that Short offered him more money than the Cardinals had paid him in 1969, Flood told Allen, "Maybe I'll start a trend of players taking a year off." Then, asked whether his one-year layoff would handicap him, he responded, "I've only been away a year. Everybody in baseball is away six months. Look at what Cassius Clay did." (Clay, or Muhammad Ali as he had renamed himself, was banned from boxing for three years from 1967 until 1970 for refusing to enter military service during the Vietnam War.) On a more serious note, Flood said that he had been under "tremendous pressure for the past year while fighting the suit." Living abroad even briefly had helped somewhat. Now he hoped that a contract with the Senators could be worked out, because "things are going so bad for me now that it would be just my luck to jump out of a window and live."[16]

Four days later, on November 4, a grim-faced Flood signed the Uniform Players Contract that made him for one year what he had said no one should be: the property of a baseball club. He did it "conditionally" because a covenant had not yet been drafted stipulating that he would play without prejudicing his case against baseball. But even the prospect of a well-drafted covenant could not save him from criticism in the media. Commenting on Flood's "conditional" contract the day after he left for Denmark to clean up his affairs, the *New York Times*'s usually

15. Flood, *The Way It Is*, 213.
16. *St. Louis Post-Dispatch*, November 29, 30, 1970.

supportive Leonard Koppett insisted that it would be difficult to devise wording that would prevent a judge from considering the fact that Flood had signed the very contract, including the reserve system, that he had earlier challenged as a form of "slavery." That was the most favorable light shed on the matter. It would not last long. Later in the month attorneys for Flood and Major League Baseball devised language for the covenant satisfactory to both: it allowed Flood to play and his case to continue. At that time, Arthur Daley, Koppett's colleague at the *Times*, argued that no matter how well the "legal beagles" had addressed the "without prejudice" issue in the covenant, "I'm positive that if I were a judge or a juror I could never erase from my mind certain inherent contradictions within the phrase. . . . Trained only by Perry Mason, I must conclude that Flood prejudices his case."[17]

Whether or not Flood had prejudiced his case, by mid-November he was obviously aboard with Bob Short and the Senators. A reporter captured him testing his batting eye at the team's "winter camp" in St. Petersburg, Florida, and interviewed him at length when he finished. The reporter then wrote a flattering piece, the first such, probably, since before Flood's miscue in the 1968 World Series. He suggested that Flood might be a candidate to become baseball's first black manager. Then he asked Flood if Ted Williams, great hitter that he had been, could help him. Flood said he thought his new manager was "such a scientist, I know he can help my hitting." Understandably, he added that he wanted to "have a good year for the Senators. They have a lot of faith in me and a lot is riding on my shoulders." But he added that, much as he had a zest for baseball, "I don't think I would play if they didn't pay me." A few days later, still in St. Petersburg, he held a news conference along with Short. He said that he would not be back in the game except for the Senators' owner and admitted that he would probably have a difficult year and "be under a microscope." He could hardly have been more prescient.[18]

Whether Flood could recover his solid batting average of the past and his Gold Glove talents were the questions on the minds of many Washington fans that fall. If they read closely, what they saw reported from the St. Petersburg "winter" camp was not reassuring. Their new

17. Leonard Koppett, *New York Times*, November 5, 1970; Arthur Daley, *New York Times*, November 29, 1970. For a grim-faced Flood, see *St. Louis Post-Dispatch*, November 4, 1970.

18. *St. Louis Post-Dispatch*, November 22, 25, 1970.

golden boy was being treated with kid gloves. Club officials were giving Flood every consideration. "Would you like No. 21 [Flood's number with the Cardinals] this season?" an official asked him. "Yes, if it's possible?" Flood answered. And of course it was. On the field the pampering continued. Short ordered that Flood should be treated to easy workouts: no calisthenics. This prompted the Senators' trainer to say, "I'm treating him like a six-month-old girl. Six-month-old boys you can treat a little rougher."[19]

It was obvious to those who watched Flood throw, go through running drills, and take batting practice that he required very tender treatment. His arm was weak and tight; he sat down to rest after flagging down just a few fly balls in the outfield; at the plate he swung hard and grunted, and for the most part he got his bat on only part of the ball and popped up. But he remained positive, at least in interviews. He told the *Washington Post*'s Gildea, "I have no weight problem. [And] you don't forget [how to play] baseball. It's like riding a bicycle." That was Flood's story, however obviously at odds it was with what a baseball coach or perhaps even a fan would see. He said it would be difficult playing up to the level of his years with the Cardinals given that he would be playing center field in American League parks whose angles he did not know, but he was "going to try like hell."[20]

While Flood waited for spring training and his second chance, he watched while his counsel, Arthur Goldberg, presented his appeal from Judge Cooper's ruling the previous August and sportswriters and the public responded to the publication of his life story, *The Way It Is*. There was little or nothing he could do but hope his book sold well.[21]

Publicity efforts had given Flood's life story something of a head start. In December 1970, shortly after Flood left the Senators' winter camp, his publisher, the Trident Press, sparked a flare-up in the baseball world. Trident gave a certain-to-be-controversial excerpt from the galley proofs to nationally influential sports columnist Red Smith. The excerpt focused on Flood's negotiations with Senators' owner Bob Short. Taking the excerpt at face value, Smith quoted Short informing Flood, "I

19. William Gildea, "Curt Flood—Baseball's Angry Rebel," *Washington Post*, January 25, 1971.

20. Ibid.

21. *New York Times*, January 6, 1971, Koppett noting that Goldberg would present oral argument in Flood's appeal to the Second Circuit Court of Appeals; "Baseball's Angry Rebel."

promise you that I won't trade you. And I guarantee you the full year's pay no matter what happens. And at the end of the year if we don't agree on terms for the following season I'll make you a free agent so that you can work out a deal with another club. But I can't put any of this in writing. And if anybody says that I agreed to such an arrangement, I'll deny it." To this exchange, Smith added, "Kuhn refused to permit such an agreement. . . . So they made their pact orally."[22]

Three days later, Short responded. "The written contract is what governs our relationship. . . . It doesn't include the stipulations he requested about not having the reserve clause in the contract." Asked by the Associated Press if there was anything to an oral pact, Short answered, "The hell with verbal agreements. There is a written agreement, and I stand behind it. The only thing not standard about it is that it says it won't prejudice his case against baseball."[23]

Smith had cited the book's claim that Short would deny the existence of an oral agreement; after Short in fact did deny any such agreement, Commissioner Kuhn added that any oral agreement exempting the reserve clause, even if made, would not be binding. Kuhn may also have told Flood that he could not play in the 1971 season if he did not delete the offending passage from the published version of *The Way It Is*. The passages Smith quoted did not appear in the book when the slim volume was published later that winter. Instead, the section dealing with the negotiations quoted Short as saying to Flood after hearing that the commissioner adamantly opposed any exceptions to the reserve clause in the contract, "I made good-faith assurances, and I'll keep them." What, exactly, Short meant by "good-faith assurances" is not recorded.[24]

The contretemps over who assured whom of what was relatively insignificant (and eventually moot) compared with the sharp reaction to *The Way It Is* when it appeared on the bookstore shelves in January 1971. According to Richard Carter, he penned only what Flood had told him, and Flood carefully reviewed every passage before the manuscript went to press. And there is no reason to doubt Carter. He was, at last contact, totally sympathetic to Flood's life story. He accepted Flood's description of his childhood neighborhood, his family, and his career, altering it only through the stylistic changes for which he was hired; he

22. *St. Louis Post-Dispatch*, December 16, 1970.
23. Ibid.
24. Flood, *The Way It Is*, 213.

made no effort to check out and, if necessary, modify his friend's characterizations. He presented Flood's story as dramatically and sympathetically as his considerable skills would allow. It is hardly to be wondered, then, that the book did not emerge as balanced or even critically sympathetic, but as an apologia, the story of Flood as the justifiably angry victim of persecution.

Of the relatively accessible reviews of Flood's book from outside the St. Louis area—three in number—all were more than sympathetic. A book review in the *New York Times* praised Carter's "spurts of beautiful prose and Flood's perception of what makes Sammy athlete run," but pointedly insisted that "the book's major value lies elsewhere:" "Power concedes nothing without a demand. . . . Flood is the one who has done the struggling, made the demand, and written an insightful book to explain his position." Two shorter reviews in the *Library Journal* stressed Flood's personal qualities: he was an "admirable man, intelligent, well-read, artistic, and tolerant." For example, he favored black pride but not black racism. A second review in the same journal praised Flood's book for its "marvelous account of the life of the black ballplayer in the minor leagues and a detailed description of the union movement within baseball." Such were some of the warm words for Flood's story, from reviewers who approved his challenge to baseball's reserve clause and who probably knew him only from a distance.[25]

Closer to the scene in St. Louis, one reviewer, Rich Koster of the *Globe-Democrat,* followed suit. However, his review was a thin piece, focusing only on the positive and the trivial. The positive consisted of Flood's persistent efforts, along with Gibson's, to bridge the gap between the team's southern-raised whites and its blacks. Koster avoided the chapter entitled "The Winning Spirit," probably because Flood discussed how owners and managers, broadcasters and sportswriters manipulated the players, and each other—a story that would not play well with those he named or with Cardinals fans. But he found more than adequate space for the somewhat trivial, if possibly titillating, chapter, "The National Pastime's Pastime," where Flood described, if in generic terms, how he and almost every other player had bedded the many women who clamored for their attention. Nicely conscientious, though, Koster noted that Flood assured players' wives that their own

25. Excerpts from five consumer reviews of Flood, *The Way It Is*, on www .amazon.com.

husbands were missing from this last form of revelry common on the road. Obviously, Koster was not interested in critically examining Flood's story. His review, if it deserves that designation, asserted that "much of Flood's tome concerns matters that have already been explored in the daily press"; as for the rest, he found Flood's philosophical views too "weighty and boring" to discuss." Koster apparently wanted only to publish a juicy column.[26]

Much in contrast, at least three other commentators in St. Louis took a sharply critical view. Harry "The Hat" Walker, once the Cardinals' hitting coach and still quite appreciative of Flood as a player, told the *Sporting News*, "He gives it 100% on the field. . . . But it burns me up to read some of the tripe he's written." Reacting to Flood's sharp criticism of Busch's clubhouse speech just before the start of the 1969 season, Walker said that the Cardinals' owner was justified: some players had failed in their contractual obligations, at times shouldering fans aside and refusing to sign autographs. Then, too, Flood complained about his salary, but his $90,000 contract was astronomical, surely out of line for a singles hitter. Furthermore, Flood ignored the fact that the Cardinals, far from being tightwads, had the biggest payroll in baseball—more than a million dollars. Worse, Flood was an ingrate who had failed to acknowledge that Busch gave his wife a modeling job when the family needed the money, that he bailed Flood out of several financial jams, and that once he reversed a front-office decision to trade him, saying, "You can't trade away my boy." As for Flood's challenge to baseball's reserve system, Walker found it a childish reaction to his failure to get his way. Referring to "Flood's overall attitude about baseball's rules and laws," Walker asserted that Flood could have accepted his trade or rejected it, "But I can't stomach his crying that baseball mistreated him."[27]

Walker was not the only former Cardinal to take umbrage at Flood's life story. Stan Musial, arguably the greatest player in the team's history, a former teammate of Flood's, and, so he thought, a friend, could not have been angrier at Flood's story of being denied admission at his restaurant. He told Robert Burnes, the *Globe-Democrat*'s sports editor, "What he doesn't say is that it was twenty minutes to one in the morning. . . . Our kitchen closes at twelve thirty. I was the one who told him

26. Ibid.
27. *Sporting News*, February 3, 1971.

he couldn't come in and why." Anyway, "that was a long time ago. Why is he bringing it up now?" Walker, of course, could have told him.[28]

Bob Broeg, who knew Flood as well as anybody except, possibly, his family and a few men in Oakland, also could have told Musial why. The tone of his *Post-Dispatch* review of *The Way It Is* closely matched Walker's and Musial's bitter critiques. No doubt this could have been foreseen: just the year before, Broeg had asked rhetorically in his column whether Flood was challenging baseball out of "principle or principal," leaving little doubt that he believed the latter motive was the real reason. Whether that was Broeg's actual personal view or that of the club owners who controlled his access to the clubhouse is not clear. But there can be no question that he found Flood's memoir bitter, hard, and cynical. In one illustration of this, he challenged Flood's assertion that the "black experience teaches that the American white is guilty until he proves himself innocent." Broeg wrote, accurately enough, that these words reversed a central concept of American justice, the presumption of innocence, and were "discouraging . . . to all who think they've learned to accept a man for what he is and does, not for what he looks like." And in the best of all possible worlds, he would have been right. However, in fairness to Flood, Broeg did not live in the black man's (or woman's) world. In that context, several questions put (by the author) to even such a courteous and ostensibly moderate black woman like Flood's sister Rickie Riley revealed that great bitterness lurked. Consequently, Broeg was on safer turf—writing about baseball rather than race relations—when he chastised Flood for his harshness toward Hemus. Broeg acknowledges Hemus's faults: Hemus had been wrong not to play Flood regularly and wrong to repeat in the clubhouse the racist words he had used on the field in the incident with Bennie Daniels when, if anything, he should have apologized. However, there was no proof that Hemus was a racist and, if he had been, there was evidence that he had changed. After Flood's failure to catch Northrup's drive in the 1968 World Series, Hemus went out of his way to write to him. He told Flood of his great regret that he had misevaluated him and complimented him on being a gentleman and a superb outfielder. At this point, Broeg thought Flood should have accepted Hemus's regrets with a measure of grace. Instead, he gratuitously wrote of his former

28. *St. Louis Globe-Democrat*, March [n.d.] 1971.

manager's letter, "Every time I look at it, I get sore." No wonder Broeg found Flood's continuing bitterness unworthy and said so in his review.

Broeg also expressed his displeasure with Flood's behavior on the eve of and during the 1969 season, the turning point in his previously solid relationship with the Cardinals and especially Gussie Busch. He noted that Flood had been Busch's pet until his "bristling ultimatum" "waved a red flag in the boss's face," and that Flood had minimized the size of the contract he was demanding: Flood said he asked for $90,000, which he eventually received, whereas Broeg placed the ultimatum as being for $100,000. Then, as if to establish his independence, while Broeg agreed with Flood that Busch should have appealed to the team privately in March rather than with the press present, he asserts that afterward Flood did not speak darkly about the boss, his lecture, and the probably disastrous consequences, but rather discussed Busch with those present in an obsequious manner. Also, Broeg argues that as the 1969 season was nearing its end, Flood "churlishly" criticized the Cardinals' front office for wanting to look at "raw, young players." Finally, recalling Flood's charge that playing rookies meant the difference between third- and fourth-place money—a thimbleful of difference—and his statement, "I want everything that's coming to me, even if it's only a dime," Broeg ended his review on a sadly critical note: "I never knew he was so damned unhappy."[29]

Broeg had clues to Flood's unhappiness: he knew Flood to be an alcoholic, a womanizer, a bad businessman, a man reeling from his brother's incarceration, and in general "a troubled person." But Broeg might also have discussed Flood's presentation of himself as victim; that was central to the book. In several chapters it portrays multiple oppressors, not only Hemus, Busch, and the Cardinals' front office, but also the white establishment in general and the baseball establishment in particular. Surely Flood's book was designed to elicit sympathy and sales, but was it honest? Was it fair? Was Flood looking outside when he should have been looking within?[30]

There is no need to repeat the challenges raised by the devastating commentaries of Walker, Musial, and Broeg. But it is fair to ask whether in Carl's case, Flood was victim or enabler. Also, did he consider the

29. *St. Louis Post-Dispatch*, March 4, 1971.

30. Recollections of Reilly (divorced from Jones), June 19, 2003. Also Whitfield, *Kiss It Goodbye*, 160, where the Washington Senators broadcaster writes, "Curt seemed to take pride in revealing his exploits with white women."

morality of forgoing a significant salary for a quixotic battle against base-ball when he owed back payments on spousal and child support, not to mention support to his mother whom he encouraged to move into a house saddled with debt that only he could afford? Then, too, did he recognize that he might be little more than a pawn in the Players Association's efforts to eliminate baseball's exemption from the antitrust laws? And why does he say that he only heard about the lawsuits filed against CFA while in Denmark, when he surely fled to escape from the embarrassment and financial consequences? In sum, was Flood a victim of not only villains from without but also demons from within?

Almost certainly, Flood did not truly understand the source of his problems: he was small for a major-leaguer, an overachiever paranoid about failing himself and his team, who, after he failed to catch North-rup's drive in the 1968 World Series, as he thought he should have, fell apart. Flood's long-submerged demons took charge. Unable to accept his failure and seeking to restore the fans' esteem and his own with an ultimatum coupled with a promise, he blew his warm relationship with Busch and the Cardinals. But he might have been traded anyway. Rumors of what Devine would call a "business decision" had been floating for a year. Thus Flood knew, especially after he failed to hit well in 1969, that he might be traded. It did not come as a surprise, and he might well have accepted it, or at least not have challenged baseball's reserve system in the courts, but for other very crucial factors. Sensitive man that he was, he bitterly resented being informed of his trade by "a middle-echelon coffee drinker in the front office" rather than the general manager. His resentment, doubtless stoked by Marian, festered as he sat in bars and in his hotel room while essentially alone in Copenhagen. And when he returned to St. Louis he found a sympathetic ear in an attorney who not only identified with him but also thought he had a strategy that made his cause winnable. Unfortunately, the need for powerful financial support and legal acumen forced Flood and Allan Zerman into the apparently helpful but controlling hands of the Players Association and a strategy that turned out to be unwinnable. Possibly, even probably, Flood, influenced by alcoholism and demands for spousal and child support, did not fully understand the forces driving him to disaster, but even had he understood them, he could not admit them to the public record. *The Way It Is* had to be an apologia that would justify his lawsuit; it had to portray him as the victim he believed he was and, just possibly, breed sympathy with Washington Senators' fans and boost his "second chance" in the coming season. For the sake of his ego as well as his finances, he needed to succeed. The next few months would tell the story.[31]

Unfortunately for Flood, his "second chance" bombed very quickly, and this time he did not have anyone to blame but himself. From the day he arrived at the Senators' spring training camp he was pampered by Bob Short and Ted Williams. And he needed it. The team doctor was quoted as saying, "Flood has to have the oldest 33 year old body I've ever examined." The winters spent boozing and painting, without exercise, had taken their toll in the form of preternaturally slowed reflexes and lack of muscle tone. And one did not have to be a doctor to see it. *Washington Post* sportswriter George Minot, although sympathetic to Flood's efforts, reported his doubts. One day after Flood dropped an easy fly ball, Minot wrote, "Flood's Comeback Springs a Leak." Another day he heard that a ball Flood threw from medium center field to the catcher bounced three times before rolling dead at the plate. He was not reassured when Flood said he would strengthen his arm by swinging a heavy ball. Neither was he reassured when he discussed Flood's hitting with Williams—Flood had not hit the ball well in eight games to date—and the manager offered a mixed response. Williams hoped that Flood would hit ".280 or .290, a heck of a year," but when he would start hitting was another matter. Williams was not stupid and did not want to appear stupid, so he added, "I'm sure he's beginning to wonder when he will. We're just going to have to play him every day to get him going." As for Flood, he told Minot, "Spring training is always tough." Flood expected that his performance would improve during the regular season.[32]

Coddling was the order of the day, as the Senators' trainer told Minot that Flood needed just a little more time to get into shape and "the basic thing is that he not hurt himself," but at least one sportswriter did not think time was the answer. *St. Louis Post-Dispatch* writer Ed Wilks asserted that "the best bet . . . is that [Flood] doesn't give the Senators half a season as a regular." And with spring training camp about to close, Minot reported that Flood "has been struggling to regain his touch" and asserted that Short had traded away too much to get him, chiefly to sensationalize some of the team's players and to sell more season tickets.

31. Vaughn "Bing" Devine, telephone interview, June 18, 2003.
32. *Washington Post*, March 17, 1971.

Unfortunately for Short's faith in sensational players, the former Cardinal was only hitting .210 when the club left for home.[33]

After opening day, *Washington Post* sportswriter Shirley Povich wrote, mockingly, "Curt Flood got himself one hit, and it was a $10,000 beauty, a bunt down the first base line so superbly artistic it was unplayable." In the following three games Flood went 1 for 12. But his failure to hit was not his only problem. On April 12 he mangled a fly ball so badly that, after the inning ended, he was replaced in center field. And it was not for just one game. Flood did not start another game until April 17, when he managed an infield hit. The next day he singled in the first half of a doubleheader, but after that Williams benched him for several days. He was hitting only .167. No wonder Povich wrote that Flood was "an outstanding flop." And apparently, Short agreed with that assessment. He said nothing, but he was seen watching with "a forlorn look" as the regulars took batting practice while Flood shagged balls in the outfield. Even so, Short had not given up on Flood, possibly because Flood had charmed him, or perhaps because he had to pay him for the season whether Flood played or not. But Flood was obviously unhappy with his distinctly limited role. It was embarrassing. On April 24, after singling in the tying run in a game the Senators later won, he told a *Washington Post* reporter, "People look for perfection; they look for it in everyone except themselves." Then, after two players interrupted the interview to congratulate him on salvaging the game, he said, as so often was his way in the past, "It delights me to be able to contribute something to the team." But his last words hid an undeniable bitterness. Perhaps it also hid a recognition that he had given all he could.[34]

Three days later, three weeks into the season, with seven hits in thirty-five at bats, Flood's attempt at a comeback ended. He took his clothes out of his locker, left the clubhouse, checked out of his hotel, and headed for New York. No member of the Senators' team or front office knew that he had left until just before that evening's game with Minnesota. Then Short hastily called a press conference. There he read a telegram Flood had sent from John F. Kennedy International Airport: "I tried. A year and one half is too much. Very serious personal problems mounting every day. Thanks for your confidence and understanding."[35]

33. *St. Louis Post-Dispatch*, March 24, 1971.
34. *Washington Post*, April 14, 25, 1971.
35. For Flood's wire, see *Washington Post*, April 28, 1971.

Short knew more than he said. Just before the press conference he phoned Joe Reichler, then assistant to Commissioner Kuhn and long a friend of Flood. He had asked Reichler to go to Kennedy and tell Flood that he was making a big mistake in abandoning his baseball career a second time. Reichler replied that Flood had called him about his situation a few days earlier. Flood had told Reichler that he was embarrassed and humiliated by his failure to play at a major-league level, and he had been a star too long to sit on the bench. He could not handle the punishing private "chats" with his manager and the bitter jokes and disdainful commentaries in the press, in the clubhouse, and even by outsiders. One scout watching him go hitless against a rookie pitcher had scoffed, "God, they don't even waste the curveball on him any more." Worse, he was deeply humiliated by his failure, as a seven-time Gold Glove winner, to play center field successfully. Altogether, he had told Reichler, it was too much to take, and he was thinking very seriously of abandoning his comeback. Reichler told Short that he asked Flood to postpone his decision: "I tried to explain to him that he shouldn't be discouraged, that fans didn't expect him to come back and hit .400. For a while I thought I convinced him. Then he told me: 'I owe Bob Short a great deal. He stuck his neck out for me.' However, quickly after he blurted: 'No, no. I'm not going to do it. I've reached the end. I'll go crazy if I don't get out.'"[36]

Despite what he had heard from Flood, Reichler respected Short's request and reached Flood at Kennedy at 7:15 p.m., but with Flood's plane scheduled to leave in forty-five minutes, they had little time to talk. Flood said he had to catch his flight to Washington, but Reichler peeked at the ticket and saw that it was marked "Barcelona," the Catalonian city on Spain's Costa Brava. When Reichler mentioned that he had seen the ticket, Flood just laughed and boarded his plane.

Many Senators were bewildered by Flood's departure, and a member of the Short family said some years later, "We all felt he had a nervous breakdown." Shelby Whitfield, the voice of the Senators on radio station WTOP, recalled two years later that Flood, despite a few reluctant, testy words to the press, never truly committed himself to being part of the team or to playing baseball. On the road he ate alone, in his room. In Washington he lived in one of the "swinging downtown sections . . .

36. On Short's desire to keep Flood and to help him with his financial problems, see *Oakland Tribune,* April 28, 1971, and *Washington Post,* May 1, 1971. But Whitfield, *Kiss It Goodbye,* 90–92, insists that Short was a publicity hound who was very unlikely to help anyone other than himself.

nursing his vodka martinis beginning at noon and wooing his women at all hours." Flood had not changed since Broeg had lectured him in the Cardinals' batting cage a year and a half before. "Tormented" was Whitfield's description of Flood's behavior while with the team and when leaving it. Fair enough, but why was Flood tormented? At the very least, one must assay the varied reasons that Flood felt such pressure that he left not only the Senators, but the country. Was it his inability to play at a major-league level? Was it being ridiculed? Or must his financial problems be factored in? And if so, how serious were they?[37]

That Flood had major financial problems is clear enough. Some are outlined in a deposition he filed in December 1970, but that document poses as many questions as it answers. Supposedly, he was to receive $50,000 when his manuscript was finished, but he did not record it in his deposition. It may be that the money was actually due him from the book's royalties, which he had not yet begun to receive; or it may be that he received the money in the form of a stated loan of $50,000 from an unidentified Barbara Sawyer. (This last is plausible as a means of avoiding garnishment by the IRS.) Otherwise, he declared about $10,000 in cash and stock offset by about the same amount in credit-card debt and bank loans. Flood also stated that he owed his ex-wife, Beverly, $20,000, but did not explain how he arrived at that number. According to the lawsuit filed by Beverly Flood Heath against his estate in July 1997, he had not paid her since October 3, 1968, and, although that suit overlooked a few dollars he sent her in 1982, he should have owed her somewhat more than $20,000 in December of 1970. Whatever the proper amount, Shelby Whitfield asserts that Beverly was hounding Flood, even that she had handed him a subpoena, but that cannot be confirmed. Indeed, Flood's deposition is riddled with unanswered questions—"Delmar Printing Company—Unknown," "Withholding Taxes—Unknown," and other significant issues, chief among them his problem with the IRS, that are not even addressed.[38]

Flood assumed that he owed the Delmar Printing Company, which was now alleging not only that CFA was deeply in arrears on its payment

37. Whitfield, *Kiss It Goodbye*, 152–53, 162; Kevin Short, telephone interview, early 2005.

38. Deposition of December 23, 1970, *Delmar Printing Company vs. Curt Flood Associates, Inc.*; Dick Young, "Will We Have to Pay the Bill," *New York Daily News*, Special, April 30, 1971, writes that Short advanced Flood "about $10,000, for back alimony and 'walking around money.'"

for "finishing" photographs but also that Flood himself was guilty of fraud. Zerman was handling the case, which had opened in early February. He did so, apparently, without compensation, as he always did with Flood. In federal district court in St. Louis he argued that his client was only a shareholder in CFA, that he played no part in running the business and was guilty of nothing. That argument contained a strong promise of success given Flood's absentee relationship with CFA. However, the same cannot be said about Zerman's arguments in the suit filed in January 1971 by Howard and Nancy Foster, from whom Flood and Jones had bought their photography business in the summer of 1969. The Fosters alleged that Flood and Jones owed them $34,000—the repayment of a promissory note both signed in July 1969 that they had failed to pay. The two trials continued well into 1971. With Zerman's help, Flood eventually was absolved of all liability in the Delmar case, but not in the clearly unwinnable Foster suit.[39]

Although Flood did not know the outcome of either the Delmar or Foster lawsuit in April, he probably knew he would lose the latter and that it would cost him at least $17,000. That proved to be the case after the judgment against him in July 1971 (the money may never have been collected). In total, Flood's debts, those he acknowledged and those he did not, those at the time and those looming, exceeded $100,000. Of course he might have expected royalties from his memoir, but Whitfield, who was well situated to know what was happening, asserts that Flood "quietly passed out copies to his new teammates, then refused to talk about the book, or to promote it at all, which might explain why the book did not make a bigger splash on the sports scene."[40]

Flood's refusal to market his book may have reflected his omnipresent insecurity and, at this juncture, his tormented state of mind. Of course, he might have filed bankruptcy, as Short reportedly urged, but his attorneys—probably meaning Goldberg and his firm—reportedly dissuaded him. In any case, bankruptcy would not have permitted his mother to

39. Deposition of December 23, 1970, *Delmar Printing Company v. Curt Flood Associates, Inc.,* Supplemental Complaint of October 1, 1970, and Judgment, August 27, 1971; *Howard and Nancy Foster v. Curt Flood and William M. Jones,* file no. 71C 14 (3), January 7, 1971, in U.S. District Court for the Eastern District of Missouri, Judgment of July 28, 1971.

40. *Delmar Printing Company v. Curt Flood Associates, Inc.; Howard and Nancy Foster v. Curt Flood and William M. Jones;* Whitfield, *Kiss it Goodbye,* 159.

escape an IRS lien on the home he had bought her. This was his—and her—major problem, but why is not clear. Apparently he did not pocket the money, and he was only an absentee owner of CFA, not responsible for its debts, as the St. Louis federal district court would say in August. Even so, the IRS held him responsible. The previous December it had assessed him $14,909, and it probably began to garnish his salary then, if not soon after. And if that problem was not crippling enough to force Flood to seek asylum abroad, he had to worry about his ex-wife hounding him for long-overdue spousal and child support, even, as one story had it, pounding on his door.[41]

Apparently, Flood never mentioned his financial problems to his teammates. And he did not mention them a quarter of a century later in reminiscing. He talked about the hate mail he received not only during spring training in Fort Lauderdale but also as the team played its way north. For the most part, the letters were much the same as those he had received before and during his trial the year before. But there was an added touch in April 1971. At Yankee Stadium he found a funeral wreath placed in front of his locker. He said later, "Coming on top of everything else, it really scared the hell out of me." And he did not believe he was paranoid in worrying. Without naming names, he thought of a St. Louis broadcaster he knew well, who an owner felt was having an affair with his wife; coming out of his hotel this man was hit by a car that jumped ten stairs to reach him. "'Curt,' I said to myself, 'you can't go through the rest of your life like this.' That's when I sent the wire to Bob Short. After that awful night in Yankee Stadium, I knew I had to get my ass out of this country. I simply could not cope with it."[42]

Obviously, Flood could not cope, but not cope with what, and where? The Senators' schedule makes clear that Flood did not react because of "an awful night in Yankee Stadium," at least not just before he appeared at JFK. He checked out of the Anthony House hotel in Washington the afternoon he left for the airport and not on the spur of the moment. Fear did not spur Flood to flee. Hate mail, racist jeers, and threats to his life were nothing new. He had survived the South. His financial problems, serious though they were and, fairly, part of the

41. Record of assessment in file no. 82–087024, Alameda County Court, Alameda, Calif.; Carter interview of October 8, 1998; and Whitfield, *Kiss It Goodbye*, 152.
42. Flood and Turan, "Outside-Outside," 32–34.

equation, probably were not the reason either. They were not about to go away, and there is reason to believe he thought about returning to the United States at an opportune time.

Flood implied a different reason for leaving later when he discussed why he had left for Spain: "I'd had so much press in Copenhagen that I couldn't hide even there," he recalled. This fits with what he told Reichler just a week before he left. He had been humiliated by being taken out during a game and by punishing private "chats" with his manager. He could not take it, as several members of the Washington team and their owner saw. Williams, who supported Flood publicly, as did Short, said the evening he left, "I do remember his eyes yesterday [Monday] looked like he hadn't slept very good. . . . The guy has had a hell of a lot of problems." Flood's roommate, Elliott Maddox, also knew he had problems, "but he didn't say what they were." Flood told no one else either. But the weekend before he left Washington, he paid the equipment manager, and said while he and Mike Epstein were shagging balls, "Things are closing in on me."[43]

It seems fair to say, then, that some serious financial problems, but especially his great embarrassment and fear of ridicule at failing to play at a major-league level, put Flood on Pan Am flight 154 to Barcelona, by way of Lisbon and Madrid, on the evening of April 27, 1971.

43. *Washington Post,* April 28, 29, 1971; Merrill Whittlesey, *Washington Star,* May 15, 1971.

X

Last Act

On April 28 Flood's plane landed in Barcelona. Despite what Reichler had seen on his ticket, the city was not his final destination. Earlier, in Copenhagen, he had heard excellent reports about Majorca, an island in the Balearic chain in the Mediterranean Sea, an hour's flight from Barcelona. He was told the weather was pleasant year-round, the Spanish peseta was weak—which meant that his dollars would stretch farther—and Palma, the port and main city, was charming. Most important, Palma was home to an English "colony," and he thought it would be easy to get along with the English expatriates there. Of course, many if not most Danes also spoke English, so language was not really the issue. The problem was the press in Copenhagen; it was from the press that he wanted to escape. Majorca, an island off the beaten track, looked like just the place to do it.[1]

As Palma was reported, so it turned out to be, a lovely, truly natural habitat for a man who, although he wanted to avoid notoriety, was looking for a place to drink, to play, and, if possible, to buy a nightspot or, if the last was too expensive, a small tavern. Flood's first of four years on the island went as well as he could have hoped. However, he did not settle firmly until after a foray to Copenhagen between May and August. Then he rented a beautiful, gated suburban home much larger than a single man could possibly need. Why he did so is not known, but in that era rents were cheap.[2]

The evidence regarding Flood's years in Majorca ranges from the hard—State Department documents—to the soft—the very limited memories of English expatriates still in the city, and Flood's own reminiscences

---

1. Flood and Turan, "Outside-Outside," 34.
2. Belth, *Stepping Up,* 189–90, whose sources probably were Bob Gibson and Lou Brock.

a quarter of a century after he left. When he discussed his time in Palma, Flood told of finding a congenial drinking hole, the Rustic Inn. Probably he saw it when he first arrived. It was located in the very-soon-to-be-fashionable Plaza Mediterraneo. Then only an offbeat, hard-to-find square a brief elevator ride up from his seaside Melia hotel, the plaza was bounded on three sides by pubs that English barkeepers leased from their Spanish land owners. Flood was seen tending bar at one of those pubs—the Rustic Inn—just after his return from Copenhagen, and by October he was looking for money to purchase it. He expected to use the $10,000 severance that he thought available from the major-league pension fund, but he soon found that a player had to wait twelve months after retiring from the game to get it. So he wrote Arthur Goldberg seeking a loan he promised to pay back in April, saying, "I wasn't very carefull [sic] with the money I had saved. I find myself in a tight situation." Goldberg's answer is not available, but he probably responded in the negative, if at all. In any event, Flood had a right to ask. However, the same cannot be said of the $5,000 he asked for and received from his half sister, Rickie Riley.[3]

He wanted the "emergency money" he had left under her name. He asked despite his knowledge that she faced a serious burden taking care of his mother, a burden for which he was chiefly responsible. Rickie had phoned him the previous spring to inform him that on May 12, two weeks after he left the country, the IRS had placed a lien on his property at 2907 55th Avenue, the house he purchased for his mother. Doubtless with good intentions, he had insisted that his mother move there, asserting that she could pay the mortgages and taxes from the rent on the two apartments in the triplex that she rented out. Now, Rickie had told him, his mother was forced to turn over the rent payments to the IRS. He responded rather curtly, "Do what you can so that mother does not have to move," but send the money.

Somehow, Rickie did both. Over time she saved her mother's home, paying the mortgages and taxes, and in 1982 she eliminated the IRS lien. How she accomplished this, other than having Flood relinquish the

---

3. For Flood's early movements in Palma, see Jimmie Angelopolous, a sportswriter for the *Indianapolis Star*, in a letter to Ted Williams, August 7, 1971, in author's possession; Flood to Goldberg, autumn 1971, following a letter from Marvin Miller to Flood of October 18, 1971, stating that he was not eligible for severance from the "Benefit Plan" (Arthur Goldberg Papers, Manuscripts Division, Library of Congress); Interview with Richard Carter, October 2, 1998.

property to her, only her real-estate lawyer might explain. Meanwhile, she had sent the $5,000 to her brother. Asked why years later, she offered a bit of insight into his appeal to many people before, during, and after his time in baseball. First she said, "He had a soft heart, even for dead-beats, he probably had given some people money that he should have kept, and he might have given some to Beverly." Rickie's assessment of her brother's soft heart is surely accurate—it is confirmed by Jody Kramer, his former mistress in St. Louis—except that he almost certainly did not send money to Beverly. On another occasion Rickie said of the check she sent her brother, "it was his money." It probably was, although hidden in her bank account. In any case, Rickie herself, always a mother surrogate, was too soft-hearted and selfless not to send it. As for Flood, however severe the distress that caused him to flee abroad, he dubiously left his mother with a lien on her home, and he left his sister to pick up the pieces. As for the check Rickie sent, it was not large enough to buy the Rustic Inn. But that problem was soon solved.[4]

As Flood said many years later, he "met a young lady from the states" while tending bar at his favored tavern. Either he could not recall the woman's name or he did not want it known, so he said, "Let's call her 'Anna.'" She had "a lot of money," so they bought a major interest in the Rustic Inn from its Spanish owner, who also owned outright the land beneath it. In Spain their partial ownership was known as a *trespasso*. For some time this was to be a distinction without a significant difference. The inn made money as sailors from the (American) Sixth Fleet came in regularly. Many of the Sixth Fleet's five thousand men came because they were black and Flood was black. Many others came because Flood was a celebrity in spite of his efforts to remain out of the limelight; many more because after he bought the inn, American movie stars and well-known political names began to crowd the plaza, and he was something of a celebrity as well as a compatriot. But the Rustic Inn had another very special attraction: Howard Cosell of ABC's *Wide World of Sports*, who was always supportive, sent Flood video

4. This story is based on interviews with Rickie Riley from 1998 to 2006; also Curtis C. Flood, Trustor, to Israel Gold and Sarah Malakoff, Trustees, October 23, 1968, Western Title Company, Records, Alameda County Courthouse; Notice of Default, Failure to Pay Taxes, by Curtis C. Flood, September 3, 1971, Western Title Co., Records, Alameda County Courthouse; Western Title Company to Harold J. Riley (Rickie's husband), Trustees Deed, January 3, 1972, copies in author's possession. Notice of Federal Tax lien forwarded from St. Louis, assessed December 11, 1970, applied to 2907 55th Ave., May 12, 1971, records, Alameda County courthouse.

tapes of the latest fights, which could be shown to an eager audience. Thus, for about four years Flood enjoyed an easy, carefree life. Perhaps that is why the English pub owners with whom he partied in the wee hours after closing did not speak of his drinking too much. Flood might have stayed fairly sober during this stress-free period. He even played a bit of baseball. According to the English bar owners still in Palma, one day Flood was challenged by the nearby El Terreno barrio to put together a team of bar owners and anyone else he wanted to recruit for a game. How much was bet on the game, no one recalled. It was recalled, however, that Bob Gibson and Lou Brock were in town—it was the off-season for baseball—and both men were recruited to play. No more needs to be said about the game's outcome or the bet.[5]

No wonder Flood enjoyed himself in Palma. At least he had a bar, even if it was not the Playboy Club, and apparently he had a very acceptable woman to live with, money, and a Porsche convertible in which to run around the island. Furthermore, he did not appear embittered by the Supreme Court's rejection of his appeal. Goldberg had argued the case in March, employing a brief that has been both criticized and praised and an oral argument that was too long to leave time for an adequate rebuttal. But what was written and said probably made no difference. Justice Harry Blackmun's majority opinion upholding the lower courts' decision did not rest solely or even largely on the case's merits—it was recognized that the reserve system was an "anomaly" and an "aberration"—but rather on "the confusion and retroactivity problems" that overturning *Federal Baseball* and *Toolson* would cause and, not least, their affection for the National Pastime. This last was reflected by Blackmun's writing into the opinion his personal Hall of Fame.[6]

5. Flood and Turan, "Outside-Outside," 34–35; for Flood's move to a new house, see his passport renewal, November 15, 1973, secured through FOIA; lunch interview with English expatriate Maureen Rowland (Africa bar owner) and Johannes Cornelius-Tringham, consular agent, July 3, 2001, Palma de Majorca; baseball story courtesy of Wendy Potyrala, resident of Palma and wife of Chuck Potyrala, writer for *Talk of the Town*, a local gossip magazine.

6. *New York Times* and *Washington Post,* June 29, 1972; also Robert Woodward and Scott Armstrong, *The Brethren: Inside the Supreme Court,* 189–92, for the alleged inside story. Of two lawyers in Goldberg's firm, one liked his brief, the other was critical, according to notations in Topkis's office. Of the decision, Topkis wrote to Goldberg on June 30, 1972, "the Supreme Court screwed us," and Goldberg replied on July 11, 1972, "I was not surprised . . . although I did expect better opinion writing" (Topkis papers).

After the Supreme Court's decision, Bruce Howard and Chuck Potyrala, interviewing Flood for the *Talk of the Town,* an English-language gossip sheet, found him a "happy man" despite the loss. Flood believed that his case had awakened Americans to the fact that "the reserve system was a throwback to slavery." He had no regrets. As for his future, he was "contented and optimistic." As the story's authors wrote, "his effervescent personality had turned his posh bar in Plaza Mediterraneo . . . into an oasis for Americans, Spanish, and Europeans of every stripe." And they concluded, "We left with a feeling that 'Curt Flood' . . . is very much alive and very well in Majorca."[7]

For four years, then, Flood did well in Palma. Then, one day in early or mid-1975, he disappeared from the city. Three decades later no one could say why with any certainty. Some speculated, probably very closely to the truth, that the other owner of the Rustic Inn, who was owner of the *trespasso* as well, disagreed with Flood over the rent and eventually incited the Guardia Civil (police) to withdraw his license. Flood in later explaining his disappearance did not mention an argument but did talk about the Guardia, whom he portrayed as the Spanish counterpart of the Nazi SS. He said later they could not understand how he was making so much money in his little bar and assumed—presumably wrongly—that he was selling drugs or laundering money, possibly even dealing in women. Accordingly, after watching him and his bar for a long time, they took advantage of a technicality to lift his liquor license, which had cost him $65,000. And that was not the end of the matter. As Flood explained, "They accused me of all kinds of ugly things and ended up giving Anna and me 48 hours to get out of town."[8]

Whether those "ugly things" were conjured up by the owner of the *trespasso* surely will never be known. Flood said later that he and Anna went to Andorra, a city-sized country in the Pyrenees, because "its extradition laws would prevent the Spanish police from messing with us." Then, too, at least some Andorrans spoke a Spanish dialect, a language Flood could adapt to because of his experiences playing in Latin America. However, Flood and Anna did not stay long, together or separately. At some point, but probably in the late summer, Anna disappeared from Flood's side: he had little or no money, and, probably

7. Bruce Howard and Chuck Potyrala, "Curt Flood—A Study in Courage," clipping, no date, in author's possession.
8. Flood and Turan, "Outside-Outside," 36; interviews with English bar owner, American consular agent, and their friends in Palma.

because of his problems, he began drinking heavily again. He also broke his arm. Later, he either did not remember much about his life in Andorra or did not want to, and probably both. A quarter of a century later he partially explained his situation: "I was getting deeper and deeper into a spiral into serious alcoholism that nearly killed me. My mother was ill, and I hadn't seen her in five years. It was time to come back. . . . And, deep down in my soul, I guess I really wanted to heal myself."[9]

One might gather from Flood's words that he came home of his own volition. But this is clearly at odds with readily available official documents. On October 1, 1975, the U.S. Consul General in Barcelona informed the State Department that Flood, "a former baseball player . . . well-known in the media," was in police custody in Andorra, held for drunkenly trying to rob a store. Later that very day the Consul General learned that because Flood had not actually taken any merchandise from the store, an Andorran judge would forgo charges; then, with mixed feelings, he heard that Flood would be put on a bus for Barcelona in two days.[10]

When Flood arrived in the Consul General's coastal domain, he was placed in a psychiatric ward to dry out. But that result did not please either Flood or the Consul General. Flood wanted to go back to Oakland as soon as possible, and the Consul General was anxious that he do so. The Consul General informed the State Department that Flood was a major embarrassment "because of his lawsuit against the baseball commissioner," and asked the department for instructions in handling Flood's debt and getting rid of him. The former ballplayer owed the hospital in Barcelona $300; he would owe more by the time he had dried out, and he was "destitute."

Shortly, it turned out that the hospital costs would not be a problem; the city would pick up the costs "if funds not available." Getting Flood home was, at least superficially, more complicated. The Consulate wanted the State Department to phone his mother to seek the airfare. If she could handle the cost, that was fine. If not, the Consulate recommended "approval of USG loan." That meant $330 for the fare to New York, apparently from State Department funds, and assistance from the

9. Interviews with English bar owner, American consular agent, and their friends in Palma.
10. Five total pages, dated October 1, 1975, to November (no date), exchanged between Consulate in Barcelona, Spain, and U.S. State Department, U.S Department of State, case no. 200202860.

Department of Health, Education, and Welfare for the flight from New York to Oakland.[11]

In short order the Consulate received an answer from Secretary of State Henry Kissinger reading, "Father informed Department that he would be sending prepaid ticket." It may be that Herman sent the ticket, but Rickie recalls paying for it. One way or the other, then, Flood was on his way home, back to the Oakland triplex he had purchased for his mother and where he would live off and on with her and Rickie, who was alone now that her husband had died.[12]

Flood did not tell his sister or anyone else in Oakland the real story of his return. He said that he was driving from Andorra to Barcelona on a motorcycle, accompanied by his dog. En route he fell and broke his arm, and when the police found he lacked the proper documentation for his cycle, they took it away. Fortunately, he continued, he was able to trade his dog for a ride to Barcelona. There, penniless and for some reason without clothes, he had asked the Consulate to phone his father.[13]

Although Flood's story of his return was not convincing, no one in the Bay area appears to have challenged it. If they had, Flood would probably have told them what he admitted twenty years later: his drinking had left him too "hazy and misty" to recall exactly his last days abroad. "I was putting away as much as a fifth a day. A lot of booze." But this should have been obvious to anyone who followed his tracks in the aftermath of his return. Not only did he frequent Oakland's bars, but he fractured his skull within the year following. According to the ever-protective Rickie, he fell off a ladder while getting on the triplex's roof. But three months later, Flood told Murray Chass of the *New York Times* a different story: he fell "down some stairs [after having] a few beers too many." Chass found Flood ready to joke: "They gave me a brain scan, and they found nothing." Flood's next few sentences further reveal his despondent state of mind. First, "The ability just to get up and do nothing is a delight to me." Then, "It's a little difficult to find a job for a used center fielder. You can't look in the want ads."

But being an ex-ballplayer without the skills demanded in the want ads was surely not the prime reason for Flood's bitterness. It may be recalled that during the first months of his battle for free agency, the

11. Ibid.
12. Ibid.
13. Riley interviews, 1998 to 2006.

Major League Baseball Players Association had negotiated a Second Basic Agreement with the club owners. It provided that all grievances except those involving alleged corruption should be handled by an independent arbitrator rather than the commissioner. And in December 1975, just two months after Flood returned from Europe, Peter Seitz, the new arbitrator, had newly interpreted Section 10A. In the past it had meant that even if a player did not sign a new contract, his old contract was automatically renewed, and this contractual process obviously could be repeated annually. However, as Seitz saw it, a contract was not automatically renewable, and when pitchers Dave McNally and Andy Messersmith, who had not signed contracts, appealed, he made them free agents. What Flood had fought for, if with a more extensive strategy, and lost, others had now won. No wonder he was bitter. Although he admitted that he had sued Major League Baseball "for me," publicly he appeared to be pleased with the number of players who now benefited from his fight against the reserve system. However, he also told Chass that he felt very bitter about fighting that battle alone. "I spent six weeks in New York during the trial," he told the reporter, "and not one player came to see what was going on." Worse, now when some of those highly paid players walked by him in a hotel lobby, they not only did not recognize him on sight, they did not know him even after he identified himself. If, as Flood told Chass, this was the case, it is no wonder that the reporter was prepared to give serious credence to the possibility, suggested by some in Oakland, that Flood's fall "down some stairs" was not an accident.[14]

Flood's apparent desperate drinking and bitterness, coupled with a desire for privacy on the one hand and an opportunity to tell his story on the other, reappeared in an interview with Richard Reeves little more than a year later. Reeves asked for the meeting to help prepare an article for *Esquire* about four men who had "stood up to the system." Flood seemed to resist: "Please don't come out here. Please. Don't bring it all up again. . . . Do you know what I've been through? Do you know what it means to go against the grain in this country? Your neighbors hate you. Do you know what it's like to be called the little black son of a bitch who tried to destroy baseball, the American Pastime?" It may have been the first time that Flood publicly, fully vented his feelings about the part he

---

14. Ibid.; Flood and Turan, "Outside-Outside," 37; Murray, *St. Louis Post-Dispatch*, reprint, September 12, 1976.

felt his color had played in his case against baseball. Then, after Reeves agreed to hear him speak at a Martin Luther King Day assembly in Sacramento, eighty miles away, he said the writer could interview him.[15]

At the high school assembly Flood did no more than repeat the story of his victimization at his trial: "I suddenly realized it was just me against nineteen millionaires." He said that no active player had shown up for his trial; that if he had been in their shoes, he probably would have been afraid of being seen there, too; and that no free agent had thanked him for his sacrifice. So, despite Flood's initial insistence that he did not want to "bring it all up again," that is precisely what he did when the opportunity presented itself, as it did in Sacramento. Moreover, he was willing to discuss his story with Reeves, so his story would spill over to a large audience via a popular magazine. But during a whole day's talking, he added nothing more than a few statements that don't pass the truth test. He said he returned to Oakland of his own volition, when State Department documents said otherwise. He said that he had spent $100,000 on legal fees, although he did not pay Zerman a cent, and his battle for free agency was paid by the Players Association. And he said that he had put money away, which was patently false: Rickie had sent him "his money" seven years before. What he lived on in his first two and half years back at home, Flood did not say, and Reeves did not ask. In fact, the writer told Flood's story as sympathetically as possible. He reported a friend of Flood's telling him before their interview, "Maybe you should leave him alone. Look, he took on something very big, and it broke him."[16]

Fortunately for Flood, the patrons of his youth were more than willing to help him in every way possible, including an attempt to repair his apparently broken spirit. Even today it passes understanding how far a very successful businessman like Sam Bercovich would go out of his way to help Flood get back on his feet. However, Bercovich warmly recalled the hard-working young man who dressed windows at his store and became a star on his American Legion teams; who then fought his way to the majors despite his size; and who had, more recently, fought a gallant battle against the powers that ruled Major League Baseball. Besides those intense memories, Bercovich was still impressed by Flood's charm and felt the least he could do was help him get on his

15. Richard Reeves, "The Last Angry Man," 41–48.
16. Ibid.

feet. Nominally, he made Flood a public relations consultant to his furniture company. However, this was a cover for Flood's coaching the same American Legion team he had played for twenty-five years before with Frank Robinson and Vada Pinson. Asked about his new job and what he was paid, Flood implied that it was unimportant, saying only, "I've not made that much money" over the least seven years. "I've been stripped of my security." That he had contributed to stripping himself, Flood could not acknowledge. But whether asked or not about the case he fought, he admitted, "You always have a little selfish thing in the back of your mind which asks 'did I give up too much to do this?' I'll never know."[17]

Bercovich's efforts to help Flood extended well beyond the lengths one might think likely, even given their friendship. In April 1978 Bercovich bought the radio rights to the Oakland A's games from Charles Finley, the club's owner, and lined up a major AM radio station in Oakland to carry the broadcasts, all this so Flood could do the color commentary alongside Bud Foster, a prominent Bay Area sports broadcaster. This prompted Flood to say to the *Oakland Tribune*, "I'm absolutely delighted to have a chance to be back around baseball games." And probably facetiously, he said it might be better than playing because he could go to the games without having "to hear about going 0-for-4, be considered an expert and get paid all at the same time."[18]

Unfortunately for Flood, on his first day a sportswriter from the *Los Angeles Times* syndicate, who was sent specifically to evaluate him, took a dim view of Flood's ability to communicate. By definition, a color commentator should enrich a baseball game for his audience. He should describe some of its more subtle points, and do so quickly, fluidly, and—at risk of stating the obvious—colorfully. Flood did none of those things. At times he answered Foster's prompts with "I beg your pardon," or "I haven't the slightest idea." At better moments he came up with meaningless comments. Asked what he thought of a bunt single, Flood did

17. Broeg, in *St. Louis Post-Dispatch*, June 21, 1972, argued that Flood was not in the pension plan because he had taken his severance; Marvin Miller responded (reported by Jack Herman in the *St. Louis Globe-Democrat*, June 23, 1972) that Flood had not lost it, that what he had taken was a loan repayable at 6 percent. It is possible that late in his life Flood repaid the loan, if there was such, and obtained his pension, but evidence to that effect was not available. For Flood's job or jobs with Sam Bercovich, see *Oakland Tribune*, October 16, 1977.

18. Composite of *Oakland Tribune*, May 1, 1978, and Charles Maher, St. Louis Globe-Democrat–Los Angeles Times News Service, May 9, 1978.

not describe its superb placement or discuss the art of bunting, but said only, "I liked it." It is no wonder the *Times*'s reporter covering Flood's new venture could only hope that his good radio voice, his real intelligence, and his knowledge of baseball would bring substantial improvement in the course of the A's season. Bercovich, who was risking $150,000 to put the A's and Flood on the air, could only hope that Flood improved very quickly.[19]

Flood's work did improve during the 1978 season; at least Bercovich said so. But it would be the last year in broadcasting for him and for Flood. However, 1978 was significant and positive for Flood in one respect. He received an invitation from the Cardinals to participate in a commemoration of twenty-five years of the club's ownership by the Anheuser-Busch brewery. Suddenly, bygones were bygones. By mid-June Flood was in St. Louis with Gibson, Brock, and other former teammates, absorbing a noisy welcome by 45,000 fans, and talking to sportswriters at length. In the main his behavior generally reflected his great pleasure at being back in Busch Stadium. He did not smoke or drink when cameras were present, and he joked with the press but said nothing that was provocative. Quite the contrary. He asserted that "Mr. Busch treated us like sons." As for General Manager Bing Devine and (believe it or not) Jim Toomey, the "middle-echelon coffee drinker in the front office" whose call about his trade had so deeply offended and tormented him, "they're super, super, super individuals. They paid me a half a million dollars to do that funny thing over there [in Busch Stadium]. We were a family. We won, we lost, we were up and we were down. We were so emotionally involved." So far so good; Flood was diplomatic. But then he lost it: the gates of his pent-up bitterness crashed. "And suddenly it [his Cardinals career] no longer existed. In 30 seconds, 12 years of life were gone. How would you feel?" Of course, everyone reading his words knew what he meant.[20]

Flood's return to St. Louis marked a lone bright spot in what was otherwise a dark, decade-long span in his life that began with his departure from Majorca. Although he had failed as a baseball commentator, he retained two connections with the game. Bill Patterson, his mentor at DeFremery twenty-five years earlier, was now general supervisor of

19. Ron Bergman, *Oakland Tribune*, May 4, 1978.
20. Joe Castellano, *St. Louis Globe-Democrat*, June 10, 1978.

sports and aquatics for the City of Oakland, and he found Flood a job in his department as commissioner of Youth America Baseball, which was the title of the Little Leagues in the city. But finding Flood a job involving children and getting him into it were two different things. Mayor Lionel Wilson, brother of the Harold Wilson who had helped Flood when he was an adolescent, knew that Flood was an alcoholic and viewed his employment by the city as questionable. However, he was satisfied when Patterson assured him that he had been working on rehabilitating Flood and that Flood was no longer drinking. That problem "resolved," Flood went to work forty hours a week during the spring and summer at $500 a week. The money was far from what Flood had been accustomed to in his years with the Cardinals, but he poured as much time and energy into it as if it were the major leagues. He enjoyed working with some 3,000 boys and a few girls. And with the aid of films of great major-league hitters such as Rod Carew and, in Flood's view, Detroit slugger Willie Horton, along with equipment supplied by other major-leaguers like future Hall of Famer Reggie Jackson and donations from still others, among them Joe Morgan, also a future Hall of Famer, he often provided personal instruction. Presumably, given the support Flood received from these men, they remembered him fondly and well. Perhaps it was because he had been a great player and a good friend, but beyond that they presumably felt that, although he had lost his challenge to the reserve system, his battle for free agency had been at least inspirational, and possibly material, in the realization of free agency five years later.[21]

Meanwhile, Flood continued to benefit from his close relationship with Bercovich. The furniture man used his friendship with Charles Finley to find Flood a place in the A's front office handling public relations. Ironically, despite the title, Flood again found himself handling matters of the same import as had Toomey, whom he scorned in his memoir. Among other duties, he worked as a go-fer for Finley. Often this meant rounding up members of the A's who slipped away for a bit of fun, and one such trip took him to Las Vegas. There, in a Riviera Hotel elevator, he ran into Marc Risman, a local lawyer and very avid sports fan, who recalls somehow becoming a very good friend fairly quickly and keeping a close eye on Flood ever after.[22]

21. Patterson interviews, 1998 to 2005.
22. Bercovich interviews, 1998–2004; Marc Risman interview, August 9, 2000; Riley interviews, 1998–2006.

Risman knew Flood only from photos he had seen, but thought he looked "horrible, a shadow of his former self." He saw "sunken eyes" and some other characteristics of a man he felt certain was ravaged by alcohol. Risman's memory of Flood does not corroborate the picture of a rehabilitated Flood that Patterson had painted for Oakland's mayor. Possibly, Patterson was blinded by many years of friendship, or by seeing Flood so often that he failed to note the changes, although for a brief span of time after he was hired, Flood probably was sober.

Shortly before his 1977 interview with Reeves, Flood's sister Barbara introduced him to the woman in Alameda who apparently was at least the primary source of Snyder's information about Flood's portrait work being fanciful. Karen Brecher was from a middle-class family. She worked for the Alameda Welfare Department. She tried to help Flood restart his portrait business, and, not least, she took him to Alta-Bates Medical Center in Berkeley in 1980, where after thirty days he sobered up. How long Flood remained sober is not clear. Indeed, the exact nature of his relationship with Karen is disputed, as is the reason he left her. One newspaper referred to her as Flood's wife; Snyder implies that he lived with her until 1983, when he received his pension (the last a matter that cannot be confirmed because the MLBPA will not release the information). Rickie insists that Flood lived in his mother's apartment during the entire six-year period, staying at Karen's a night or two or more every week, and that he left her when he learned that his father was terminally ill with cancer. Whichever story is correct about Flood's relationship with Karen, Flood admitted shortly before his death that his "drinking problem" in the early and mid-eighties was "terrible," and everybody in his hemisphere knew "except me and Pete Rose."[23]

Beginning in 1983, when he learned of his father's illness, Flood often flew to Los Angeles to comfort Herman as best he could. Apparently he flew to see his father countless times, a mode of travel that he had always feared and which may have sparked his heavy drinking again. It is also likely that his father's death in 1985 prompted in him a new sense of his own mortality and contributed to his desire to further secure what he believed his legacy: his inspirational battle that had led to the liberation of all baseball players from the game's reserve system. Although he now

23. Riley interviews, 1998–2006; Flood and Turan, "Outside-Outside," 40; *Oakland Tribune*, June 12, 1983; Snyder, *A Well-Paid Slave*, 325, 333; *St. Louis Post-Dispatch*, May 26, 1981.

complained that, unfortunately, higher salaries had led to higher prices at the ballpark, he coupled this regret with even greater displeasure that too many players walked by him in hotel lobbies and did not speak to him of his contribution to their well-being. Not only that: he thought baseball fans throughout the country ignored what he had accomplished, although he never said whether that was stirring the consciousness of other players or in a more tangible sense contributing to the Second Basic Agreement. In any event he felt unappreciated. He was honored for his (unspecified) "contribution" by Oakland's NAACP in 1980, but that was important only in the Bay area. Flood wanted national recognition, and sometime in the mid-eighties he began working with a screenwriter on a movie script that would highlight his battle against baseball's reserve system. One day in 1985 this screenwriter, while thinking about a woman to cast for the projected movie, asked him, "Didn't you used to date Judy Pace when you were younger? Wouldn't it be interesting if we got her to play a part in the movie?" Flood agreed that it would and, after setting up a luncheon date with her, off they flew to Los Angeles.[24]

What might have been only a brief visit with the actress instead dramatically changed Flood's life. The lunch, as Flood recalled happily years later, "turned into a three day affair and, two or three weeks later, I moved back to Los Angeles." No wonder—as Rickie points out, no one had ever taken Judy's place in his heart. Thus he and Judy renewed the intimate relationship severed fifteen years earlier, after their trip to Puerto Rico and his decision to challenge baseball's reserve system. That had been a life-changing decision for both of them. Despite four years of a loving relationship, she had to recognize the dire prospect of life with an alcoholic who was on a quixotic mission that would leave him without a decent future, while her career was about to flower. She would receive excellent reviews in 1970 for her performance in *Cotton Comes to Harlem*, and she appeared in *Brian's Song* a year later. However, she did little acting other than for television after that. Perhaps this was because in 1972 she married Donald "Don" Mitchell, best known as detective and lawyer Raymond Burr's aide and bodyguard in the television series *Ironside*, and raised two children. However, by the

24. Flood's award ceremony, *Oakland Tribune*, March 9, 1980, multi-page program courtesy of Bill Patterson, who chaired Flood's induction as a member of the NAACP; for Flood's decision to fly to Los Angeles, see Flood and Turan, "Outside-Outside," 40.

mid-eighties she had divorced Mitchell and was free except for an ongoing legal battle over ownership of their house. Then, out of the blue, Flood turned up, and the candle of their love, clearly never snuffed, burned brightly again. To be sure, Flood was still an alcoholic and was drinking heavily, but Judy was now a mature forty-three and, as her legal battle with Mitchell and various later legal battles makes eminently clear, a determined woman and a tough fighter. In 1985 she was prepared to fight for Flood. She could deal with his alcoholism. So, after a lunch that obviously did more than renew their earlier affair, Flood moved to Los Angeles, and they were wed.[25]

Flood needed Judy desperately. He insisted later that he could not have stayed sober without his wife's help, although for several years he did not stay sober. And their relationship was not an easy one. He said later they "kind of hung on each other and scuffled right through it." Surely, intense financial stress was the bane of their existence. Judy recorded her income in 1987 at $800 a month, and Flood's income (pension or no) added on did not begin to meet their needs. A private investigation firm hired by Beverly after Flood's death found that they defaulted on their mortgage payments twice and on loans three times; one of the loans was for just a little more than $1,000. Apparently, Judy handled money no better than her husband or, for that matter, Beverly, whose spending had so incensed Flood. No wonder he was stressed and as always continued to drink heavily, although later in the decade he stated that his drinking had "a lot to do [with] the paranoia that was stored up in me." What, exactly, that meant he did not explain, but he did say he was still bitter because "organized baseball . . . has kept me at arm's length [because] I truly pissed them off." Whether Flood really suffered from paranoia or was just intensely bitter, he finally realized that he had to stop drinking. Probably he was hard-pressed by Judy, but in the early nineties he entered a hospital, and after spending what he called "21 days of sheer agony . . . gained sobriety." Of course, even then he had to deal with his alcoholism on a day-to-day basis; there is no cure for the disease.[26]

25. *St. Louis Post-Dispatch*, January 24, 1987. For Judy Pace's fight with Mitchell, see Los Angeles County record D14155304.25, 1985, Los Angeles County Court.

26. For Judy Pace's income and the Floods' litigations and defaults, see TransWest Investigations, Inc., 3–5 (copy in author's possession), and Flood and Turan, "Outside-Outside," 40.

Flood insisted later that his marriage was the decisive factor in his battle to stay sober. But there were other factors. Beginning in 1985 or 1986 he became one of several former major-leaguers invited to participate in a "fantasy baseball camp" organized by Dr. Andy Cameron in Reno, Nevada. As is typical of such camps, the major-leaguers mixed with the "campers," many of them baseball fans wishing to meet their favorite pros, but some very much interested in instruction and playing. This was the fantasy camp's main attraction, but there were also after-dinner lectures, including one of significance by Flood. One evening he lectured on bigotry. In doing so he commented that he had fired a potential biographer who was "short, fat, and Jewish." This remark rightly offended a Jewish camper, a dermatologist from St. Louis. He challenged Flood from the floor, asking if he fired the writer because he was short, because he was fat, or because he was Jewish. Flood responded that he did not realize that what he said was anti-Semitic. However, after the lecture he walked over to the camper, and they discussed the issue at some length. Flood repeated that he did not realize his words might be seen as anti-Semitic; he had fired the writer because he was not empathetic—whatever that meant and why or why not—and he apologized for having given offense. The St. Louis–based dermatologist accepted Flood's explanation, and the two became friends, exchanging letters until Flood's death. He might have wondered, though, as the reader with an extensive knowledge of Flood's mentors and friends might, why Flood was so lacking in sensitivity when he not only knew so many Jews but readily accepted so much critical help from Bercovich, Zerman, Miller, Cosell, and Topkis, all of them Jewish. Richard Carter, Flood's ghostwriter, questioned about Flood's possible anti-Semitism some years later, labeled it as nothing more serious than an atavistic reflection on the numerous Jewish landlords in West Oakland where he grew up. But as always, whatever Flood's reason for his admitted blunder, he still had the natural saving grace that had served him so well, so often: an ability to charm and evince goodwill, and to reach out and to develop a tight, lifelong friendship.[27]

Judy notwithstanding, probably no friends were more crucial to Flood's mental health in the late eighties than Oakland's Bill Patterson, Mayor Lionel Wilson, and Joe Morgan, men who had saved him during

27. Dr. Jerome Aronberg interview, June 18, 2003, Aronberg e-mails, November 17, 18, 2005; Richard Carter to author, November 10, 1998 (copies in author's possession).

his darkest period in the preceding decade. In 1989 they produced another honor for Flood: the city of Oakland dedicated the Curt Flood Sports Complex, an elaborate affair that included three softball fields, a soccer field, a field house, and paved, lighted parking. At the same time, Flood received an honor that also contributed, albeit briefly, to his always tender self-esteem. In 1989 the newly organized Senior Professional Baseball Association appointed him its commissioner. He was now charged with supervising eight Florida-based teams composed of players thirty-five and older. Flood told Sean McAdam of the *Providence Journal* that he saw a bit of irony in being a member of management. In that context, he reflected on salaries. He thought he could be sensitive to both management and labor. He wanted it known that it had not been his intention, in his lawsuit, to bankrupt owners, only to secure the right for a player to negotiate for his fair worth. Then he added, perhaps without thinking it through, "I was being a little selfish for myself and for my family." No one asked him how free agency would have helped his family when he had not paid alimony and child support for a year before he plunged into his lawsuit. As for the Senior League, unfortunately for Flood it collapsed after two years.[28]

Flood was unemployed and, worse, had lost a position of some prestige. But he stayed busy and apparently was a contributing member of the community in the City of Angels. In either the 1980s or early 1990s he founded the Curt Flood Youth Foundation. The organization and its work thereafter seem to have benefited from the cooperation of Tom Bradley, the mayor of Los Angeles, who was introduced to Flood by Patterson. But whatever its origins, a private investigation in 1997 found that the organization was financially minuscule; its office was lodged in the Flood home; Judy, her sister, and a friend helped administer it; and Judy paid her home's utility bills from its funds. Unfortunately, the only available measure of the Curt Flood Youth Foundation's achievements is to be found in a 1994 letter Flood wrote to his new fantasy camp friend in St. Louis, in which he noted that the foundation "placed 35 Foster Care kids in jobs" that summer.[29]

If Flood left the management of the foundation to his wife, possibly it was because he was too busy flying to engagements well beyond Oak-

28. McAdams column, *St. Louis Post-Dispatch*, September 30, 1989.
29. TransWest Investigations, Inc., Regarding Judy Pace Flood, October 27, 1997 (copy in author's possession); Flood letters to Dr. Jerome Aronberg, Christmas 1994 (copies in author's possession).

land. Clearly, he had emerged from the anonymity of the years just after his return from Europe. Times had changed. As free agency became accepted—in 1986 the *St. Louis Post-Dispatch* called it "a part of baseball"—Flood's stature grew. Increasingly, he was in demand. He attended Cameron's Reno fantasy camp, but others as well. In 1986 he joined other former Cardinals at a fantasy camp in Mesa, Arizona. And after that he received requests to speak, not only about baseball, but also as an artist: in 1990 he gave the commencement address at Savannah's College of Art and Design. Then, too, he was honored in 1993 at a black-tie dinner in New York hosted by the Rawlings Company and attended by one of his sons, probably Curt Flood, Jr., and his daughter, Debbie. Former Cardinals teammate Bill White, now the president of the National League, presented Flood with his Gold Glove for the 1969 season, a presentation that had been aborted by Flood's decision to sue baseball; Flood called attention to the delay by saying, "A strange thing happened to me on the way to receive that Gold Glove." He did not add that earlier he had called White's or Rawlings' attention, and perhaps both, to the oversight.[30]

Early in 1995 Flood received another honor, one surely significant for him: he was inducted into the Bay Area Hall of Fame. Arguably, there was no other regional Hall of Fame with as many stars in so many sports. Flood's presenter that night was Vada Pinson, who had driven from South Florida to honor his close friend. And Flood expected to return the favor when he heard that Pinson was to be inducted into the Bay Area Hall of Fame in 1996. But it was not to be for either man. Sometime before October 21 Pinson was found on the floor of his home, dead. Flood did not know when exactly Pinson had died; no one did. However, Flood knew, sorrowfully, that he could not attend his friend's funeral. He was suffering from throat cancer and had begun his second cycle of chemotherapy, meaning, of course, that he was diagnosed and treated earlier. This time the chemotherapy was coupled with radiation, and his doctors told him he could not leave. He told the press that his prognosis was good—that he had not been sick—he meant that he had not lost his hair or his "testiness"—and his doctors said his illness was 90 to 95 percent curable.[31]

Flood's doctors were wrong. On Monday, January 20, 1997, he died. On a Monday, seven days later, he was buried. People once famous and in

---

30. Clarence E. Wilson, Jr., "Curt Flood's 9th Inning," a partial clipping; Joseph Durso, *St. Louis Post-Dispatch*, February 6, 1986, and November 19, 1993.

31. *St. Louis Post-Dispatch*, October 26, 1995.

some instances still famous arrived for his preplanned funeral. Judy had sent out invitations, and positive responses flew in from across the country: Flood's family came from Oakland; Bob Gibson from Omaha; Bill Patterson, Joe Morgan, and Sam Bercovich from the Bay Area; Lou Brock from St. Louis; and a variety of celebrities came from Washington, New York, Chicago, and Las Vegas, including Marc Risman—all men who had known Flood well. Curiously, two other men who had known him well and played absolutely critical roles in his life, Marvin Miller and Allan Zerman, did not attend, Miller because he had a serious heart problem (he sent a eulogy), Zerman because he was not invited and, surprisingly, one might think, did not know his onetime client had died. Even so, the First African Episcopal Church, or FAME as the beautiful church was known, was full for what Flood's sister Barbara later disdainfully labeled a "production."

Entering the church, the mourners received a colorful multipage "programme." Curt's 9th Inning, as its title read, portrayed Flood in his Cardinals' uniform with his number—21—emblazoned front and back. Inside was a full-page poem by Judy's brother-in-law, the 23rd Psalm, a summary of Flood's achievements on and off the field, his honors, notice of a fifteen-minute Spike Lee and Bryant Gumbel movie about the departed hero soon to be shown on HBO, and notice of legislation a Michigan congressman and a Utah senator had recently introduced that would, if passed, remove baseball's antitrust exemption. Then the brochure asserted, if inaccurately, that Flood's lawsuit "changed the face of professional sports by opening the door to free agency." That ignored the already-opened door in other premier professional sports, and it did not say how Flood's challenge in 1970 led to free agency in baseball in 1975. Neither did Reverend Jesse Jackson's eulogy, in which he argued that "Curt Flood must go into the Hall of Fame." Nor did Jackson's assertion that today's players "must be challenged to pay a reward for all he did." What kind of reward, and to whom? Of course, Jackson may have been right in asserting that "Because Curt won, baseball is better, people are better. America is better." But the only thing fairly certain is that baseball players' wallets, especially those of the stars, have grown much thicker, their bank accounts and investments much fuller, and their many other accoutrements much more numerous, larger, and fancier since free agency.[32]

---

32. Ibid., January 28, 1997. This bill, introduced by Congressman John Conyers of Detroit and Senator Orrin Hatch of Utah, the Curt Flood Act of 1998, removed baseball's antitrust exemption only as it involved labor relations.

Six days before Flood's funeral, in the morning-after obituaries and those in the weeks following, most columnists echoed Jackson: Flood was a hero approaching the proportions of the civil rights leaders of the sixties. To nationally read political pundit and baseball fan George Will, who spoke at Flood's funeral and later wrote a brief essay about him, Flood was a martyr in the lineage of Dred Scott, an inspirational figure in the model of Rosa Parks. Then and later, the retired players who attended the funeral—no active players attended—and columnists alike projected the same theme: Flood "paved the way" for free agency. But none specified how. Neither did his widow then nor, as best can be known, later. But it might have been argued that Flood's December 1969 letter to Bowie Kuhn seeking his freedom to negotiate with any club that he wished publicly exposed the injustice of a commissioner appointed and paid by the club owners dealing with players' grievances, and that this exposure led quickly to the Second Basic Agreement. However, even if Flood's letter led directly to an independent arbitrator who in 1975 would declare two players—Andy Messersmith and Dave McNally—free agents, establishing this right for all ballplayers after them, his role would not necessarily confirm him as a hero. It would not unless he stepped up for ballplayers' rights, as two recent biographers have asserted, with sharply focused, reasoned judgment, and standing on firm moral ground.[33]

Did he? Alex Belth in *Stepping Up: The Story of Curt Flood and His Fight for Baseball Players' Rights* and Snyder in *A Well-Paid Slave*, both published almost a decade after Flood's funeral, assert that he did. So the eulogistic words read at Flood's death persist. But while Belth emphasizes Flood's fight as a battle for basic civil rights for all ballplayers, only hinting at race as a factor, Snyder's more widely researched and more richly detailed appraisal clearly portrays Flood as a black activist in the mold of Jackie Robinson. However, Snyder, unlike Belth,

33. George Will, "Dred Scott in Spikes," 276–79; Thomas Boswell, *Washington Post,* April 22, 1997; John L. Mitchell, *Los Angeles Times,* January 28, 1997, for "sowed the seed." Among other obituaries, Joseph Durso, *New York Times,* January 21, 1997, is notable because in a three-column story, he devoted three paragraphs to Flood's miscue in the 1968 World Series; Mike Eisenbach, *St. Louis Post-Dispatch,* January 26, 1997, also spent ink on it; as for Bob Broeg, *St. Louis Post-Dispatch,* January 27, 1997, he mentioned it only in passing; while Rick Hummel, *St. Louis Post-Dispatch,* January 21, 1997, did not mention it at all. A list of some who attended Flood's funeral are named in the color brochure, "Curt's 9th Inning," available to mourners; some others are listed in the *St. Louis Post-Dispatch,* January 28, 1997.

humanizes his hero. He admits that Flood had feet of clay, but he depicts those clay feet almost exclusively in the aftermath of the trial, when Flood was deep into alcohol and expectably bitter. More important, he reports that while Flood at that time told many reporters he was pleased with his fight for free agency, he told Karen that if he had known his fight would leave him impoverished, he would not have fought it. This admission forces the response that Flood had to realize before he sued that he would face crippling problems if he sued Major League Baseball. Zerman and Miller had warned him. He had shrugged them off and plowed ahead.

It must be reasserted, then, that Flood was not thinking in a focused, reasoned manner when he agreed to challenge baseball's reserve system. The evidence is substantial. His decision must be viewed against his sensitive, brooding temperament and failure to handle pressure, as well as his alcoholism, quick temper, and at times irresponsible behavior, as they and his sense of being a victim interacted with his failure to catch Northrup's line drive in the 1968 World Series. Whether he should have caught it is not the issue. Errors are part of the game, as of life, but the truly successful accept their failures and move on. Flood could not. He admitted at one time or another to being "completely bushed" and slipping on wet turf, but he did not admit to misjudging the ball, which, it appears, was his real problem that afternoon. Why Flood misjudged it is the question. No answer can be certain, but there is good reason to believe that Beverly's mid-September demands in Alameda for more alimony and child support effectively distracted him then, as it did at other times when he slipped up during the series. This explanation is reinforced by his failure to send her the bimonthly check due a week later and, with an exception many years later, and that a brief one, his refusal to accept his legal and moral obligations to her and, especially, their children.

Flood's failure to accept his responsibilities meant that he saw himself, as always, as a victim. Such is his self-portrait in his 1971 memoir and in his interviews after his return from exile abroad. First, he was a victim of the dark "West Oakland Ghetto," then of "the Peckerwoods." After that it was manager Solly Hemus, who could not see him because he was black; later, it was Gussie Busch, demoralizing him and the team; after that it was the front office hounding him about his business enterprises, and, at last, it was Jim Toomey, a flunky in the Cardinals' front office simply carrying out his orders. The only flaw Flood admits is failing to notice that Carl was on drugs and dangerous to his career, not to mention to himself and others, and even this he excuses. At the same time, also in 1969, he ignores his March salary ultimatum, Carl's arrest and conviction, and any failures of conduct on his part or that of other Cardinals prior to Busch's March clubhouse lecture. He also denies having done anything to incur his "persecution" in the season following. It seems clear, then, that he was, as Broeg told him, the problem, part of it too much Bacchus and too little Morpheus, but this warning Flood apparently rejected. And beyond all else, Flood boiled at being informed of his trade to Philadelphia by "a middle-echelon coffee drinker" rather than by Bing Devine, the Cardinals' general manager.

As Flood reacted to what he saw as a deliberate insult, even worse than the unfair trade itself, bitterness festered. In short order Marian Jorgensen, his manipulative confidante, suggested if not prodded: "Why not sue?" Thinking about it in Copenhagen, he concluded that the trade itself was not only unfair but wrong, and he returned home wondering what could be done about those who persecuted him. Allan Zerman, his lawyer and friend, offered some answers. Flood might sue, but he could not sue the Cardinals as they were following the rules of Major League Baseball. However, Flood could attack the root of the rules, the reserve system, by suing baseball and having the courts overturn the system as an unconstitutional infraction of the Sherman Antitrust Act. And Zerman seems to have thought that Flood might win without taking his case to the upper reaches of the judicial system. But Zerman did not have the resources for such a suit and instead sent Flood to Marvin Miller and the Players Association, which did have the money and a law firm but also a more extensive strategy. All this time Flood was warned, first by Zerman, then time and again by Miller, that his case was extremely chancy, that in St. Louis Busch would be able to hurt him, that it was very unlikely that he would play again, and that he would probably get no money from the case even if he won. And yet he went forward, pushed surely by the sense of injustice that stemmed from what he felt was his persecution. But even if he was acting righteously, stepping up for all victimized ballplayers, he was acting irresponsibly. If he did not play ball again, he would not make a decent income. Without it he could not pay court-ordered alimony and, surely more important, child support. If he was "stepping up," as Belth contends and Snyder agrees, it was to the chopping block, and he was forcing others who lacked any choice to join him.

However, Flood's lawsuit was not the only field in which he acted irresponsibly. He ignored CFA, Inc. Too late he saw that it was failing and could not pay Delmar Printing Company for its services. Worse, he ignored the danger involved when he and Bill Jones signed a promissory note; worse yet, he did not make certain that his corporation's FICA taxes were paid; and, worst of all, he left for Spain knowing that the IRS would slap a lien on his mother's home. What could have been more irresponsible and immoral than to leave his mother in the lurch?

What, then, shall we say of Curt Flood? Was he a hero, later a martyr, for trying to modify the reserve system? Was he a rogue for failing to fulfill his obligations to his ex-wife, his children, and his mother? Twenty-five years earlier, Bob Broeg had insisted that Flood was fighting for principal, not principle. If Broeg meant a "pot of gold" should Flood win his lawsuit, doubtless he was wrong. But making money was not altogether beyond Flood's mind. He told the *Post-Dispatch* in 1989, and Snyder acknowledges that he told *Sport* some years before, "I was a little selfish for me and my family. I figured if I could negotiate with two teams . . . it would put more bread on the table. No way in the wildest stretches of my imagination could I have seen what was going to happen."[34]

Of course that was not true; he had been forewarned. It is true that putting more bread on the table is a fair motive when one has a family to feed, but it is not consonant with a man who did not take care of his family and at the same time sang the song of civil rights. So the myth of Curt Flood as a heroic, principled, self-sacrificing martyr to free agency has to be modified. It emerged because he was a great center fielder and an often charming man whom the St. Louis Cardinals traded with good reason, but threw out in a cruel manner, only to have him fight back, even though it cost him the game he loved, his livelihood, and much of his future and those of others.[35]

This is not to say that Flood's story as written here is the be-all and end-all. Probably it will not satisfy many people in a number of respects,

---

34. Belth leaves references to important aspects of Flood's personal life to a chapter titled "Aftermath," when probing them more deeply and integrating them earlier might have impaired his thesis. Beyond that there are errors of fact, among them that Flood's ghostwriter was not black (63), Flood's "business ineptitude" landed him not in small claims court but a federal district court (174), and Flood was not diagnosed with cancer in the spring of 1996 but almost a year earlier (199). Snyder, *A Well-Paid Slave*, 331. *St. Louis Post-Dispatch*, September 30, 1989.

35. Snyder, *A Well-Paid Slave; St. Louis Post-Dispatch*, September 30, 1989.

from its explanation of Flood's failure to catch Northrup's drive and on to his ultimatum, his differences with the Cardinals' front office in 1969, and his response to Jim Toomey's phone call informing him of his trade. Perhaps there is no absolutely satisfactory answer either to Marian's influence on Flood's decision to challenge baseball's reserve clause. We also cannot know with any assurance what made him an alcoholic or how his alcoholism affected his decisions in late 1969 and over the next year and a half. Even the reasons why he gradually dropped a measure of his post-1971 bitterness are uncertain, although it is clear that he was greatly pleased by the Cardinals' invitation to come to Busch Stadium for the ten-year reunion of the 1968 team, and by the way that baseball continued to flourish after free agency in 1975. Perhaps it was his belief that his battle contributed to free agency that helped improve his spirit, the lack of recognition by other players notwithstanding. It appears, also, that by the mid-eighties, perhaps earlier, he began to feel that his battle was truly important. Over time applause for his battle came his way; he was *somebody* once again.

In the end, as with anyone, Flood's achievements and his failures may be seen as a combination of his nature and nurture, including their setting in a transitional, very difficult era for a black man. He was fortunate to have parents who bequeathed him artistic and athletic talent, ambition, and the gift of charm. Unfortunately, they also bequeathed him an unusually sensitive, brooding temperament, a family history of alcoholism, and a tendency to place the blame for his problems on others—at times this meant individuals he encountered; at other times it was the white establishment, despite his many white friends who went out of their way to help him and who might have been members of that establishment were they not Jewish, and even then were often powerful figures. Flood would have done better, as well, had his parents been able to provide him with more height and strength, and with it greater confidence. The last he needed desperately. Too often he worried too much over too little, making others, most notably his first wife, bear the burden of the pressures he faced. And too often, his insecurity, perhaps linked to his size, made him see himself as a victim. Surely this last was a crucial factor in his eventual decision to sue baseball: disregarding his future and those of others, he insisted on seeking vengeance, and as he could not get it against the Cardinals, then he would get it against the baseball establishment.

But there are no definitive answers to Flood's life story, any more than there are to the lives of other men and women. Too many questions remain. What did he mean when he wrote at the end of the first chapter of his apologia, "I am pleased that God made my skin black, but I wish he had made it thicker"? Why did he need what seemingly were mother surrogates, from his sister Rickie to Marian Jorgensen, Karen Brecker, and even his wife, Judy? There are these and more questions to be asked about a man's life, and perhaps in time more will be asked about Curt Flood, the man behind the myth.

Those who look for Flood will find complexity. If he was not the mythical hero his eulogists have portrayed, he was surely one of the best center fielders to play the game, as well as, unusually, an artist, guitarist, and engraver. He was also a charitable man, and to some, particularly his team, he was intensely loyal. And to his credit—and their own—his friends and mentors from his childhood remained loyal after his fall from baseball's graces, truly going out of their way to sustain him after his return from Spain. Unfortunately, by his late fifties no one could help Flood to any measurable degree. He had to fight the unbelievable pain of throat cancer, but he did it with unusual courage. Even though he was unable to speak, he was not speechless. He wrote letters to the last. Fortunately, in his last decade he had again found—and this time married—Judy Pace, who first helped him deal with his alcoholism and then to cope with his last, deadly disease. If later she did what she could to perpetuate his myth, appearing in movies and attending events that lent it credence, it is to be understood. But she was not the only person to endorse his life: there were both Bill Patterson, Flood's mentor at DeFremery and helpful friend later, who keeps Flood's picture next to that of Hall of Famer Joe Morgan in his foyer, and there was Sam Bercovich, who did so much to boost Flood's career, tried his best to help him later, and set aside a room to memorialize him. Those three, at the least, did what they could to sustain if not enhance the Curt Flood they knew: a charming and gracious man, a superb center fielder, a self-sacrificing pioneer of free agency, and a martyr to Major League Baseball's reserve system.[36]

36. For Judy Flood's contribution, see chap. 2, note 18. Curt Flood Memorial Field Dedication, July 3, 1997, William B. Patterson, Chairperson.

Bibliographical Essay

This book deserves a bibliographical essay because it originated in a quite unusual manner and the research followed accordingly, a bit unorthodox. Furthermore, a long list of citations would suggest only that I might have read the sources mentioned, not whether I had, and it would not reveal their value. Then, too, I had no idea of writing a book when the research began. I was a retired university historian, lacking any subsidy and, no less important, any idea of writing anything. I knew that in 1970 Curt Flood sued Major League Baseball and lost in the Supreme Court, but only because a friend from the St. Louis area mentioned it at a spring training game when telling me that Flood had died on January 20, 1997, about a month earlier. Thus reminded, I asked myself why he lost the case when his lawyers' argument seemed correct: the reserve system that Flood challenged required collusion among the club owners, what the Sherman Antitrust Act called "a conspiracy in restraint of trade." The answer (it seemed) lay in a precedent from a 1922 Supreme Court case (*Federal Baseball Club v. National League,* 259 U.S. 200, 1922). Later, I again read Bob Woodward and Scott Armstrong, *The Brethren: Inside the Supreme Court* (New York: Simon and Schuster, 1979). It stressed the sentiment in Justice Harry Blackmun's majority opinion. But the Supreme Court's decision did not provide useful information. Neither Woodward and Armstrong nor the Court's decision told me why Flood sued Major League Baseball when he was well paid and players were always being traded or bought and sold from one club to another. What was different about Flood? I decided to probe a bit, but I would not readily spend the children's inheritance in doing so.

Naturally, I went to the Internet. There I found many Web sites, several only with Flood's statistics as a ballplayer but a few describing his battle in heroic, self-sacrificing terms. One site, "Blasphemy"

(http://xroads.virginia.edu/~class/am483_97/projects/brady/flood
.html), last modified on January 21, 1997, and maintained by Pat Brady,
enthusiastically endorses Flood's cause in an introductory essay and
several links, then suggests additional reading. One book that seemed
essential was Flood's memoir, *The Way It Is* (New York: Trident Press,
1971). Ghostwritten by Richard Carter, it was likely to be an explanation,
even a justification, of Flood's case because it was published just months
after a federal district court ruled against him. However, as a copy was
not then available to me, there was no way of knowing. But a paperback
copy of John Helyar's *Lords of the Realm: The* Real *History of Baseball*
(New York: Villard Books, 1994), with the word "Real" italicized, was
also on Brady's list, and it was in the bookstore, so as I was leaving on
a trip to Europe, I bought the book and began to read it immediately.

There was little new about Flood in Helyar's book, but it did place
his lawsuit in context, that being the Major League Baseball Players
Association's efforts to modify the reserve system and to end baseball's
age-old exemption from the Sherman Antitrust Act. Helyar also reintro-
duced me—Brady's Web site being the first—to Marvin Miller, the Players
Association executive director when Flood sued, and also to Miller's
autobiography, which contributed a chapter to the Flood story: *A Whole
Different Ball Game: The Sport and Business of Baseball* (Secaucus, N.J.:
Carol Publishing Group, 1991). Curiosity had already prompted me to
make an appointment to see Miller in his New York apartment before
leaving the country. So, too, would I visit Jay Topkis of the New York law
firm of Paul, Weiss, Rifkind et al., who handled much of Flood's lawsuit
in court.

When interviewing Miller, questions and answers did not matter. He
displayed his charismatic power at eighty years of age. It left an indeli-
ble—and critical—imprint: thirty years earlier he surely dominated any
discussions in his office, such as those with Flood. As for Topkis, he did
not recall details about the case but invited me to return to look at such
materials as his firm still had on the case.

Meanwhile, at my wife's behest, I found myself in Los Angeles on
March 4, 1998, for an early visit to the Getty Museum. Having a free afternoon and recalling that Flood had died in the Los Angeles area, the
thought occurred to me: for what it's worth, find his death certificate.
And I did, in a Los Angeles County repository for such in a Norwalk
court. I also found an address for Flood's widow, Judy Pace, and a

record of a lawsuit filed against Flood's estate for child support for more than half a million dollars by his first wife, Beverly (*Beverly A. Flood, aka Beverly A. Heath, Petitioner and Obligee, vs. Curtis Charles Flood, Obligor, now deceased, C/O Judy Pace Flood, surviving spouse,* Support Order, filed in Bureau of Child Support Operations, Case no. BL028957, Los Angeles Superior Court, July 28, 1997.) (An addendum of December 8, 1997, listed the Flood children from the dates of their birth.) From what I saw then, I had no idea of the significance of this document for a book about Curt Flood, which I as yet had no intention of writing. It seemed no more than a lead to underlying documents in Oakland, hundreds of miles away. But there was an address for Curt Flood's adopted daughter, Debbie, which Beverly Flood had given as her address as well.

Later that day, in interviewing Debbie at her home in nearby Altadena, I heard both favorable and unfavorable comments about the father who had adopted her. While these were interesting and useful, our second meeting in 1999 with her brother, Curtis, Jr., was more important by far. She gave me two significant documents. One was a transcript of her father's late-in-life reminiscences (Curt Flood and Kenneth Turan, "Outside-Outside: A Life That Changed Baseball," undated, but seemingly sometime in the mid-1990s); the other was a lengthy investigation of her father's estate and of his and her stepmother's liabilities, assets, and litigation ("Beverly Heath," file no. 100897–15-054, TransWest Investigations, Los Angeles). Meanwhile, I had found *The Way It Is* at a rare-book Web site and given it a reading, the first of several, and decided to do a little more research.

In late May 1998, I went to Oakland, where Curt Flood grew up, and where the Alameda County courthouse held the records supposedly supporting Beverly's child-support lawsuit. The microfilms of the Floods' battle (*Beverly A. Flood, Plaintiff, v. Charles Curtis Flood, Defendant,* case no. 356589, Superior Court of the State of California, Alameda County, Oakland, from February 7, 1966, through 1969 [thereafter Charles Curtis became Curtis Charles and Beverly Flood became Beverly Heath-Flood in 1983]) proved fascinating. What I did not know then was how valuable a source the microfilms would prove to be—so I spared myself the expense of photocopying a hundred pages unless and until I had more context.

A telephone call to Dave Newhouse, *Oakland Tribune* sports editor, at May's end proved helpful. He told me which people to see and said he would send me photocopies of some Flood stories in his newspaper's archives (which he did). After that interview, I took a look at the area in Oakland where Flood grew up, which I did not find the dark "ghetto" he described in *The Way It is,* a book which I was coming to believe was an apologia (a justification of his lawsuit) posing as a memoir. But half a century had passed; I could not know what the area was like when Flood lived there. I undertook my appointments with that in mind.

The first interview brought me to Bill Patterson, once Flood's black mentor at an Oakland recreation center; the second to Sam Bercovich, once the sponsor of the American Legion team on which Flood played. Both greeted me in their homes. Patterson was an obvious admirer of Flood even after his friend's loss in court, his self-imposed exile, and his alcoholism, and the picture that emerged in interviews over the next four or five years reflected it. So did a book he gave me: Dorothy W. Pitts, *A Special Place for People: The DeFremery Story* (Memphis: Better Communications, 1993). But the book also revealed that the West Oakland ghetto was not closed; it offered an opening to a larger world. My next appointment took me to the home of Bercovich, whose room memorializing Flood clearly bespoke his admiration. Like Patterson, he testified to Flood's ability to charm; otherwise, he provided narrative context for Flood's pre– and post–major-league years. Meanwhile, Patterson had made an appointment for me to see Harold Wilson, in Flood's time a black probation officer who had known the Flood family well. I listened to Wilson's anecdote about young Curt Flood and his brother, Carl, then moved on.

The most important person I saw was Iola "Rickie" Riley, Flood's stepsister, who dubbed herself the family historian. It was the first of four or five interviews in "Rickie" Riley's home that informed me of the family's origins in Louisiana and Texas, as well as of their life in Oakland—and more. She had lived with her husband on the first floor of her much younger stepbrother's childhood home, then, as it is today, a substantial house; she supplied anecdotes that suggested her parents' problems with alcohol, their personalities, and their financial situation, as well as those characteristics which their son, Curtis, inherited. Rickie spoke easily and intelligently, but at eighty-five she could not recall exactly when her mother was born, although she knew it was sometime in the late 1890s. The answer was not vital, but a look at Charles Curtis Flood, "Request for Inspection of Passport File," by the Internal Revenue Service, Passport Office, U.S. State Department, November 26, 1974, gave it as October 1897, and the citation was useful later because it provided Flood's address when in Palma de Majorca. Rickie also led me to financial records regarding her stepbrother's purchase of his mother's home and what followed (Internal Revenue Service assessment for unpaid taxes on 2907 55th Ave., Oakland, CA, December 11, 1970, IRS lien May 12, 1971, and Release of Lien, July 7, 1982, Records, Alameda County courthouse, Oakland; also mortgages on home, Western Title Guaranty Co. to Israel Gold and Sarah Ann Malakoff, October 23, 1968, Deed of Trust to Curtis C. Flood, and Notice of Default, by Curtis C. Flood, failure to pay interest, principal, and taxes, and sale to Harold and Iola E. Riley, Western Title Guaranty Company, September 3, 1971, Alameda County courthouse). It should be noted that in a last interview with Rickie she said that beneath her true gentility and apparent moderation on racial issues lurked great bitterness, an insight that may have influenced my sense of her stepbrother's views on the subject. As for Herman, another of Rickie's stepbrothers, he was sometimes present, but he was by nature quiet. At any rate, I left Oakland believing that Flood had overstated the harshness of the West Oakland ghetto, and that his parents were not the impoverished victims of the white establishment that he had wanted his readers to believe; instead, they were alcoholics with conflicting and difficult characteristics that left a mark on their youngest son, though they could afford to send him to baseball camp and to games out of town.

Three months after my first interview with Rickie, on June 29, 1998, I ate lunch with Flood's widow, Judy Pace. She knew about my interview with Debbie and quickly accused me of taking Beverly's part in the lawsuit against her husband's estate. I told her she was wrong, but she said she would ask "the baseball community" not to talk with me and, with one important exception (an interview by telephone with Flood's former teammate Bill White in October 1998), they would not. Curiously, considering her distrust of me, she talked about how she and Curt Flood first met in 1965; told me that they had split in December 1969 or soon after, but not why; then recounted how they met again in 1985 and married. After these anecdotes (placed in a memo the next morning), I wondered why she would ask Flood's teammates not to talk. Was it fear of what I might learn: that she had an agenda I might undermine? And did the same apply to Beverly and Debbie Flood? Undoubtedly. Beverly Flood would not talk then, and after the lawsuit was settled or had collapsed, Debbie would not answer questions, but in 2006 her son said, in an accidental meeting, "we disrespected him."

By early October 1998 I decided, in part because Judy Flood did not want a book, to do more research. Flying to Dulles International Airport in Washington, D.C., and renting a car, I saw Richard Carter at his home outside Ossining, New York, and listened to him speak of his sympathy for Flood and his cause. But Carter said that he only wrote down what Flood told him (subject, he must have meant, to styling) and had checked nothing. The next day was spent at Topkis's office, sorting through files and copying letters. Then it was off to High Point in North Carolina, where Flood had played for the Hi-Toms, the local minor-league team. There the sports editor of the *High Point Enterprise,* Tom Berry, let me look through the newspaper's files on Flood, some of which I photocopied, then drove me to the boardinghouse where Flood had lived. After that, he took me to the office of George Erath, who was the Hi-Toms' general manager when Flood played for them, and after that to the office of Jim Sumner, from whom I bought a copy of his *Separating the Men from the Boys: The First Half Century of the Carolina League* (Winston Salem, N.C.: John F. Blair Publisher, 1994). Then we visited for a few minutes with Joanne Black, a white friend of Flood. Busy at work then, the next day she not only spoke of her and her boyfriend's friendship with Flood but also showed me a photograph of the three of them together.

One day later I drove to Savannah, Georgia, where Flood played for the Savannah Reds, Cincinnati's Class A farm team. I was not quite as lucky as in High Point, but I did have a useful talk with Al Jennings, who in Flood's time had broadcast the team's home games. He gave me the address of a white ballplayer who had befriended Flood—"Buddy" Gilbert, as I knew him then—and soon we would correspond. Then it was back to Dulles and home, only to fly to Phoenix to see baseball Hall of Famer Frank Robinson. The meeting with him was a fiasco; he had nothing significant to add. It was time to do more reading.

Having just returned from the South, I picked up a book by William H. Chafe, *Civilities and Civil Rights* (New York: Oxford University Press, 1980), which provided a broad view of the mid-fifties racial climate in North Carolina when Flood played. Then I read Jules Tygiel's *Baseball's Great Experiment: Jackie Robinson and His Legacy,* expanded edition (New York: Oxford University Press, 1997), which placed Flood's experience with racism in the context of the broader experience of black players in the South. After that I phoned the *St. Louis Post-Dispatch*'s library, where I found a man willing to pull and send all the Flood stories he could find. So, too, with the St. Louis Mercantile Library, which held the now-defunct *St. Louis Globe-Democrat*'s back issues and was willing to send me stories about Flood. Both newspapers would provide many absolutely crucial details about Flood's baseball career with the Cardinals. Suddenly, the records in the Alameda County courthouse that I had seen but not photocopied became of the greatest significance. I had a context for them now, and if I went to Oakland again, I would pay to copy them. Meanwhile, I found important elements of the Flood story in the *New York Times, Washington Post,* and the (often derivative) *Sporting News,* as well as to a lesser extent in the *Philadelphia Daily News, Washington Star, Oakland Tribune, St. Petersburg Times,* and *New York Daily News.* There were also several pertinent magazine articles of greater or lesser value within easy reach.

The most useful article, Al Stump, "Curt Flood in the Midnight League," *Sport* (March 1965), 33, 78–79, offered essential insights into Flood's temperament as well as his commitment to the Cardinals. Of somewhat lesser importance was William Leggett, "Curt Flood of St. Louis: Baseball's Best Centerfielder," *Sports Illustrated* (August 19, 1968), 18–21. Other magazine articles included Phil Pepe, "How Flood Finally Made It," *Sport* (1962, n.d.), 44–45, and John Devaney, "Why I Am Challenging Baseball, by Curt Flood," *Sport* (March 1970), 11–12, 62. There were also books dealing with the gradual death of the reserve system, such as Charles Korr, *The End of Baseball as We Knew It* (Urbana: University of Illinois Press, 2002), especially chapter 5. Another book of some interest was Lee Lowenfish, *The Imperfect Diamond: The Story of Baseball's Reserve System and the Men Who Fought to Change It* (New York: Stein and Day, 1980).

By 1999 it was clear that all the books and articles, photocopying, and interviews were significant in terms of their insight into Flood's decision to sue baseball only when connected to his performance during a World Series game, his ex-wife's demands for alimony and child support, and his responses to that pressure as I recalled them from the records of *Flood v. Flood,* which at that point I had seen but not copied. With those records in mind, I returned to Oakland to have them photocopied. Furthermore, I copied the documents related to the house Flood had bought for his mother in his name, as noted earlier.

Meanwhile, fortuitously, I met Allan Zerman, the St. Louis lawyer with whom Flood first discussed suing baseball. He was so cautious about discussing the suit and its origins that he needed constant coddling. Eventually, he heard me say that Flood was an alcoholic, and that loosened him up. From that time and until 2003 we exchanged e-mails and talked in his office, and he mailed me documents—Morris Oliphant Papers, 1955–1964—that led to David Oliphant, the man who prompted Flood to write his memoir, and subsequent correspondence and telephone interviews from October 1998 to 2001. Meanwhile, Zerman opened the door to two civil actions involving Flood: *Delmar Printing Company, Plaintiff, v. Curt Flood Associates, Inc.,* Civil Action, 70 C, 209, United States District Court for the Eastern District of Missouri, Eastern Division; and *Howard and Nancy Foster, Plaintiffs v. Curtis C. Flood and William M. Jones,* no. 71 C, 14, Civil Action, United States District Court for the Eastern District of Missouri, Eastern District.

By 2001 my research had gone so far as to recommend a trip to Majorca, where Flood spent four years in exile. Early in 2001 I was able to contact Johannes Cornelius Tringham, our consular agent in Palma, by e-mail. That summer we had lunch, and through her I met two women who had known Flood: Maureen Rowland, who owned a tavern, and Wendy Potyrala, whose husband published *Talk of the Town,* a local gossip publication. Inquiries into when and why Flood left Palma or where he went produced no information, but through the Freedom of Information Act I was able to find U.S. Consulate in Barcelona to the U.S. State, and State Department to Consulate, case no. 200202860. They were of some importance to the Flood story, although not close to the caliber of *Flood v. Flood.*

Two years after returning from Majorca, I learned more about Zerman in speaking with his former secretary, Connie Reilly, once Connie Jones, the wife of Flood's business partner Bill Jones. On that trip I also saw Ruth Sutterfield, manager of a Flood studio, in her apartment; it was the second time I had met with her, the first being in 2002. I also went through the City Directories for Flood's years in St. Louis, glanced at the Parkway Hotel where he lived for a year, looked closely at his last fine apartment, an opportunity made possible by the doorman, and interviewed Dr. Jerome Aronberg, with whom I later corresponded via e-mail. There were other telephone interviews, too, as I attempted to check sources—to the NAACP in Danville, Virginia, and also the Danville newspaper, the *Register and Bee.*

Throughout five years of somewhat happenstance research I interviewed William Gildea of the *Washington Post* when I was in the area, and also in Washington I found the Arthur Goldberg Papers at the Library of Congress, which were of only limited advantage. I also telephoned Jody Kramer, a St. Louis woman who responded indirectly to my *St. Louis Post-Dispatch* personal ad seeking information about Flood. Further, I read more books, articles, and newspapers when they seemed even slightly pertinent. These sources included, most significantly, Brad Snyder, *A Well-Paid Slave: Curt Flood's Fight for Free Agency in Professional Sports* (New York: Viking, 2006); Shelby Whitfield, *Kiss It Goodbye* (New York: Abelard-Schuman, 1973); the Web site www.baseballlibrary.com; Bob Gibson and Lonnie Wheeler, *Stranger to the Game: The Autobiography of Bob Gibson* (New York: Viking Books, 1994); Alex Belth, *Stepping Up: The Story of Curt Flood and His Fight for Baseball Players' Rights* (New York: Persea, 2006); the *Baseball Encyclopedia,* tenth edition, revised and updated (New York: Macmillan, 1996); and, of less value, James N. Giglio, *Musial: From Stash to Stan the Man* (Columbia: University of Missouri Press, 2001); Geoffrey Ward and Ken Burns, *Baseball: An Illustrated History* (New York: Knopf, 1994); Tim McCarver and Danny Peary, *Tim McCarver's Baseball for Brain Surgeons and Other Fans* (New York: Villard Books, 1998); Bowie Kuhn, *Hard Ball: The Education of a Baseball Commissioner* (New York: Times Books, 1987); Gerald Scully, *The Business of Major League Baseball* (Chicago: University of Chicago Press, 1989); and Peter Golenbock, *The Spirit of St. Louis: A History of the Cardinals and the Browns* (New York: Spike, 2000); and George F. Will, *Bunts* (New York: Touchstone, 1999). Useful articles were Richard Reeves, "The Last Angry Man," *Esquire* (March 1, 1978), 41–48, of value for Flood's life after his return from exile, as was an article by Murray Chass, reprinted in the *St. Louis Post-Dispatch.* Video tapes include "Spike Lee Presents a Profile of Curt Flood," HBO's *Real Sports* (episode 11, March 10, 1997); and "A Fire in the Night," also known as "City on Fire: The Story of the '68 Detroit Tigers," HBO (July 30, 2002). Also helpful was an interview with Marc Risman, Las Vegas, 2005. Last on this list, but deserving special mention, is the *St. Louis Post-Dispatch*'s sports editor, Bob Broeg, who may at times have reflected the interests of August Busch and the St. Louis Cardinals front office, but who wrote matchless columns about Flood over many years, one in particular including an invaluable interview with him.

Yes, I scavenged other books and newspaper articles about Flood and the reserve system, and corresponded with other men not mentioned, but they added nothing and are not cited for that reason. This bibliography was designed to distinguish sources that offer access to the most significant documents—for insights into Flood's temperament, "Curt Flood in the Midnight League"; *Flood v. Flood,* microfilm that I was reluctant to purchase but that was surely the most crucial source material for discussing the very heart of the story, the pressures that Flood could not handle; Flood's late-in-life reminiscences with Turan; and the interviews with Rickie Riley, without which there would have been no beginning. Several of the other sources, especially the Oliphant papers, father and son, Marvin Miller's *A Whole Different Ball Game,* and Shelby Whitfield's *Kiss It Goodbye* developed interesting and essential aspects of the story, while still other sources provided context, moved the story along, or both. As for Alex Belth in *Stepping Up,* he falls into a different category. His book produces some interesting anecdotes, but it relegates most of Flood's personal life, and the most important elements within it, to the book's end, as a kind of afterthought; he does not integrate Flood's personal life with his baseball career. Although Belth once went to Oakland, apparently he did not go to the Alameda County courthouse, where he might have found the alimony and child-support battle with Beverly, the business difficulties, and the problems with the IRS. How Belth might have interpreted these sources is one thing, but that he did not use any of them is or should be a serious disappointment to any reader. Although Brad Snyder's *A Well-Paid Slave* is a far more deeply researched and detailed biography than Belth's, he does not seem to have reviewed the alimony and child case in the Alameda courthouse or the Curt Flood Associates, Inc., cases in federal district court in St. Louis either. Nonetheless, it is a fine book that I should like to think of as complementing this one. If, as Snyder argues, Flood was active in the civil rights movement, or even was deeply concerned with the issue, as he probably was, it does not mean that his decision to sue was shaped with reasoned, focused clarity of purpose.

Clearly, for this book a Flood diary or extensive letters would have added much; so too would extensive interviews with his first wife and his widow, but the former refused to say anything, and the latter would say but a few words. Perhaps now that three books have been written, both women will respond to this replacement of the Flood myth by what I hope is a more realistic view of the man, of his decision to challenge the reserve system, and of those men and women who influenced that decision and otherwise shaped his life. Meanwhile, you, the reader, must decide whether the story told in the chapters you have read are strongly sourced, and whether they inform or mislead. That is why there are footnotes. That is why writers differ in their interpretations.

Index